International Environmental Agreements

D0145365

International environmental agreements provide a practical basis for countries to address environmental issues on a global scale. This book explores the workings and outcomes of these agreements, and analyses key questions of why some problems are dealt with successfully and others ignored.

By examining fundamental policies and issues in environmental protection this text gives an easily comprehensible introduction to international environmental agreements, and discusses problems in three areas: air, water and on land. It traces the history of agreements in broad thematic areas related to long-distance air pollution, ozone-depleting and greenhouse gases, ocean management, biological diversity, agricultural plant diversity and forest stewardship. Drawing on experts in their respective fields, this book provides an insightful evaluation of the successes and failures, and analysis of the reasons for this. Concluding with an insightful examination of research to show how performance of agreements can be improved in the future, this volume is a vital contribution to our understanding of the politics associated with establishing international environmental consensus.

International Environmental Agreements will be of interest to scholars, students and researchers in global environmental politics, international relations and political science.

Steinar Andresen is Senior Research Fellow at the Fridtjof Nansen Institute, Norway, and formerly professor at the Department of Political Science, University of Oslo.

Elin Lerum Boasson is Research Fellow at the Fridtjof Nansen Institute, Norway.

Geir Hønneland is Research Director at the Fridtjof Nansen Institute, Norway and Adjunct Professor at the University of Tromsø.

Environmental Politics/Routledge Research in Environmental Politics

Edited by
Steve Vanderheiden, University of Colorado

Over recent years environmental politics has moved from a peripheral interest to a central concern within the discipline of politics. This series aims to reinforce this trend through the publication of books that investigate the nature of contemporary environmental politics and show the centrality of environmental politics to the study of politics per se. The series understands politics in a broad sense and books will focus on mainstream issues such as the policy process and new social movements as well as emerging areas such as cultural politics and political economy. Books in the series will analyse contemporary political practices with regards to the environment and/or explore possible future directions for the 'greening' of contemporary politics. The series will be of interest not only to academics and students working in the environmental field, but will also demand to be read within the broader discipline.

The series consists of two strands:

Environmental Politics addresses the needs of students and teachers, and the titles will be published in paperback and hardback. Titles include:

Global Warming and Global Politics
Matthew Paterson

Politics and the Environment
James Connelly & Graham Smith

International Relations Theory and Ecological Thought
Towards synthesis
Eric Laferrière & Peter Stoett

Planning Sustainability
Edited by Michael Kenny & James Meadowcroft

Deliberative Democracy and the Environment
Graham Smith

EU Enlargement and the Environment
Institutional change and environmental policy in Central and Eastern Europe
Edited by JoAnn Carmin and Stacy D. VanDeveer

The Crisis of Global Environmental Governance
Towards a new political economy of sustainability
Edited by Jacob Park, Ken Conca and Matthias Finger

Routledge Research in Environmental Politics presents innovative new research intended for high-level specialist readership. These titles are published in hardback only and include:

International Environmental Agreements

An Introduction

Edited by
Steinar Andresen, Elin Lerum Boasson,
and Geir Hønneland

Routledge
Taylor & Francis Group

NEW YORK AND LONDON

First published 2012
by Routledge
2 Park Square Milton Park Abingdon Oxon OX14 4RN

Simultaneously published in the USA and Canada
by Routledge
711 Third Avenue, New York, NY10017

*Routledge is an imprint of the Taylor & Francis Group, an informa
business.*

British Library Cataloguing in Publication Data
A catalogue record for this book is available from the British Library

Library of Congress Cataloging-in-Publication Data
International environmental agreements : an introduction / edited by
Steinar Andresen, Elin Lerum Boasson, and Geir Hønneland.
p. cm. -- (Environmental politics / Routledge research in environmental
politics ; 19)
Includes bibliographical references and index.
1. Environmental policy--International cooperation. 2. Environmental
management--International cooperation. 3. Environmental
protection--International cooperation. 4. Environmental law,
International. I. Andresen, Steinar. II. Boasson, Elin Lerum, 1978-
III. Hønneland, Geir.
JZ1324.I56 2011
333.7--dc23
2011019506

ISBN: 978-0-415-59825-5 (hbk)
ISBN: 978-0-415-66462-2 (pbk)
ISBN: 978-0-203-18145-4 (ebk)

Typeset in Times New Roman
by Integra Software Services Pvt. Ltd, Pondicherry, India

Contents

Contributors

Regine Andersen is a Senior Research Fellow at the Fridtjof Nansen Institute. Her work focuses on the effects of multilateral environmental and economic agreements on the management of plant genetic resources for food and agriculture in developing countries. She is the author of *Governing Agrobiodiversity: plant genetics and developing countries* (Ashgate, 2008).

Steinar Andresen is a Senior Research Fellow at the Fridtjof Nansen Institute. Among his books are *Science and Politics in International Environmental Regimes: between integrity and involvement* (Manchester University Press, 2000) and *Environmental Regime Effectiveness: confronting theory with evidence* (MIT Press, 2002). He has published articles in a number of journals and was recently guest editor of *Global Environmental Politics* and *International Environmental Agreements: politics, law and economics*.

Elin Lerum Boasson is a Research Fellow at the Fridtjof Nansen Institute. She is currently working on her PhD thesis in political science at the University of Oslo and is mainly interested in the energy and climate politics of the European Union. She has published several articles and book chapters. For the academic year 2009–10 she was a visiting scholar at the Department of Sociology, University of California, Berkeley.

Lars H. Gulbrandsen is a Senior Research Fellow at the Fridtjof Nansen Institute. He studies international environmental politics with a particular focus on market-based policy instruments, non-state governance and corporate social responsibility. He has published a number of journal articles and is the author of *Transnational Environmental Governance: the emergence and effects of the certification of forests and fisheries* (Edward Elgar, 2010).

Geir Hønneland is Research Director at the Fridtjof Nansen Institute and adjunct professor at the University of Tromsø. Among his books are *Russia and the West: environmental co-operation and conflict* (Routledge,

2003), *Implementing International Environmental Agreements in Russia* (Manchester University Press, 2003), *International Cooperation and Arctic Governance: regime effectiveness and northern region building* (Routledge, 2007) and *Borderland Russians: identity, narrative and international relations* (Palgrave Macmillan, 2010).

Øystein Jensen is a Research Fellow at the Fridtjof Nansen Institute. He is an international lawyer specialising in the law of the sea. He has published several articles on law of the sea issues in the Arctic Ocean and is currently working on a PhD thesis related to the Commission on the Limits of the Continental Shelf.

Kristin Rosendal is a Senior Research Fellow at the Fridtjof Nansen Institute. She studies international environmental politics, with a particular focus on biodiversity, forestry management, biotechnology and genetic resources. She has published a number of journal articles and the book *The Convention on Biological Diversity and Developing Countries* (Kluwer Academic Publishers, 2000).

Peter Johan Schei is Director of the Fridtjof Nansen Institute. He has headed several Norwegian delegations to international meetings and conferences between 1979 and 2004 under the auspices of, among others, CITES, the Bern Convention, CBD, Ramsar and Biosafety protocol negotiations. He is series editor for CABI Publishing's *Environmental Risk Assessment of Genetically Modified Organisms Series*.

Jon Birger Skjærseth is a Senior Research Fellow at the Fridtjof Nansen Institute. Among his books are *North Sea Cooperation: linking international and domestic pollution control* (Manchester University Press, 2000), *Environmental Regime Effectiveness: confronting theory with evidence* (MIT Press, 2002), *Climate Change and the Oil Industry* (Manchester University Press, 2003), *International Regimes and Norway's Environmental Policy* (Ashgate, 2004) and *EU Emission Trading: initiation, decision-making and implementation* (Ashgate, 2008).

Olav Schram Stokke is a Senior Research Fellow at the Fridtjof Nansen Institute. His books include *Governing the Antarctic: the effectiveness and legitimacy of the Antarctic system* (Cambridge University Press, 1996), *Governing High Seas Fisheries: the interplay of global and regional regimes* (Oxford University Press, 2000), *International Cooperation and Arctic Governance: regime effectiveness and northern region building* (Routledge, 2007) and *Managing Institutional Complexity: regime interplay and global environmental change* (MIT Press, 2011).

Jørgen Wettestad is a Senior Research Fellow at the Fridtjof Nansen Institute. Among his books are *Designing Effective Environmental Regimes: the key conditions* (Edward Elgar, 1999), *Science and Politics in International Environmental Regimes: between integrity and involvement*

(Manchester University Press, 2000), *Clearing the Air: European advances in tackling acid rain and atmospheric pollution* (Ashgate, 2002), *Environmental Regime Effectiveness: confronting theory with evidence* (MIT Press, 2002) and *EU Emission Trading: initiation, decision-making and implementation* (Ashgate, 2008).

Preface

This book is a joint effort by researchers at the Fridtjof Nansen Institute at Lysaker, Norway, all working in different areas of international environmental politics. It is a heavily revised and updated version of the Norwegian textbook *Internasjonal miljøpolitikk*, which was published by Fagbokforlaget in 2008. Although this English version is structured by theoretical discussion and builds on fresh academic research, students – more than academic peers – are still our primary audience.

Thanks to Chris Saunders for translating the Norwegian text into English and to Maryanne Rygg for help in preparing the manuscript. We are also indebted to Routledge editors Heidi Bagtazo and Hannah Shakespeare and three anonymous reviewers, who all helped define the direction of the English version of the book.

We have used few acronyms, but have instead shortened the titles for most agreements. We write, for example, Biodiversity Convention instead of CBD and Law of the Sea Convention instead of UNCLOS.

Steinar Andresen
Elin Lerum Boasson
Geir Hønneland

Part I

Introduction

1 An international environmental policy takes shape

Steinar Andresen, Elin Lerum Boasson and Geir Hønneland

Important years

1872 The world's first national park established
1900 The first international convention for the conservation of nature signed
1948 The International Union for the Protection of Nature established (name changed to International Union for Conservation of Nature and Natural Resources in 1956, with the acronym IUCN)
1961 World Wildlife Fund (WWF) established
1962 The book *Silent Spring* published
1972 The Stockholm Conference on the Human Environment
1972 United Nations Environment Programme established
1987 United Nations report *Our Common Future* published
1992 Rio Conference on Environment and Development
2000 UN Millennium Declaration
2002 World Summit on Sustainable Development in Johannesburg

International environmental problems have now been on the political agenda for more than thirty years. The traditional approach to deal with these problems is to establish multilateral environmental agreements (MEAs). There has been a tremendous growth in these agreements and several hundreds now exist. Although some of them have had a positive effect on the problem at hand, overall progress has been limited and existing environmental problems are formidable. In this book we explore the emergence of the environment as an international political issue. The main focus, however, is on the working and effect of these agreements. Why are some problems dealt with rather effectively while there is little or no progress within other issue areas? Also, what can be done to improve their problem-solving ability?

Although a few scattered conservation agreements had appeared in the early years of the twentieth century, the 1972 Stockholm Conference on the Human Environment is generally considered the watershed event sparking a truly international approach to the environment. The conference resulted in several international agreements in the field of what is

usually referred to as 'classic' nature conservation – the protection of
endangered species for example. As the 1970s progressed, treaties targeted
air and water pollution, usually within a demarcated part of the globe. By
the 1980s, pollution was a worldwide concern and initiatives promoted an
international programme to reduce emissions of substances known to deplete
the ozone layer. The UN Convention on the Law of the Sea, concluded in
1982, was followed a decade later by another epoch making event, the 1992
Conference on Environment and Development held in Rio de Janeiro,
Brazil. Several important agreements came out of the summit, including
conventions on biological diversity and climate change. The 2002 World
Summit on Sustainable Development in Johannesburg did not produce the
same kind of substantial output. More recently, environment, particularly
climate change, has been on the agenda of more exclusive high-level
international political forums like G-8 and G-20.

Changing international relations and trends affect perceptions of environmental problems and the options for dealing with them. In this book we
discuss the most important multilateral arrangements set up to address
environmental problems in three areas: air, water and nature protection/
biological diversity. This threefold division informs the structure of the
book as a whole. The part on air deals with long-distance air pollution,
ozone-depleting gases and greenhouse gases. The section on water examines
the international stewardship of the oceans, including ocean law, marine
pollution and fisheries management. The section on soil and diversity in
nature addresses biological diversity, agricultural plant diversity and
forest stewardship. Under each heading we look at international systems
of collaboration and achievements to date. To conclude we compare
approaches and discuss possible ways forward to improve performance
and outcomes of international environmental policy.

We approach these issues from a political science angle, a main topic being
the political bargaining over diagnoses of the ailment and appropriate
cure – perceptions and conceptualisations. Science teaches us about natural
processes and nature's response to human interference: both of which are
an essential background for discussing substantive policy options. It is not
surprising that scientists were the first to 'discover' the threat facing environment, and came up with methods for dealing with it. Political science, for
its part, can help explain why some environmental problems are solved
relatively quickly and others are suspended in a semi-permanent state of
political contention, with no conclusion in sight. Insofar as the problems
themselves differ, policy must obviously be designed around the particular
issue in question. Bringing the issue to international attention is sometimes
an effective approach, sometimes not. Further, the form or configuration
of the international response will vary; some approaches may be fruitful
while others may fail.

The international collaboration on environmental matters interferes
with national and local problem-solving efforts. Sometimes MEAs may

enable and promote national and local problem-solving efforts, while in other instances it may hamper such efforts. In any case, increased knowledge of the international policy framework will make it easier for national and local actors to select fruitful strategy and tools.

In this introduction we explain what we understand by international environmental politics, the book's main contentions and theoretical grounding. This leads to an account of international cooperation on the environment, its origins and history. We stay with history when we turn to the emergence of a truly international approach, before concluding with a review of the ensuing chapters.

Theoretical approach

The prefix 'inter-' means 'between' or 'among'. Hitched onto 'national' it becomes 'international' and signifies the presence or involvement of two or more states. 'International' in this literal sense is too narrow a concept for our purposes. In the field of the environment, numerous non-governmental organisations and transnational corporations operate outside their country of origin. International, in our rendition, will therefore include relations between governments and non-governmental organisations, and between the latter organisations themselves. *Politics* is understood just as broadly. Any process or situation impinging on the creation and implementation of multilateral environmental agreements will be considered relevant.

In this book we shall be looking in particular at the political practices of parties to relatively stable treaties and conventions. Usually based on some kind of written settlement or pact, both the degree and type of commitment taken on by governments can vary. We shall use the terms 'accord' and 'regime' interchangeably with the term 'international environmental agreement', which includes the institutional arrangements surrounding the agreement itself. Bilateral agreements, between two individual nation-states, are the least complicated. Agreements can have a specific regional or geographical focus, generally the home region of the signatories. When governments from different regions and continents come together for a common purpose, the resulting approach is global. Our interest in this book lies mainly with arrangements at the regional and global levels, that is with MEAs.

Each chapter asks the same set of questions:

1 What is the nature of the particular problem?
2 What is the history of the MEAs that are developed to cope with the problem?
3 How do the MEAs operate?
4 How effective have the MEAs been in solving the problems they were set up to deal with?
5 What explains the performance of the MEAs?

Our first question concerns problem identification, that is, the reason why this particular multilateral arrangement was created. We inquire into the type of problem, its magnitude and significance. How far does its geographical impact extend? Is it a local, regional or global problem? In the event of environmental damage, do the harmful processes take place in water, in the soil or in the atmosphere?

We are interested in more than the technical and scientific aspects, however. If we want to understand the political discussions, we need to know how environmental problems challenge conventional mindsets, behaviour and actors. How far does the scientific community agree on the causes of the problem? Is one particular sector of society affected, or several? Will taking action result in piecemeal political concessions, and are powerful constituencies likely to feel threatened? Finding answers to these questions will tell us a great deal about the problem itself and not the least how difficult or easy it will be to solve the relevant problems. We will therefore get back to this aspect under question five where we explain performance.

The second question addresses the creation and history of the MEA. When was the problem identified? How long did it take before the international community responded? Who helmed the work? Did new states join or current members leave the negotiations? Could certain episodes in all the rounds of negotiations be characterised as particularly momentous? Where is the arrangement in terms of its 'life cycle'? Is it young and healthy, or already passed its 'sell by date' in respect of the initial cause?

Our third question explores how the MEAs operate. To grasp the potential of a collaborative effort, we need to analyse it substantively. According to sociologist Richard W. Scott (1995) social structures may be understood as being normative, cognitive or regulative. This may also work as a template for describing the key content of the various MEAs. The normative dimension covers the values and moral principles that are promoted. One manifestation will be the urgency with which the problem is viewed relative to other pressing issues. Strongly normative regimes will be at pains to establish and communicate clear goals and values. What do they ultimately hope to achieve in addressing this environmental problem? What should be the moral principles of their work? Which values should take precedence? Surveillance mechanisms can be created for monitoring compliance. If countries violate the normative principles of the regime, they run the risk of alienating the public; if they uphold the principles, however, they will be applauded.

The cognitive aspect concerns how the problem is perceived and how remedies are presented. The key factors are the main causes of the problem, the degree to which something can be done about it, whether economic or regulatory action seems the best approach. When the cognitive element is central, the regime will encourage scientific studies and release considerable resources for research on likely solutions and procedures. Mapping cognitive content also means establishing the causes of the environmental problem and its impact. Which principles are likely to shed light on effective solutions? Some regimes will be strong enough to influence a state's perception of the problem, by bringing scientists and bureaucrats on board, providing training programmes and manuals for those engaged in addressing the problem.

Regulatory aspects are formal sets of rules governing the arrangement. The crucial thing here is whether the agreements contain legally binding commitments on the participating states. How rigorous, far-reaching or ambitious are these commitments? Are they rendered in clear, lucid, easily understood language? Oversight and enforcement mechanisms tend to be built into the more rigorous treaties, including some form of punitive action for non-compliance. Here it is pertinent to ask whether surveillance and dispute mechanisms are sufficiently robust. Are states likely to lose rights for breaking the rules? Are economic penalties a real possibility? Does the regime have the muscle to enforce punitive measures?

While some MEAs are strong on the normative aspects, others rely on the cognitive or regulatory ones. Some agreements utilise all three dimensions more or less equally. Regulatory measures are usually practised by parties to the agreement in a top-down direction. The normative and cognitive elements work – without necessarily invoking governmental intervention – by encouraging the media, private sector, experts and interest organisations to examine and change if necessary attitudes and opinions. Historically, political science has laid most weight on the regulatory pillar. Carefully, precisely worded provisions were therefore expected to have greater effect in practice than loosely formulated, airy commitments. However that may be, the regulatory strength does not as such tell us much about what the treaty means in practice. Strict and precise rules and regulations increase the potential for higher effectiveness, but it is no guarantee that it happens.

In the 1970s and 1980s, social scientists wanted to explain how and why treaties came into existence (Young 1989; Haas 1990; Benedick 1991). By the late 1990s, the performance or effectiveness of treaties was attracting attention (Victor *et al.* 1998; Weiss and Jacobson 1998; Young 1999); by then, many had 'come of age'. Had they done well? Had they made a tangible difference? The problem with performance questions is the difficulty involved in assessing it. The most obvious method is to compare performance with official goals. If the goals are plain and clear, uncontroversial and easily measured, this can be a useful approach. But targets are frequently vague, with governments and observers harbouring very different ideas about what they boil down to. The essential question we nevertheless shall try to answer is whether the multilateral institution has succeeded in solving the problem that occasioned its creation.

Thus, in question four we set out to evaluate the relevant MEAs. Up until quite recently there has been a considerable debate among scholars on how best to measure the performance of MEAs. More recently, however, there is an emerging consensus that a distinction should be made between *output*, *outcome* and *impact* (Underdal 2002). Output is the rules and regulations constituting the MEA, thereby similar to the regulatory aspects described above. This indicator is fairly easy to measure and is much used by students of international law. Strict rules and regulations normally indicate a more effective MEA, but we do not know that until we find out what actually happens on the ground. That is, output tells us about *potential* effectiveness more than *actual* effectiveness. That is why additional measurement criteria are needed. Outcome deals with the set of consequences flowing from the implementation of the rules and regulations laid down in the relevant cooperative arrangements. That is, the more successful the state-parties are in actually implementing the regulations, the more effective the MEA in question. A key element in this process is to get the key target groups to change behaviour in the direction described by the regime. The final indicator, impact, deals with the consequences that materialise as changes in the state of the environment itself – as a result of the relevant MEA.

To measure output is a fairly straightforward process, but there are severe challenges in measuring the two others, particularly the impact indicator. This is so because of the difficulty in establishing a *causal link* between the relevant components of the MEA and the behaviour of target groups as well as effects on nature itself. Ideally, the one indicator we would like to use most is the impact indicator as it gives the best measurement on the 'real' effect on the problem caused by the MEA. However, due to the influence of a host of other factors, this indicator is very difficult to use; many other factors impinge on the state of the environment apart from a treaty or convention. Isolating the effects of a treaty from other phenomena such as natural variation, or economic, technological or social change, is extraordinarily complicated.

To illustrate challenges regarding the application of the outcome indicator, it is not enough, for instance, to point to a drop in emissions or reduced catches: they could just as easily have completely different causes. Two examples illustrate the difficulty. In the early 1960s, there was a noticeable slide in the numbers of great whales caught. But it was not because the International Whaling Commission had tightened the rules; after decades of over-exploitation the whale population was decimated and, naturally, harder to find. And when emissions of greenhouse gases fell steeply in Europe in the early 1990s, the main cause was not the Climate Convention, but the sudden slowdown in industrial output following the Soviet Union's collapse. But as various studies show, the impact of many agreements is both immediate and strong on participating countries' behaviour. One of the clearest examples is the Montreal Protocol under the ozone regime.

Altogether this leaves us with five indicators on how to measure or evaluate the performance of the MEAs described and analysed in this book: normative ('strength'), cognitive ('strength'), regulative (or output), outcome and impact. It is fairly straightforward to measure the first three of these indicators. We will apply the two latter and more methodologically challenging indicators only when analysing the more 'mature' MEAs. Many treaties and conventions analysed are relatively young: it would be quite unrealistic to expect them to have solved a complex environmental problem within the space of a couple of decades or so. It takes time to induce behavioural change and even more so impact on nature. However, in the concluding chapter we will investigate closer the possible inter-linkages between the different indicators. For example, will a high score on the 'softer' indicators (norms and cognition) also render a high score on the harder indicators (output and outcome)?

Turning then to question five, how do we explain the performance of the various MEAs and why some are much more successful than others? These questions have been approached in different ways (Victor *et al.* 1998; Miles *et al.* 2002; Breitmeier *et al.* 2006). Here we apply a simplified version elaborated by Underdal (2002). Coming to grips with the causes of the detected changes is a formidable explanatory challenge as an MEA is only one of several factors that may induce changes. This is why Miles *et al.* (2002) take as a point of departure the *nature of the problem* that the relevant MEA is set up to deal with.

A main explanatory factor of the effectiveness of the cooperative venture can be traced to the nature of the problem. The more 'malign' a problem is, the more difficult it will be to solve. A malign problem is characterised by deep-seated political conflicts, incongruity, asymmetries as well as uncertain or/and disputed science. As we shall have more to say about later, biodiversity is a typical malign political problem while the ozone regime has faced much more 'benign' challenges. In itself it seems as a rather trivial observation to postulate that difficult problems are harder to solve than easy problems. However, to control for the underlying problem structure when assessing MEAs is often forgotten by policy-makers as well as analysts. Some international agreements are hailed as a great success, but the reason may be that it is set out to deal with a benign problem. It may be more of an accomplishment to move a thorny issue a small step in the right direction. Both practice and research have shown us that some MEAs are highly successful while others fail. The large majority, however, end up somewhere between these two extremes (Breitmeier *et al.* 2006). The nature of the problem is therefore a natural starting point when evaluating the various MEAs. However, from an analytical and policy point of view, this aspect is of more modest interest as it tends to be a given characteristic, often rather stable and hard to change.

This is why more emphasis should be given to another explanatory factor, the problem-solving ability of the MEA at hand (Underdal 2002). This variable then focuses explicitly on characteristics of the relevant MEA and how this may explain its effectiveness. The argument is that some problems are approached with more political and institutional energy than others. To simplify, problem-solving ability is seen as a function of three factors, power, leadership and institutional set-up. A few words are warranted on each of these dimensions. Power essentially deals with the distribution within an agreement between powerful state pushers and laggards. The more powerful the pushers are, the higher the chances for a more effective MEA, and vice versa. This perspective draws on a school of thought that long dominated the study of international relations, realism. The emphasis on the significance of leadership, in contrast, draws on the liberal school of thought, having a more positive attitude to the independent significance of the MEAs than realists have. The logic is that various kinds of leadership, pursued by different individuals and non-state actors involved may increase the chances of higher effectiveness (Skodvin and Andresen 2006). The institutional aspects include a host of factors such as voting rules, the strength and independence of the secretariats associated with the MEA and not the least the institutionalisation and strength of the knowledge-producing process. This latter perspective, particularly the weight on knowledge and learning, draws on a third main school of thought within international relations, the social constructivist perspective.

Research has indicated that the aspect of power is particularly important when it comes to dealing with malign problems. We will therefore be sensitive to how power plays out in malign problems like climate change and biodiversity. Although the institutional aspects may not be that decisive in explaining performance, it is particularly interesting in the sense that these variables may be manipulated or changed. This therefore involves the question of *institutional design* of MEAs (Wettestad 1999) as well as learning and diffusion between various cooperative ventures. For example, will effectiveness vary depending upon how the science-policy interface is organised (Andresen *et al.* 2000)? Finally, we will also look into how two explanatory perspectives interact, particularly the effect of the problem-solving capacity on the problem at hand. Is it possible that strong political energy and smart institutional design can break the vicious circle of a classical malign problem?

International cooperation on the environment – a short history

A coordinated international response to the problems besetting the natural environment was not really seen until well into the post-Second World War era, from about the early 1970s. But people have been worried about the environment since nineteenth-century Romanticism. Wildlife, some believed then, should be protected as a legacy of mankind. Starting in Europe, conservationism grew into a tangible force in the US where the world's first national park, the Yellowstone, was designated as early as 1872, and the world's first environmental organisation, the Sierra Club, established in 1892. By the turn of the century, natural resource management was increasingly informed by scientific principles. The International Council for the Exploration of the Sea (ICES) was set up in 1902, for instance. While the focus of environmentalists and conservationists in America remained on the domestic front, Europe hosted the first attempt to organise an international response to the issues, that is, the protection of endangered wildlife species. Reflecting contemporary mores, colonial powers were increasingly concerned about the preservation of fauna in Africa, not least because they wanted adequate stocks of big game for their own hunting parties. A conference was convened in 1900 of European governments with a colonial presence in Africa, and the first international convention was signed: Convention Designed to Ensure the Conservation of Various Species of Wild Animals in Africa Which are Useful to Man or Inoffensive. By the 1930s the Convention Relative to the Preservation of Fauna and Flora in their Natural State was in place. Although the practical implications of these two conventions were limited, the latter was notable for its inclusion of a 'red list' of threatened and endangered species – still an important management principle in our own day and age. In short, what was later called 'classic conservation' – protection of habitats and threatened wildlife species – was at the centre of attention in this early phase, with the major Western countries setting the tone.

The establishment of the United Nations (UN) in 1945 accelerated a more systematic push towards international cooperation in many areas, including the environment. Although considered in the 1950s to be little more than a technical exercise, the UN Food and Agriculture Organization (FAO) and UN International Maritime Organization (IMO) were created in response to specific resource management problems rather than wider environmental and developmental challenges. Industrialised countries still called the shots, but although the UN was an important stage, events outside the organisation were at least as important. Consolidation of international environmental movements accelerated with the founding of the International Union for the Protection of Nature in 1948. (The organisation changed its name to the International Union for Conservation of Nature and Natural Resources in 1956, with the acronym IUCN.) Management of the natural environment was now established as an international priority. The participation of governmental and non-governmental organisations was also of great importance to this process. The IUCN issued its first red list in 1960. Concern for wildlife was the driving force behind the 1961 formation in the UK of the World Wildlife Fund (WWF): it was the first environmental organisation with an overtly international ambit. Tethered to neo-colonialist principles, it was a mirror of its time. Decolonisation, it was feared, would wreak havoc with habitats on the African continent, even threatening the survival of some species. The establishment of WWF was a milestone in the history of international environmental politics simply because the organisation relied so much on international lobbying, campaigns and active relations with the media. WWF remains an important player, but is less of a campaigner or activist nowadays. Those functions were taken over by Greenpeace, established in 1979.

The 1960s heralded a wider approach to environmental issues. Rachel Carson published her seminal account, *Silent Spring*, in 1962, and some of the results of the post-war rush to regenerate industry and manufacturing were beginning to tell in the form of polluted water and air. International environmentalism faced problems affecting the oceans and industrial sector. Critics of economic growth were gaining traction, and warnings were sounded that the world might run out of the very resources on which economic growth depended. Informed controversies fanned growing popular concern for the environment and involvement in environmentalism. It was, however, a typical expression of post-materialism – limited in other words to the affluent West. Neither Eastern Europe nor developing countries shared these sentiments or conception of the issues.

But it was on the basis of this otherwise broad consensus that the Swedish government offered to host what became the 1972 United Nations Conference on the Human Environment in Stockholm. Developing countries were originally against the conference – it was not considered a matter of urgency by any means, and the response of many developed nations was pretty lukewarm. But 120 nations did attend, and the conference marked a breakthrough for international cooperation as one element of a wider social and economic framework. The Stockholm conference introduced several key principles, including 'polluter pays', and adopted the United Nations Environment Programme (UNEP). It spawned moreover a plethora of issue-specific agreements during the 1970s and 1980s. The dominant players were still the governments of the Western world, and the issue was the environment – development did not make much of a showing. Conservationists and environmentalists still played a relatively minor role.

Although international agreements covering environmental issues continued to grow in number, the state of the environment was not a prominent issue on the international calendar until the mid 1980s. The Third UN Conference on the Law of the Sea (1973–82) was one of the few international events to attract political attention. The 1982 conference on the environment hosted by the UNEP went virtually unnoticed by the wider public. Two dramatic events set off the warning lights: the 1986 Chernobyl nuclear reactor accident and news of a hole in the ozone layer over Antarctica. Both occurred just as the UN was in the process of publishing *Our Common Future*, in 1987, in all probability the most important report on the environment ever to come out of the UN system. Heading the UN commission was Gro Harlem Brundtland, prime minister of Norway at the time. By unveiling the idea of *sustainable development* a message was sent to developing countries that the developed world was ready to accommodate calls to approach the stewardship of environment and development as two sides of the same coin. *Sustainable development* speaks equally to the environment, to welfare and to development: a healthy environment depends on a healthy, growing society, and welfare and growth on a healthy environment. The ambiguousness of this phrase has not made it very useful as a precise guiding device for behavioural change. Nonetheless, it is clear that the sustainable development concept contributed to easing the process of persuading countries in the South to step up and engage in the global environmental discourse. The idea of 'common, but differentiated responsibilities' was another concession to developing nations. It placed in effect the responsibility for the environmental problems on the developed world, which moreover was best placed to address them. Developed countries should provide developing countries with the means to undertake counter-measures and build necessary technological know-how. To this end, the Global Environment Fund (GEF) was established in 1990.

Not surprisingly, sustainable development was the key theme of the 1992 Rio Summit. Agenda 21, signed at the summit, is the most ambitious international document on the environment ever adopted. The Climate Convention and the Biodiversity Convention were also adopted and the Commission for Sustainable Development (CSD) was established as well. This Summit marked the environmental movement's breakthrough on the international stage. It was the largest international conference ever launched and its apparent success was due not least to the widespread optimism of the early 1990s. The East–West conflict was over; economic prospects looked good; and people were generally confidant in the international community's ability to find ways of working together on policy. A further upshot of the Rio Summit and Brundtland Commission was the establishment and expansion of national and international governmental and non-governmental environmental institutions.

After the media spotlight focused elsewhere, however, so did the political will and capacity to follow through on the pledges made at Rio. Still, many local, national and international projects got off the ground. But the tenor of public policy remained the same, despite what observers were led to expect by the discussions of 1992. Those that expected the rich countries' readiness to extend a helping hand to the poor eventually saw the error of their ways. The enthusiasm that had driven the great environmental project forward petered out, and the 1997 New York Earth Summit+5, convened by the UN to review progress since 1992 was, to put it bluntly, a fiasco. It produced no new agreements, and sustainable development failed to fire the imagination of either the global public or the international political class. Increasing distrust between developing and developed countries contributed to stalling the process.

After the US fell victim to the terrorist attacks of September 2001, politicians had even less time for environmental problems. So when the UN's third 'mega conference', the 2002 Johannesburg World Summit (Rio+10), got under way, no one expected much from it. Unlike its predecessors, this conference examined the issue of poverty and development, partly at the expense of purely environmental issues. Poverty alleviation is basically about trade and aid, usually the business of other, much more practically inclined bodies than UN conferences. While the 'greens' noted success in Rio, the business community left its mark on the Johannesburg meeting. This was connected to the increasing focus on partnerships and multi-stakeholder processes involving the business community, environmentalists and governments. Whether initiatives like these actually promote sustainable development is contested. But the summit produced somewhat more than the pessimists expected, even if it was to all intents and purposes largely a repackaging of the UN Millennium Declaration of 2000, presently the most important benchmark of progress in environmental and development terms (Andresen 2007).

Attitudes towards environmental problems have changed considerably over the years. We understand more today about the problems separately and how to go about tackling them. From being an 'eccentric' pursuit of a few green activist groups in a few countries, it is now a major item on every government's agenda and on the agenda of an increasing number of non-governmental organisations too. Much of the impetus to integrate environmental and developmental thinking has come from the developing countries, and some of their demands have met with success, at least on paper, within the global conference system. Environmental problems are increasingly seen as problems for the international community. During the first decade of this century there was strongly renewed interest in the environment, particularly in the developed world, and particularly related to climate change. The peak was reached in 2007 and the first half of 2008. Then came the financial crisis. Some see this as an opportunity to build a new 'greener' world economy, while others maintain that the effect will be that the environment once more will be on the back-burner of the international agenda.

We turn now to a review of the international treaties and agreements concerning the environment. This is where high-minded ambitions are supposed to translate into practical measures and outcomes in specific areas, the chief concern of this book. It is easy for governments to swear allegiance to forward-thinking policies at international conferences because their pledges are not binding. International treaties are different. They are binding under international law on the signatories, and often require governments to initiate specific measures. The number of international treaties depends rather on how you count them, but there are several hundred, and most of them appeared in the last twenty to thirty years. The great majority are bilateral. There is a sizeable number of regional treaties as well, but far fewer global ones because environmental problems can usually be dealt with more effectively at lower levels. Nevertheless, the global treaties tend to get most attention both by policy-makers and the media. This is because they represent the environmental problems that are most difficult to solve. They also generate the most interesting political and economic debates. In the next section we take a closer look at the multilateral agreements and how they work in practice.

Organisation and development of international environmental agreements

The organisation of MEAs

As a rule, international environmental agreements build on a legally binding agreement between states, that is, a treaty or convention. There is no substantive difference between these concepts, but global agreements are more likely to be termed conventions. A convention or treaty is a starting point, a shell, to which rules and specifications – protocols or appendices – can be added to define and delineate the main principles. It helps to streamline operations, and allows for meetings at regular intervals for progress assessment, rule modification or supplements. For a convention to be binding in international law on the signatories, it needs to be ratified under the domestic laws of each state-party. Whether a treaty is put before a parliament or other representative assembly is also a matter for domestic legislation. A convention will generally stipulate the minimum number of ratifications for it to enter into force, that is, for it to acquire the force of law. If the agreement carries few liabilities for the state-party, ratification can often be fast tracked. But if the commitments are far-reaching or controversial, or both, ratification can take years. More than seven years were needed, for example, before the Kyoto Protocol on Climate Change came into effect. Parliamentary systems of government tend to work faster than federalist systems, such as the US, which proceeds very slowly indeed.

Multilateral arrangements will usually have a permanent secretariat tasked with preparing negotiation proceedings for the individual governments. The secretariat's capacity varies from treaty to treaty, but at a minimum it will organise inter-party negotiations. States-parties generally convene at annual or biannual Conferences of the Parties (COPs), the supreme decision-making body. Given the importance of these events, governments tend to despatch senior government officials, ministers or other political envoys. Governments maintain regular contact at lower levels, meeting counterparts more frequently than the annual conference of the parties provides for.

Many multilateral arrangements enjoy close ties to UN organisations, such as the United Nations Environment Programme, the Global Environment Fund and the UN Economic Commission for Europe. Membership of some of the global treaties is truly global, comprising virtually every state in the world, nearly 200 countries. But while the strongest nations deploy enormous teams of negotiators and staff, poor countries will often have to get by with a single delegate. A treaty will often appoint specialist bodies to compile and disseminate information of a technological and scientific nature. The number of specialists can reach several hundred. Lobbyists of every complexion are represented, such as the environmental and business lobbies. The media will usually have a prominent place as well. Overall, several thousand individuals performing various roles and functions are involved in negotiations, the sessions of which often last for weeks at a time. When so many countries convene to discuss issues of far-reaching importance to the way society is organised, consensus will often prove elusive. And despite the enormous cost of the exercise, it often results in unclear, watered-down half-measures. That many observers question the efficiency of the international community's environmental ventures, should therefore not surprise us.

The development of MEAs

The development of MEAs starts with the problem being identified, usually by scientists. Not all environmental problems make it to the level of international politics. Environmental problems may simply be ignored because the warnings promulgated by the scientific community are incomprehensible to non-scientists, and fail to ignite the blue touchpaper of political action. In many cases, the environmental movement contributes to 'translating' and simplifying the scientific message before urging politicians to do something about a given problem. When an issue reaches the agenda stage, very few governments will be in a position to take immediate action, usually because the action in question is expensive or departs from established practices.

Although multilateral treaties as a whole have been unable to overcome the great environmental challenges, it seems as if the situation would have been even worse without them. And treaties are becoming more ambitious and sophisticated. The first treaties, back in the 1970s, did little more than acknowledge a problem's existence and set out ambitious plans, but did not set targets or prescribe actions. The most important accomplishment of these agreements was waking the political establishment up to the problem and instigating systematic efforts to learn more about it.

During the 1980s, a new generation of agreements came into being. They were more enterprising in setting numerical targets and deadlines for emission cuts. The Montreal Protocol, a key document of the ozone regime, was one of the first agreements to adopt the approach, which quickly found its way into other agreements on air and sea pollution. Targets were often rather random, and not always well founded. But these agreements represented nevertheless a significant advance over the first generation, not least because progress (or lack of it) could now be measured. On the other hand, the one-size-fits-all approach was not always meaningful. The adverse effects came to light partly because economists were increasingly influential in these multilateral arrangements. Eyes pinned to the bottom line, they urged cost-effectiveness: decision-makers should make cuts where it cost least. As a mindset it informed the design of many agreements on the environment, marked increasingly in the 1990s by differentiated targets. Differentiation is also connected to another variable, nature's capacity to absorb or tolerate harm. The impact of acid rain is one well-documented example.

Protocols began to proliferate as supplements to the general treaties. If a new substance proved dangerous, it could be added to the protocol. Targets could be tightened and objectives delineated more precisely. The principle of fair treatment also encouraged differentiation. It is fair to give developing countries more time to reach the targets than the developed world. The principle has since been worked into many environmental agreements. The latest innovations are market and incentive mechanisms, incorporated in agreements such as the Kyoto Protocol. Long controversial, the approach has made headway of late. Not all issue-areas are amenable to a market philosophy: biological diversity is but one example.

Following on the rapid proliferation of treaties in purely numerical terms, social scientists have recently turned their attention to linkages between them (Oberthur and Gehring 2006). Do treaties overlap, pull in opposite directions or complement one another? Studies so far suggest there are as many synergy effects as problems stemming from treading the same ground or pulling in opposite directions. There has been a great deal of interest in what is viewed as a potential conflict between environmental treaties and trade, that is, regulations and standards issued by the World Trade Organization. As the MEAs become more ambitious and sophisticated they may challenge the rules of free trade. So far, this has not hampered the international efforts to promote a better environment, but the potential for conflict between the two sets of regimes is an undeniable fact.

As we have already remarked, international collaboration is more than formal regulations; it has cognitive and normative aspects. And international collaboration takes place across a wider spectrum today, with organisations and businesses setting up dedicated forums for pooling resources and designing joint initiatives. No longer do the government-dominated treaties and conventions discussed so far control international environmental policy alone. New policy tools emerged in the past decade, prompted not least by the increased pace of economic, political and cultural globalisation. In a parallel development, governments have forfeited influence in international politics and non-governmental actors of various hues have increased theirs. Within some issue areas, stakeholders that used to glare ominously at one another from either side of the environmental divide have engaged in partnerships: business, environmentalists and governments. While some observers are dismayed by what they conceive as the private sector's greenwashing and posturing – trying to convince the world of their innocence, instead of making a real effort – some are more inclined to welcome these new alliances as useful additions to the international web of treaties and conventions.

The rest of the book

Apart from an introduction and conclusion (Parts I and V), the book is structured, as we have said, around three thematic areas: air, water and nature protection/biological diversity. Each area has three chapters, dealing with a specific multilateral arrangement. In some cases the three selected arrangements have close ties, in others they are more or less solitary ventures. Part II deals with air pollution. Some of the substances discussed act in the lowest layer of the atmosphere (troposphere), while others affect higher levels (stratosphere). Chapter 2 looks at one of the major issues confronting international environmental politics in the late 1970s, that is, acid rain. The author examines the 1979 treaty on long-range transboundary air pollution and later protocols. This is one of the most sophisticated MEAs developed to date. Chapter 3 selects the most important environmental issue of the 1980s, the ozone hole and efforts to reduce ozone-depleting emissions. As a model of international diplomacy it was highly successful, and there were attempts to emulate it when a new environmental crisis loomed in the early 1990s, human-induced climate change. The Climate Convention was signed in Rio in 1992, and the Kyoto Protocol, signed five years later, introduced the first binding emission reduction targets. This we explore in Chapter 4.

Part III presents regimes tasked with the stewardship of the seas. Underlying both Chapter 5 on the protection of the marine environment by the law of the sea, and Chapter 7 on fishery management, is the 1982 Convention on the Law of the Sea. In the areas of pollution and resource management, it is supported by regional and more specialised global agreements. In Chapter 6 we examine in detail a regional regime for the protection of the marine environment, that is, efforts to stem pollution in the North Sea. In the area of fisheries management, the Convention on the Law of the Sea was joined by the 1995 Agreement Relating to the Conservation and Management of Straddling Fish Stocks and Highly Migratory Fish Stocks (Fish Stocks Agreement) which helped to strengthen regional fishery management regimes and the establishment of new ones. Chapter 7 reviews the work of these regional arrangements in the fisheries sector.

Three chapters on international policy on protecting the diversity of earth's flora and fauna follow in Part IV. Chapter 8 spotlights the 1992 Biodiversity Convention, but also discusses some of the classical con-servation agreements of the early 1970s. Chapter 9 devotes itself to work being done to preserve genetic diversity of agricultural plants. Key here is the Plant Treaty, adopted by the UN Food and Agriculture Organization in 2001. In Chapter 10 we take a detailed look at global forestry man-agement. There are many and diverse arrangements in place here, but as a whole, the regime is relatively spineless. Where governments have failed to agree on binding commitments, market-based systems of certification have been established. We summarise our discussion in Chapter 11 and ask whether MEAs have actually done anything to narrow the gap between ideals and reality and briefly discuss if and how performance can improve in the future.

Bibliography

Andresen, S. (2007) 'The effectiveness of UN environmental institutions', *International Environmental Agreements: politics, law and economics*, 7: 317–36.

Andresen, S., Skodvin, T., Underdal, A. and Wettestad, J. (2000) *Science and Politics in International Environmental Regimes: between integrity and involvement*, Manchester and New York: Manchester University Press.

Benedick, R.E. (1991) *Ozone Diplomacy: new directions in safeguarding our planet*, Cambridge, MA: Harvard University Press.

Breitmeier, H., Young, O.R. and Zürn, M. (2006) *Analyzing International Environmental Regimes: from case study to database*, Cambridge, MA and London: MIT Press.

Haas, P.M. (1990) *Saving the Mediterranean: the politics of international environmental cooperation*, New York, NY: Columbia University Press.

Miles, E.L., Underdal, A., Andresen, S., Wettestad, J., Skjærseth, J.B. and Carlin, E.M. (2002) *Environmental Regime Effectiveness: confronting theory with evidence*, Cambridge, MA and London: MIT Press.

Oberthur, S. and Gehring, T. (2006) *Institutional Interactions in Global Environmental Governance: synergy and conflict among international and EU policies*, Cambridge, MA: The MIT Press.

Scott, R.W. (1995) *Institutions and Organizations*, 2nd edn, Thousand Oaks, CA and London: Sage.

Skodvin, T. and Andresen, S. (2006) 'Leadership revised', *Global Environmental Politics*, 6: 13–28.

Underdal, A. (2002) 'One question, two answers', in Miles, E.L., Underdal, A., Andresen, S., Wettestad, J., Skjærseth, J.B. and Carlin, E.M., *Environmental Regime Effectiveness: confronting theory with evidence*, Cambridge, MA and London: MIT Press, pp. 3–46.

Victor, D.G., Raustiala, K. and Skolnikoff, E.B. (eds) (1998) *The Implementation and Effectiveness of International Environmental Commitments: theory and practice*, Cambridge, MA and London: MIT Press.

Weiss, E.B. and Jacobson, H.K. (eds) (1998) *Engaging Countries: strengthening compliance with international environmental accords*, Cambridge, MA and London: MIT Press.

Wettestad, J. (1999) *Designing Effective Environmental Regimes: the key conditions*, Cheltenham and Northampton, MA: Edward Elgar Publishing.

Young, O. (1989) 'The politics of international regime formation: managing natural resources and the environment', *International Organization*, 43: 349–75.

——(ed.) (1999) *The Effectiveness of International Environmental Regimes: causal connections and behavioral mechanisms*, Cambridge, MA and London: MIT Press.

Part II
Air pollution

2 Reducing long-range transport of air pollutants in Europe

Jørgen Wettestad

Important years

1968 Seminal article on long-range transport of air pollutants published
1979 Long-range Transboundary Air Pollution Convention adopted
1982 Germany changes from policy laggard to leader
1985 First sulphur protocol signed
1999 The integrated multi-pollutant Gothenburg Protocol signed
2010 Deadline for meeting obligations under the Gothenburg Protocol

Economic growth following the Second World War exacerbated the problems of air pollution in Europe. One method of reducing local problems in major emission countries like the UK and Germany was simply to make the smokestacks at coal-fired power stations higher in order to spread the polluting emissions over a wider area. This, however, created long-range transboundary air pollution which was particularly damaging for countries like Norway and Sweden, both of which began working in the 1970s for the establishment of effective international mechanisms that could address the acid rain problem. The effort led to the creation in 1979 of the non-binding framework agreement known as the Long-range Transboundary Air Pollution Convention (ECE/CLRTAP 2010) (hereafter Air Convention). When Germany discovered 'Waldsterben', that is, forest damage believed to stem from acid rain, within its own borders in the early 1980s, the international cooperation gained pace. The Gothenburg Protocol of 1999 is the most recent of a series of protocols to have reduced the problems significantly.

This chapter provides an overview of this exciting and dynamic process. First, the nature of the problem is discussed. What causes long-range air pollution, what is its impact, and what are the feasible abatement mechanisms? Six main substances are identified, each with somewhat differing central sources and hence differing abatement options and policy responses. This is followed by a chronological review of the collaborative effort which started with the 1979 Convention. Reflecting the variety of substances involved, eight main regulatory protocols have been adopted along the way. These have successively built upon each other and added up to a complex organisational structure. The next question concerns how actual emissions have developed and which main causal factors have been at work. Performance is found to be good overall, but still a bit uneven. Although these results are partly due to factors clearly not related to the collaboration grounded in the Air Convention at all, this collaboration has also mattered, not least in its contribution to knowledge improvement. The chapter winds-up with a concluding discussion and identification of some key research challenges ahead.

What's the problem?

By the end of the 1960s concern was rising especially in Sweden and Norway over increasing acidity of lakes and rivers resulting in higher fish mortality rates. There were reports of dead fish in southern Norway. Water acidity tends to be around 6 pH. Precipitation of sulphur dioxide emissions (SO_2) lowers it below 5 pH, a level that is lethal for fry and fish. In 1968 a Swedish scientist published an influential article on the phenomenon (Oden 1968). After citing evidence of damaged forests he posited a direct link between long-range air transport of SO_2 from the UK and Central Europe and acidification. As mentioned above, taller smokestacks discharged pollutants at greater heights in the atmosphere. Since the prevailing winds in Europe travel from the southeast to northwest, those emissions could be transported along the same route. However, at first, this was a theory with limited evidence to back it up. Initial scientific and political concern focused on sulphur emissions; they stemmed principally from power stations and factories (McCormick 1997). With regard to reducing the emissions, the principal mechanism was to install filters and purification systems. The technology was readily available at an early stage, but came of course at a cost. In the early days, leading emitters like the UK cited lack of scientific certainty as a reason for not installing the technology. A different approach to dealing with the impact of acid rain was to add lime to affected lakes and rivers.

As described in the following section, concern over long-range air pollutants would soon include emissions of nitrogen oxides (NO_x) (Gehring 1994). In addition to power stations and manufacturing plants, the transport sector (sea and land) is responsible for a significant proportion of NO_x emissions. Some also derive from oil extraction. NO_x emissions contribute to environmental acidification and damage. But they also affect local air quality and health of urban dwellers. In addition to filtering and purification technology in manufacturing, emissions from cars and boats need to be cut. This can be done by way of filtering technology (installing catalysers) or reducing traffic speed and volume (by, for instance, lowering speed limits and introducing toll payment schemes).

And as was becoming increasingly clear, emissions of volatile organic compounds (VOCs) represented an additional problem. VOCs stem from many of the same sources as NO_x emissions (i.e. land and sea transport and evaporation in connection with oil extraction), and contribute to problems both via long-range transport of air pollution and more local pollution in urban areas. They create together with NO_x a 'lethal cocktail'. The main counter-measures are largely the same as for NO_x. In addition there are technological fixes to reduce evaporation from oil during loading and unloading.

The impact of SO_2 and NO_x emissions is mainly regional and local. Two other types of substances are transported across very wide areas; their impact are global, insidious and long term. These are heavy metals such as lead, and persistent organic pollutants (POPs) such as the insecticide DDT and dioxins (Selin 2010). These pollutants stem essentially from manufacturing – especially of plastic products in the case of POPs, for instance. Over time, these emissions can represent a significant danger to health. The main counter-measure is abatement within industry and substituting these harmful compounds with less harmful substances.

Emissions from agriculture also play a role. The main pollutant here is ammonia. These emissions exacerbate the acidification and over-fertilisation of lakes and water systems.

An international air pollution abatement mechanism takes shape

As European long-range trans-boundary air pollution was soon acknowledged as one of the essential causes of the problem, an effective response would have to be international in scope (ECE 2004). At first the countries most aware of the problem were Sweden and Norway (Wettestad 2004). At the 1972 United Nations (UN) environmental conference in Stockholm the Swedes presented a report on acidification of soils and water and the like-lihood of declining growth in Scandinavian forests. A drop in forest growth in Sweden by as much as 10–15 per cent by the year 2000 was one of the prognoses.

Awareness was raised in Norway with the publication of the Government's long-term programme for 1970–73 which said, among other things,

> One particular problem to have emerged in recent years is the increasing acidity of rainfall over the Scandinavian countries, the consequences of which for fish stocks could be serious. ... Higher rainfall acidity is attributed to emissions from large industrial areas in Western Europe. ... The Government considers it of importance to follow up the international work on the problems of air pollution.
>
> (cited in Eliassen 2002: 14)

To strengthen the scientific basis a study called 'Acid Deposition – Effects on Forest and Fish' ('Sur nedbørs virkning på skog og fisk') was inaugurated in 1972. It was essentially a joint programme involving the Norwegian

Institute for Air Research, the then Norwegian Forest Research Institute and the Norwegian Institute for Water Research (Eliassen 2002). While this was proceeding, the Organisation for Economic Cooperation and Development (OECD) initiated a large-scale international programme for monitoring long-range transport of air pollutants, an effort in which the Norwegian Institute for Air Research would come to play a key role.

The first victory for Scandinavian 'air pollution diplomacy' came in 1975, and was connected to efforts at the time to facilitate a 'thaw' in East–West relations at this point in the Cold War. The final document from the Conference on Security and Cooperation in Europe named the environment, particularly transboundary air pollution, as an important area of East–West cooperation (Gehring 1994). This East–West dimension was instrumental in making the UN Economic Commission for Europe the logical forum for addressing the work ahead. The results of the monitoring programme, published in 1977, indicated widespread transboundary air pollution in Europe. Five countries stood out as particularly affected: Finland, Norway, Switzerland, Sweden and Austria. Negotiations commenced therefore in 1979 to forge an agreement on reducing transboundary air pollution.

At that time few states apart from the Nordic countries saw any need to establish a strong international mechanism to solve the problem. Key emitters like Germany and, not least, the UK, felt little affected by damages in their own countries and cared little for the role their emissions played in causing environmental damage in other countries. They were reluctant participants in the negotiations and strongly opposed to Nordic calls for quantified reduction targets. That an agreement came out of the process and was signed by all the main actors was largely because one wanted to build confidence and further a climate of East–West détente, an objective whose environmental significance was very slight. And the result was a loose framework convention with few commitments. Its overarching objective was to 'endeavour to limit and, *as far as possible*, gradually reduce and prevent air pollution including long-range transboundary air pollution' (Art. 2 of the convention; my emphasis).

The 1979 Convention on Long-range Transboundary Air Pollution was signed by 33 parties (32 countries and the EU Commission) in Geneva in November 1979 (Levy 1993; Wettestad 1999, 2002a, 2002b). In addition to the European countries, the US and Canada were also signatories. Apart from the overarching objective set out in Art. 2, the convention specified a commitment to develop joint strategies by exchanging information, consultation, research and monitoring (Art. 3). But a proposal to include a commitment to detailed and binding follow-up protocols was voted down. A desire was expressed to employ the best available and economically feasible technology. Among the emissions to be reduced SO_2 was mentioned explicitly several times in the convention text, in addition to 'other major air pollutants'.

The UN Economic Commission for Europe was chosen as the institutional foundation for the collaborative effort, and an executive body was appointed to function as an annual meeting of the representatives of the parties. In time this organisational structure was developed to include numerous working groups, more technical/scientific expert groups and programmes (Wettestad 2000). The working groups, such as the Working Group on Strategies and Review, form the more permanent element, while the other bodies come and go. This has been a gradual development connected with the need for more scientific research, and with technological and political clarification stemming from an improved understanding of the complexity and interacting nature of the problems. The Air Convention came into force in 1983 and the number of ratifying parties as of November 2010 was 51.

In November 1979 the activist Scandinavian countries scored an important intermediate success, the establishment of an international framework agreement. But it was little more than an empty shell, as already mentioned, and the countries continued to press the international community to fill it with material substance in the shape of a more binding agreement to reduce SO_2 emissions. On this point, the activists faced an uphill struggle since a key emitter such as the UK was still disputing the adverse effects of long-range air pollutants originating from Britain in countries like Norway and Sweden.

But from around 1980, concern was increasing in Germany about forest damage, which was believed to be related to rising levels of air pollution. The press and national media carried dramatic reports of widespread forest damage. In response then to an increasingly agitated German opinion, in 1982 the Government turned 180 degrees and adopted a completely revised approach to (long-range) air pollution (Wurzel 2002). A target of reducing German emissions by 50 per cent within the decade was established, and a more binding international sulphur agreement was warmly welcomed. Hence, the looser alliance of 'sulphur activists' was suddenly augmented with a major player on the international stage.

The alliance was committed to a 30 per cent reduction of SO_2 emissions, a target motivated by practical and political considerations (Haigh 1989; Wettestad 2000). On the one hand, 20 per cent sounded too little, on the other 40 per cent was obviously too high. The Germans were instrumental in speeding up processes within the EU to widen commitments in air pollution policy. They saw it as necessary to make sure that the tighter constraints on German industry were matched by similar constraints on economic rivals. In 1983 the EU Commission issued a draft directive on the reduction of emissions by large power stations and refuse disposal plants.

The issue was clearly gaining international momentum. The 30 per cent reduction proposal was supported by ten states at a minister meeting in Ottawa in 1984 (Gehring 1994). These dynamics led in the autumn of 1984 to negotiations on a protocol to reduce sulphur emissions. While the number of countries acknowledging the need for a more binding agreement was now substantially higher, some of the major emitters were still far from convinced. This was particularly the case with the UK, but also countries like Poland.

Inasmuch as the UN operates according to a philosophy of consensus among parties, the solution to the decision-making dilemma was to allow those countries still unconvinced of the case for a 30 per cent reduction target to refrain from signing the protocol. At the end of the day, 21 countries, along with the EU Commission, signed the protocol in Helsinki, July 1985 (hereafter the Helsinki Protocol). It became the first protocol to build upon and specify the Air Convention's pious hope of emission cuts. The protocol's central element was the commitment of the signatories to reduce SO_2 by at least 30 per cent 'as soon as possible' or 1993 at the latest. 1980 was adopted as the base year on which the 30 per cent cut was calculated (ECE 2004). The protocol came into force in 1987 and as of November 2010 has been ratified by 25 parties.

As early as Helsinki 1985 a consensus had started to form on the need for another protocol, this one covering nitrogen oxides, considered then to adversely affect both rural areas and urban air quality. Since the scientific and political focus had long been on sulphur emissions, there was an urgent need to research where NO_x emissions came from, their long-range transport and impact, as well as reviewing possible emission abatement measures. To this end several working groups were set up. Negotiations began in the autumn of 1986. As far as leaders and laggards are concerned, the emerging picture was not all that different from that in connection with the SO_2 negotiations. Sweden and Germany were two of the leading campaigners. In September 1987 these two countries, together with Austria, Switzerland and the Netherlands, proposed the same approach as for sulphur, that is, a 30 per cent cut in emissions (Gehring 1994).

But unlike the SO_2 negotiations, the Nordics this time round held more widely dispersed positions. Finland and Norway were hesitant, not wanting to go further than stabilise emissions within a given time limit. Norway was worried about the feasibility of cutting emissions in the shorter term from vessels plying routes along a highly indented coastline. The UK, France and Spain were of a similar opinion. Then there was a third group of countries which basically remained unconvinced of the need for any agreement at all. It included the Soviet Union, Canada, US and Italy. At the final round of negotiations in Sofia in 1988, agreement was reached on the need to stabilise emissions at 1987 levels by 1994 (hereafter referred to as the Sofia Protocol) (Levy 1993; Gehring 1994).

During the course of the negotiations an idea was gaining traction that policy and emission cuts should be designed so as not to exceed ecosystems' critical sustainability levels (or critical load). The idea was incorporated into the protocol as a basic principle of policy development in this area. In fact, a resolution was passed to initiate negotiations on a new, improved protocol within six months of the Sofia Protocol entering into force.

Twenty-five countries signed the protocol, including even laggards like Canada, Italy and the Soviet Union. The protocol came into force in 1991 and as of November 2010 has been ratified by 34 parties.

After the official negotiations were concluded, in response to certain countries' disinclination to go further than stabilising emissions, 12 countries decided to draw up a non-binding memorandum of understanding to cut emissions by about 30 per cent by 1998 (the base year to be chosen between 1980 and 1986). Not surprisingly, the group included former policy leaders like Germany and Sweden. It was more surprising to find the signatures of hesitants like Finland and Norway on the memorandum, indeed, even former foot-draggers like Italy.

Three factors can help explain this somewhat surprising mix of countries (Wettestad 1998). First, this was a non-binding political deal. Since it would be non-binding under international law there would probably be less scrutiny of how the different countries performed relative to their commitments. Second, the agreement gave the countries more time for implementation than the protocol did, and they enjoyed more flexibility with regard to choice of base year. Third, the EU had passed the directive mentioned above on reducing emissions from large combustion plants earlier that year, aiming to cut emissions from these sources by around 30 per cent. So in a sense this figure was not a totally new target for EU member states.

Scientific research into international air pollution was revealing an increasingly complex, intricate problem. The searchlight was now increasingly focused on a third category of substances, namely volatile organic compounds (VOCs). Insofar as NO_x and VOCs are highly interactive in nature, it made good sense to address VOCs immediately after adopting the NO_x protocol.

While negotiations on a VOC protocol got under way in 1989, it soon became apparent that the scientific knowledge about these emissions was far from adequate. The division of states into leaders and laggards was not dissimilar to that obtaining in the case of NO_x (Levy 1993; Gehring 1994). Germany and EU countries wanted a new 30 per cent protocol. A small group of countries wanted a more diluted, less specific text urging parties to cut those emissions which 'gave rise to long-range transboundary emissions' by 30 per cent. This group comprised Canada, Norway and the Soviet Union/Russia. Norway probably took this position because rising emissions from the oil and gas industry and the will and possibility to reduce them were causing concern. Most of the Eastern European countries constituted a third group; they wanted a stabilisation target like the NO_x protocol's. They emphasised lack of knowledge about their own emissions and were not willing to take on commitments they might not be able to honour.

In order to achieve consensus on a protocol text it was therefore decided to let all three groups choose the commitment they felt most comfortable with. Twenty countries and the EU Commission signed the protocol in Geneva

in 1991 (Geneva Protocol). Fifteen countries went in for a 30 per cent reduction of emissions by 1999, using 1988 as the base year (EU, Liechtenstein
and the US); two countries chose the watered down 30 per cent option
(Canada and Norway) and three countries chose stabilisation by 1999
(Bulgaria, Greece and Hungary) (Levy 1993). The protocol came into force
in 1997; parties ratifying the protocol as of November 2010 numbered 24.

As we will recall, the Helsinki Protocol had set 1993 as the deadline. It was
time therefore to assess compliance and discuss further regulatory steps.
As mentioned in connection with the NO_x protocol, the scientific community was favouring a critical loads approach. This meant that emissions
did not have to be cut as much in places where the natural environment
was more robust and resilient. The philosophy was considered sensible
also by economists who emphasised the need for flexible, differentiated
abatement targets. By now cost effectiveness had emerged as one of the
major principles on which to base international environmental policy.

With regard to the Helsinki Protocol, achievements for SO_2 around
1992–3 were generally speaking quite uplifting. Seven countries had cut
emissions by 50–60 per cent (including Sweden, France and West Germany)
and six had achieved cuts of 30 per cent (among them Norway, Finland,
the Netherlands and Italy). Only three Eastern European countries had
floundered somewhat.

Negotiations on a follow-on protocol to the Helsinki Protocol could
start, then, on a relatively positive note. Since 1988 several working groups
had been working on the mentioned critical loads approach. The work
was partly scientific and partly economic. Help was on hand from the
Vienna-based International Institute for Applied Systems Analysis in the
development of a regional data model. Different actions could be fed into
the model, which then worked out the likely impact and cost. Formal
negotiations began in 1992.

In 1993 agreement was reached on a basic approach for the new SO_2
abatement measures (Gehring 1994). This approach was based on a desire
to reduce the gap between emissions in 1980 and critical environmental
loads by about 60 per cent by the year 2000. Model runs automatically
produced the different ceilings for the different countries' emissions. These
ceilings were in turn used as a starting point in the final negotiations. It
turned out that many countries were willing to accept slightly more stringent
targets than the model had given them. After all, in the field of sulphur
emission cuts the performance of many countries had been impressive. The
Eastern European countries made it plain they would need more time than
allowed by the 2000 deadline. And old frictions re-surfaced when the UK
called for a more generous timetable than the majority felt was sensible.
For instance, Norway's then Minister of the Environment, Thorbjørn
Berntsen, berated the British, calling them 'shit bags'.

The protocol was approved finally in Oslo in 1994 and signed by
28 parties (Oslo Protocol). On the basis of the ambition of a 60 per cent

reduction of the gap between 'dangerous' and 'acceptable' emission levels, half the countries adopted a variety of targets to be met by the year 2000. For example, Germany would be making an 83 per cent cut; Sweden 80 per cent; Norway 73 per cent; and Spain 35 per cent. The other half took 2010 as their deadline, with 2000 and 2005 functioning as intermediate milestones along the way. For instance, the UK aimed at reducing emissions by 50 per cent by 2000, 70 per cent by 2005 and 80 per cent by 2010 (Wettestad 2002b). In addition to greater flexibility and varying targets, another interesting organisational development of the 1994 protocol was the appointment of a special implementation committee to monitor and discuss reporting and compliance of the parties with their commitments, calling attention to non-compliance and violations of the agreement. Eight legal experts would sit on the committee (Wettestad 2007). The protocol entered into force in 1998 and by November 2010 had been ratified by 29 parties.

Now 1994 was also the deadline for NO_x freeze agreed under the Sofia Protocol, but the progress here was rather less encouraging than in the case of sulphur. Of the 24 signatories to the 1988 protocol, 15 were in compliance with the protocol's stabilisation requirement. In Western Europe, only five countries had achieved significant reductions (between 15 and 25 per cent); only Austria was anywhere near to fulfilling the non-binding 30 per cent commitment. Several countries in Eastern Europe could report reduced emissions in excess of 30 per cent, but none of them had signed the 30 per cent agreement. Five countries performed particularly badly, with emissions rising by 30–70 per cent. Ireland's performance was worst, but Norway also lagged far behind its protocol commitments, with a 21 per cent rise in emissions (McCormick 1997).

In light of increasing knowledge of how the different substances interacted and the obligations under the Sofia Protocol to start new negotiations as soon as possible after that protocol entered into force, preparations for a more comprehensive and tougher follow-up protocol to the NO_x and VOCs commitments began around 1991. But it was not until the revised sulphur protocol was ready in 1994 that work on a new protocol under the Air Convention really began (Wettestad 2001, 2002a). Although new NO_x commitments were the main issue on the agenda, the evolving science on the interaction between substances and effects made it sensible to broaden the regulatory focus. By 1994, then, the aim was to have a protocol covering not only NO_x but VOCs and SO_2 emissions, along with a completely new source of pollutants in this context, namely ammonia emissions deriving mainly from agriculture. With an integrated approach like this, three important problems caused by the mutual interaction of these substances could be addressed: the classic acidification problem; the problem of smog and poor urban air quality; and a problem which until then had attracted scant attention, the eutrophication of forests and waters (ECE 2004).

In 1995, Sweden, Finland and Austria joined the EU. One of the first things Sweden did as an EU member state was to initiate the drafting of an EU directive similar to that negotiated under the Air Convention (i.e. the National Emission Ceilings Directive). Focus remained therefore on the same four substances and the same three effects. This dual track approach would produce several benefits. The EU had more money to spend than the Convention and could pay for expensive, sophisticated model runs and calculation work of practical use to both the EU and the Convention (Wettestad 2002a).

In between model runs and early political discussions on the design of this new 'integrated protocol', time was taken in 1997–98 to negotiate protocols on two other groups of substances whose impact on the environment and on people was clearly negative, though as mentioned before of a more incremental, long-term character, namely heavy metals and persistent organic pollutants. The two protocols on heavy metals and persistent organic pollutants were approved by 28 Parties in Århus in 1998 (Århus Protocols on Heavy Metals and on Persistent Organic Pollutants [POPs]). With regard to heavy metals, the parties undertook to cut emissions to the 1990 level (or any year between 1985 and 1990), though the deadline was unspecified. With regard to persistent organic pollutants, 16 substances were selected; half were banned with immediate effect, and half were given the 'yellow light' and phased out gradually (Selin 2010). The protocols on heavy metals and persistent organic pollutants entered into force in 2003; by November 2010 they had been ratified by 30 parties.

With the protocols on heavy metals and persistent organic pollutants in place there was time and space in 1998 to concentrate on finalising negotiations on the integrated multi-pollutant protocol. Model runs had resulted in a menu of four regulatory options, ranging from fairly modest emission reduction targets to more ambitious ones. In early 1999 Austria, Denmark, Finland, the Netherlands and Sweden suggested a middle-of-the-road solution. It was a policy these countries were pursuing in a parallel process within the EU, as mentioned above. Figures were presented indicating that the benefits would far exceed the costs. After a while, this proposal gained wide approval among the convention countries.

Is it possible then to identify leaders and laggards in the Air Convention negotiations on a multi-pollutant protocol? Some countries were indeed more enthusiastic and pro-active than others, but the picture is more nuanced than on earlier occasions. One reason is that the high number of substances and themes gave almost all countries special domestic industries and interests to protect. And it is worth noting how during the negotiations' final stages nearly every country modified the emission targets this 'moderately ambitious' model would strictly speaking impose on them. For example, important countries like France, Italy and Poland proposed such less ambitious emission targets. Towards the end of the process the EU Commission launched a draft of the parallel EU directive with stricter emission ceilings than the proposals on the table so far in the context of the Convention, but that did not inspire the Convention process much. Perhaps the most important change in national positions was the far more positive attitude emerging from the UK side. In fact, the British were among those few willing to go the extra mile in the final stages of the negotiations (Wettestad 2001).

Given all the themes and complexity of the negotiations, when agreement was finally reached on an integrated protocol in Gothenburg in December 1999 (Gothenburg Protocol) it was hailed as a great victory. It was the seventh and clearly most comprehensive and ambitious protocol under the Air Convention. Set against emission levels in 1990, the different countries' different objectives and emission ceilings resulted in the following over-arching emissions cut targets by 2010: sulphur emissions should be reduced by 63 per cent; NO_x emissions by 41 per cent; and VOC and ammonia emissions by 40 per cent (Wettestad 2001, 2002a). The protocol was signed by 31 parties and entered into force in 2005. As of November 2010, it has been ratified by 26 parties.

In the EU the parallel directive on 'national emission ceilings' was approved in 2001. The ceilings here were somewhat lower and more ambitious than those in the Gothenburg Protocol, but the difference was not striking (for example, the EU ceiling on NO_x emissions was just 2 per cent lower). The most important difference is that the EU has tougher compliance mechanisms, with the ultimate possibility that countries can be sentenced by the EU Court of Justice if they fail to comply with limits and deadlines. That sort of sanction is not available in the Convention context (Wettestad 2002a).

Performance and achievements

No further protocols have been adopted under the Air Convention since the year 2000. The agenda over the past few years has principally been to ensure implementation. We are passing the 2010 deadline, and with regard to the Gothenburg Protocol status as of spring 2008 was as follows: sulphur emissions were reduced by about 65 per cent. That goal was therefore reached, even though half the parties were struggling to fulfil their own specific targets. As mentioned earlier, reaching the NO_x emission targets is fraught with difficulties. These emissions have so far been cut by about 30 per cent and well over half the countries are struggling to reach their objectives. Emissions of volatile organic compounds have been cut by 38 per cent, so one is practically across the finishing line here. A small number of countries, such as Norway and Spain, are struggling though. Ammonia emissions are down by about 22 per cent; there's still some way to go here. What about the environmental effects then? Acidification in particularly vulnerable areas such as Norway and Sweden has clearly improved, and there is clear evidence of gains in relation to fish and bio-diversity. But progress stalled somewhat a few years ago. New research indicates higher environmental vulnerability in more places than previously assumed, so the 'critical loads' are still exceeded by about 10 per cent with regard to acidification in Europe (ECE/CLRTAP 2010).

Altogether, the regime has achieved significant results, even though more needs to be done, whether we are talking about acidification, NO_x or issues to do with urban air quality. Now there are several things which cannot be attributed *directly* to the measures under the Air Convention but which have helped improve performance. First, the Scandinavian frontrunners were joined in 1980 by a major partner, Germany. Germany's radical policy revision came about mainly in response to the domestic political situation. Second, during the 1980s, the British closed or converted coal-fired power stations into gas-fired ones, mainly for reasons to do with the economy and market ideology (Wurzel 2002). This helped from the early 1990s to turn the 'leading laggard', the UK, into a constructive partner. Third, the fall of communism in the East led to the closure of polluting heavy industry and far more open and trusting East–West collaborative relations. A fourth factor is that while the Air Convention, particularly in the early 1980s, had an effect on the EU, developments within the EU have gradually acquired a momentum of their own, and have clearly helped reduce emissions in Europe (Wettestad 2002a, 2002b, 2005).

But it is also widely acknowledged that multilateral efforts under the Air Convention *have* achieved things of significance. Most would emphasise the cognitive elements. The generation of new knowledge has been important. It gradually helped change national perceptions and positions, and made it possible to adopt far more flexible agreements which have further strengthened the determination to work constructively together (Munton *et al.* 1999; Wettestad 2000). The scientific structure has had a reasonably stable core. One key element here is the working group on effects. One also has a permanent group which acts as a meeting place and discussion forum between the scientific/expert community and bureaucrats/politicians (working group on strategies). Around this core looser, more temporary programmes have come and gone, coordinated by different lead countries. At the moment six such programmes are active (ECE 2004; ECE/CLRTAP 2010).

Turning to the normative aspects of the work, a key element is the development of the idea that emissions should not exceed critical thresholds/ loads in the environment. The seed was sown in the mid-1980s, but came to fruition only in the early 1990s. The idea provided useful reference points for the negotiations and the related possibility of justifying differentiated commitments fit hand in glove with the generally increasing emphasis on cost effectiveness and flexibility in international environmental politics.

Regarding the regulatory structure, flexibility is its most important feature. The regime has been able to successively address new groups of substances as a response to alarming scientific reports, establish new scientific working groups to clarify problems and possible fixes, and incrementally negotiate and add new protocols to the regulatory core (Wettestad 1999, 2005, forthcoming). The Air Convention has been useful in several ways, but the regime has not had particularly sharp 'teeth'. But while the Convention lacks a legal sanctioning mechanism like that of EU, the Convention's implementation committee has consistently reacted since 2000 to poor reporting and compliance with the protocols. This mild form of pressure has undeniably had some effect (Wettestad 2007).

Conclusions

All in all, the multilateral partnership to emerge from the 1979 Air Convention has grown into an impressive structure with a number of offshoots and good results. Eight protocols have been successfully negotiated, each new step addressing new issues or representing tighter control on emission levels. The most ambitious of these protocols is the 1999 Gothenburg Protocol, which is also widest in scope. Most success in terms of emission reductions has been recorded in the field of sulphur abatement; emissions have dropped by 65 per cent. This has led to a significant reduction in acidification-related damage in Europe. But the critical loads in the environment are still exceeded in vulnerable areas.

Many of these results are due in part to better scientific understanding and changed attitudes of politicians, bureaucrats and other involved parties to air pollution as a problem. It is hence clearly challenging to measure the exact impact of the multinational mechanism on these achievements. For instance, much of the research has been conducted under national auspices and would probably have been carried out also in a situation without the international regime. That caveat apart, we are reasonably sure that emissions in Europe would have been considerably higher in such a counterfactual, no regime situation. But how much higher is difficult to say. And as mentioned above, important events such as Germany's crucial policy about-turn and the fall of communism cannot be credited in any significant degree to the international air pollution regime.

With regard to the more specific question of regime design, the air regime has been quite cleverly designed, not least with regard to its strong focus on knowledge development and its dynamic and gradual style of development, differentiating and strengthening commitments as knowledge has improved and better technologies have become available. This has in turn led to the problems addressed by the regime becoming less malign over time. So there has been important *internal* interaction effects (Wettestad 1999, 2005, forthcoming).

The cooperation has continuously operated in the sensitive interface between the regional and the global. The primary focus has been Europe and the regional, but the underlying East–West détente encouraged the US and Canada to join the air regime as slightly exotic partners. When the focus began to shift in the 1990s to substances capable of travelling very large distances, such as heavy metals and persistent organic pollutants, it gave the global dimension an added meaning. The role of the EU has also changed over time, from that of a 'shy little brother' in the early days of the air regime to an independent and increasingly powerful partner from the 1990s onwards. Membership of the EU today is three times what it was in the early 1980s. So 'little brother' may already have matured into 'big brother' in the work to reduce air pollution in Europe. In fact, the over time increasing interplay between policy-making in the air regime and the EU may be one of the key factors which have helped turn the story of international air pollution into one of substantial success.

This interaction effect has probably been much more important than the fact that the increasing attention to climate change in recent years has taken some political energy out of the fight against air pollution. But then again, on balance, much climate change policy also has beneficial effects for the level of air pollution, so also this particular interaction may have been on the net positive side for the fight against air pollution spearheaded by the air regime. But there are still important remaining challenges in the international cooperation, not least related to the further reduction of NO_x emissions.

As to important research challenges ahead, as discussed in more detail in Wettestad (2005), a wave of air regime implementation research was started in the mid-1990s and ended just after the turn of the millennium (e.g. Underdal and Hanf 2000). As several years now have passed, is it perhaps time for a new wave of in-depth country case studies? In the case of the Air Convention, to my knowledge, very little implementation research has been carried out both with regard to VOC commitments and the heavy metals and POPs commitments. As several countries seem to have problems with their implementation of the NO_x commitments agreed to under the Gothenburg Protocol, this is a particularly interesting topic for closer scrutiny. And detailed studies of the implementation of the Gothenburg Protocol become increasingly meaningful and important, as the target date now has passed (i.e. 2010).

Bibliography

ECE (2004) *Clearing the Air: 25 years of the Convention on Long-range Transboundary Air Pollution*, Geneva: ECE.

ECE/CLRTAP (2010) Web site information on protocols, ratification, compliance, organisation, Online. www.unece.org/env/lrtap/html (accessed 17 December 2010).

Eliassen, A. (ed.) (2002) *Sur nedbør: tilførsel og virkning*, Oslo: Landbruksforlaget.

Gehring, T. (1994) *Dynamic International Regimes: institutions for international environmental governance*, Berlin: Peter Lang Verlag.

Haigh, N. (1989) 'New tools for European air pollution control', *International Environmental Affairs*, 1: 26–38.

Levy, M.A. (1993) 'European acid rain: the power of tote-board diplomacy', in P. Haas, R. Keohane and M. Levy (eds) *Institutions for the Earth: sources of effective international environmental protection*, Cambridge, MA: The MIT Press.

McCormick, J. (1997) *Acid Earth: the politics of acid pollution*, London: Earthscan.

Munton, D., Soroos, M., Nikitina, E. and Levy, M.A. (1999) 'Acid rain in Europe and North America', in O.R. Young (ed.) *The Effectiveness of International Environmental Regimes: causal connections and behavioural mechanisms*, Cambridge, MA: The MIT Press.

Oden, S. (1968) 'The acidification of air and precipitation and its consequences in the natural environment', *Ecology Committee Bulletin* (1), Stockholm: Swedish National Research Council.

Selin, H. (2010) *Global Governance of Hazardous Chemicals: challenges of multilevel management*, Cambridge, MA: The MIT Press.

Underdal, A. and Hanf, K. (eds) (2000) *International Environmental Agreements and Domestic Politics: the case of acid rain*, Aldershot: Ashgate.

Wettestad, J. (1998) 'Participation in NOx policy-making and implementation in the Netherlands, UK, and Norway: different approaches but similar results?', in Victor, D.G., Raustiala, K. and Skolnikoff, E.B. (eds) *The Implementation and Effectiveness of International Environmental Commitments: theory and practice*, Cambridge, MA: The MIT Press.

——(1999) 'More "discursive diplomacy" than "dashing design"? The Convention on Long-Range Transboundary Air Pollution (LRTAP)', in *Designing Effective Environmental Regimes: the key conditions*, Cheltenham: Edward Elgar.

——(2000) 'From common cuts to critical loads : the ECE Convention on Long-range Transboundary Air Pollution (CLRTAP)', in *Science and Politics in* Andresen, S., Skodvin, T., Underdal, A. and Wettestad J. (eds) *International Environmental Regimes: between integrity and involvement*, Manchester: Manchester University Press.

——(2001) 'The 1999 Multi-Pollutant Protocol: a neglected break-through in solving Europe's air pollution problems?', in Stokke, O.S. and Thommessen Ø.B. (eds) *Yearbook of International Co-operation on Environment and Development*, London and Sterling, VA: Earthscan Publications Ltd.

——(2002a) *Clearing the Air: European advances in tackling acid rain and atmospheric pollution*, Aldershot: Ashgate.

——(2002b) 'The Convention on Long-Range Transboundary Air Pollution (CLRTAP)', in Edward Miles *et al.* (eds) *Environmental Regime Effectiveness: confronting theory with evidence*, Cambridge, MA: The MIT Press.

——(2004) 'Air pollution: international success, domestic problems', in J.B. Skjærseth (ed.) *International Regimes and Norway's Environmental Policy: crossfire and coherence*, Aldershot: Ashgate.

——(2005) 'The effectiveness of environmental policies', in M. Betsill, K. Hochstetler and D. Stevis (eds) *Palgrave Advances in International Environmental Politics*, New York: Palgrave Macmillan.

——(2007) 'Monitoring and verification', in D. Bodansky, J. Brunnee and E. Hey (eds) *The Oxford Handbook of International Environmental Law*, Oxford: Oxford University Press.

——(forthcoming) 'The improving effectiveness of CLRTAP: due to a clever design? in R. Lidskog and G. Sundquist (eds) *Governing the Air*, Cambridge, MA: The MIT Press.

Wurzel, R.W. (2002) *Environmental Policy-making in Britain, Germany and the European Union: the Europeanisation of air and water pollution control*, Manchester: Manchester University Press.

3 International ozone policies

Effective environmental cooperation

Jon Birger Skjærseth

Important years

1974 Problem discovered
1985 'Ozone hole' discovered over the Antarctic; Vienna Convention adopted
1987 Montreal Protocol adopted
1990 Fund established to help developing countries
1992 New substances and time limits incorporated
1999 New substances and time limits incorporated
2007 95 per cent of production and use of substances under Montreal Protocol phased out

A discovery made in 1974 showed that man-made substances could damage the ozone layer. Today, the production and use of the main ozone-depleting substances have been phased out. The international community's handling of this problem is, in other words, a story with a happy ending. It came about largely because of the innovative way international cooperation was organised, reducing scientific uncertainty, adopting ambitious international targets and securing high compliance by nearly every country in the world. But it is also because the problem was easier to solve than many of the other global challenges such as climate change and loss of biodiversity. The production of ozone-depleting substances is not a matter of life and death for any individual company, country or the global economy as a whole; good substitutes for ozone-depleting substances proved relatively easy and inexpensive to develop. However, it is important to maintain momentum in the ozone cooperation because many challenges remain before the ozone layer can recover. A full recovery of the ozone layer is not expected until the middle of the century because the lifetime of ozone-depleting substances in the atmosphere is so long.

In this chapter we shall be looking first at how scientists discovered the problem and reduced uncertainty regarding the causes and effects of the depleting ozone layer. We ask how public authorities and the business community responded to the challenge from the scientists. In the third section of the chapter we shall see how innovative the international effort under the Montreal Protocol was in several areas, especially in the way developing countries were persuaded to join although the developed countries were mostly to blame for the problem in the first place. Finally, we discuss the effect of the cooperation on the production and use of ozone-depleting substances and depletion of the ozone layer.

The problem comes to light

In 1974 two chemists at the University of California, Irvine, Mario Molina and Sherwood Rowland, found that chlorofluorocarbons (CFCs) could damage the ozone layer. CFCs did not disintegrate in the lower atmosphere but ascended to the stratosphere where they accelerated the decomposition of ozone molecules. Major chemical companies where CFCs were being manufactured were among the least thankful for the scientists' discovery. In 1995, the two scientists (together with Paul Crutzen) received the highest possible recognition for their discovery, the Nobel Prize for chemistry.

CFC gases were developed by General Motors in the early 1930s. Because they were not particularly toxic, were inflammable, extremely stable and cheap in production, they were an immediate success. It is their stability though, which is the big problem for the ozone layer. Together with halons, CFC gases were used everywhere as cooling agents in fridges and cold storage plants, as propellants in aerosols, as aerating agents in plastic foams, as solvents for cleaning fabrics and extinguishing fires (halons).

The ozone layer acts as the world's 'sun glasses', protecting all living organisms from the sun's harmful ultraviolet radiation. The layer is like a thin membrane of gas in the stratosphere somewhere between 15 and 35 kilometres above the surface of the earth. Ozone-layer depletion can harm animals and plants. Plant damage can result in lower yields and less food production. Plant plankton can also be affected and harm the ecosystem of the seas. The problem can lead to immune system deficiencies and increase the likelihood of skin cancer, infectious diseases and eye disorders, especially cataracts. Increased ultraviolet radiation accelerates the decomposition of materials like plastic. All countries will be affected because the problem is global, even though some regions like Antarctica are more exposed than others. The biggest ozone reduction observed today is over Antarctica. In 1995, the extent of the 'ozone hole' was twice the size of Europe. The ozone hole describes an annual cycle of sharp declines in the months September–November during which the ozone layer can shrink by up to 60 per cent. After two or three months the ozone layer gets back to normal before starting on the next cycle. Ozone is produced and destroyed in a natural process, but the emission of ozone-depleting substances such as CFCs has disturbed this balance.

There was considerable uncertainty during the 1970s and 1980s about the causes and effects of ozone-layer depletion. Major research projects were initiated internationally and nationally, particularly in the US where much of the expertise on the atmosphere was gathered. Uncertainty remained high until the mid-1980s. The problem was complicated and not well understood. Scientists combined data simulation and satellite surveillance data, but in the absence of tangible evidence, uncertainty remained high. Research into the ozone layer had been going on for many years, but scientists were unable to demonstrate significant levels of ozone depletion (Skjærseth 1992).

A major international scientific programme got under way in the late 1980s headed by NASA and the World Meteorological Organization (WMO) and employing 150 scientists. Their aim was to inform authorities in countries across the globe as accurately as possible on the threat to the ozone layer from human activity. The next scientific breakthrough occurred almost immediately, but in another area. An article was published in 1985 in the highly respected scientific journal *Nature* concerning a discovery later known as the 'ozone hole' above Antarctica. While the involvement of CFCs was still far from clear, and different theories were proposed to explain the 'hole', these observations provided the first clue that something was seriously wrong with the ozone layer. The theory proposed in 1974 had in other words found its first support in actual observations. Shortly after the discovery of the 'ozone hole', the WMO/NASA programme submitted its results. Although this and other reports emphasised remaining scientific uncertainty, they spoke for the international scientific community when they warned that the problem was real and its impact likely to be serious if steps weren't taken without delay. A new comprehensive report appeared in 1988: there were strong indications that man-made ozone-depleting gases were the leading cause of the observed thinning of the ozone layer (Benedick 1998).

Four expert panels were set up in connection with the 1987 Montreal Protocol, bringing together 500 scientists and other experts (see below). One of the recommendations of their first report, issued in 1989, was to phase out all important ozone-reducing substances. Fifteen years after the problem was identified, decision-makers across the globe were given clear advice on what needed to be done to save the ozone layer. In the next section we shall see how authorities and business communities responded to this challenge.

International ozone cooperation

Negotiations to hammer out an international treaty on CFC reduction were initiated in 1981 with the appointment of a working group under the United Nations environment programme tasked with drafting a global agreement to protect the ozone layer. The science was still shaky, and CFC abatement was expected to be costly. The US had banned CFCs in spray cans as early as 1978. Canada, Sweden and Norway had followed suit. After a slow start the negotiations picked up speed with the creation of the so-called Toronto Group in 1985. Headed by the US, other members were Canada, Finland, Norway, Sweden and Switzerland. They aimed at reducing CFC emissions and tabled a ban on CFCs in spray cans, similar to bans introduced already at the national level. On the other side of the fence stood the EU arguing that a ban wouldn't be effective because CFCs were being used increasingly in other areas. The EU therefore proposed a ceiling on CFC production combined with a 30 per cent reduction of CFCs in aerosols. The EU had already enacted this reduction (Benedick 1998).

The positions of the US and EU reflected the situation in the market place. Europe and North America were the leading consumers and manufacturers of CFCs. The EU exported most, while the US consumed most of its own CFCs itself. The US no longer produced CFCs for use as aerosol propellants, while the EU's production of aerosol CFCs represented more than half of the total production volume. CFC production was limited to 17 companies in 16 countries. In 1986, 35 per cent was produced in the US, 36 per cent in Western Europe, 8 per cent in the Soviet Union, 3 per cent in Latin America and 18 per cent in Asia and the Pacific (Skjærseth 1992).

The outcome of this clash of interests was the absence of specific targets in the first international treaty on the protection of the ozone layer – the Vienna Convention. Passed in 1985 the Vienna Convention came into force in 1988. Many blamed the EU for the lack of progress. The Convention was formed as a framework agreement and signed by 20 countries and the EU. It required countries to share information and work together scientifically to understand the problem's atmospheric, technological and economic challenges. Just as important was the establishment under the Convention of procedures for adding protocols further ahead to reduce emissions.

Negotiations on such a protocol to the Vienna Convention started in December 1986. These talks were essentially bilateral, between the EU and US. The main issue was how much to phase out and by when. The US approach had grown increasingly radical since 1985. The US argued in favour of stabilising production levels of CFCs and halons over the shorter term and cessation across the board further ahead. The Nordic countries, Canada, and a few others supported the US position. The EU was split, and policy at the time was decided by those who wanted least. The Federal Republic of Germany had the highest ambitions, the UK the lowest. The British went to the negotiations hoping to get a lower production ceiling through. They then agreed to production stabilisation and a 20 per cent cut. Only months before the Montreal Protocol was signed in 1987, the UN delegates were worried the negotiations were on the verge of collapsing altogether. Finally, however, the EU capitulated and in 1987 24 countries and the EU passed the Montreal Protocol. It came into force in 1989 as a protocol to the Vienna Convention (Benedick 1998).

The protocol aimed at reducing production and use of CFCs and halons in developed countries by 50 per cent by 1999 using 1986 figures as the baseline. Developing countries were given an additional ten years to fulfil their commitments. In 1988, Britain's then Prime Minister Margaret Thatcher indicated a change of policy on the ozone problem when she announced that Britain would host a meeting in 1989 to consolidate what was achieved by the Montreal Protocol. At the meeting Britain supported the US motion to bring the production and use of CFCs to a halt by 2000. The rift between the US and Britain was therefore healed only 15 months after the Montreal agreement. The call to halt all production and use of CFCs and halons by 2000 was adopted formally at the second Meeting of the Parties in London, 1990. The number of Parties to the Montreal Protocol was now at 58, representing 90 per cent of global production and use of ozone-depleting substances. The protocol has been amended several times since then. More and more ozone-depleting substances are being controlled and the deadline for halting emissions has been brought forward. The Montreal Protocol is now ratified by 191 countries.

According to Mostafa Tolba, then executive director of the United Nations Environment Programme, money more than the environment dominated the talks. The chemical industry, especially Du Pont in the US which produced 25 per cent of all CFCs in the global market place, had been developing alternatives to ozone-depleting substances since the 1970s without making significant headway. The international deals, however, increased the pace of research and development radically. Just after the 1985 Vienna Convention Du Pont announced alternatives could be on the market within five years. The Montreal Protocol clearly signalled a halving of the CFC market by 1999. Only four months after the negotiations in Montreal, the industry had begun to coordinate research on CFC substitutes. One year later, reducing CFCs and halons by at least 50 per cent was considered entirely feasible. Over one hundred experts worked on the panel set up under the Montreal Protocol to monitor technological progress. In the report they published in 1989, CFC consumption could be reduced by 95 per cent by 2000, they said.

While the interests of the developed countries converged in many respects, the differences between the interests of the developed and developing world were more sharply delineated. Many developing countries were not involved in the Montreal talks because of fears of a negative backlash on their own economies from tight regulations and probably costly substitutes, while all the benefits went to US and European chemical companies. The developed countries were responsible for 88 per cent of global CFC consumption, but had less than 25 per cent of the global population. Mexico was the only CFC-producing developing country to sign the Montreal Protocol at first. Between 1987 and 1990, 71 countries ratified the Vienna Convention and signed or approved the Montreal Protocol, most of them developing countries. The developing countries contemplated continued production and use of CFCs because the substances were important to their economic growth. The Chinese refrigerator market was rising exponentially at the time.

In addition to the extra decade for meeting targets, the developing countries insisted on setting up a dedicated fund to provide technological and financial assistance as a means of improving compliance with the Montreal Protocol. The developed countries were positive to the idea, and wanted to put the fund under the World Bank and control it through the biggest donors, the US, Japan and Germany. A solution was found at the Meeting of the Parties in London, 1990, which approved an independent fund to be set up for a limited period of time with its own secretariat. A compromise was achieved on how the fund should be organised. The multilateral fund provided a precedent on which to base compensation of developing countries and has been adopted in other international environmental deals. As we shall see below, the Montreal Protocol broke new ground also in other ways.

Organisation of a ground-breaking cooperation

In addition to the multilateral ozone fund, creative thinking informed the approach to synchronising scientific collaboration, procedures for joint decision-making and compliance, and the use of trade restrictions to make the cooperation as effective as possible. Some of these arrangements provided models for subsequent international environmental agreements, including the cooperation on climate change. Although the different mechanisms play together, we shall look at them separately (OECD 1997).

In 1988, the United Nations Environment Programme began setting up the expert panels as mandated by the Montreal Protocol's Art. 6. It was, moreover, the same year as the Intergovernmental Panel on Climate Change was created. Four expert panels were formed at the first Meeting of the Parties in 1989. The Scientific Assessment Panel was tasked with exploring the extent of ozone depletion and related scientific questions. The Environmental Effects Assessment Panel assessed the implications of ozone depletion for the environment. The technology and economic panels considered availability and cost of alternatives for the ozone-depleting substances and were later combined to form the Technology and Economic Assessment Panel. The three panels were employed to provide information for political decision-making to tighten time limits across an ever growing inventory of ozone-depleting substances by periodic knowledge status evaluations. Comprehensive reports were issued in 1989, 1991, 1994, 1998, 2002 and 2007. An annual report is also published by the Technology and Economic Assessment Panel on the availability of alternatives to ozone-depleting substances. There is little doubt that these panels have enhanced the legitimacy of the ozone cooperation by reducing uncertainty and widening consensus among scientists. They have also increased the effectiveness of the cooperation. The information in the reports from the Technology and Economic Assessment Panel are frequently used by the Parties when designing proposals to tighten the control of ozone-depleting substances.

The heart of the ozone cooperation is the deadlines for phasing out use and production of ozone-depleting substances. Both use and production were included to avoid preferential treatment of certain regions. The engine in the cooperation has been to include new substances and tighten time limits on the advice of the expert panels. The cooperation is organised through the annual Meetings of the Parties to the Montreal Protocol and Vienna Convention. Important amendments to the protocol, including more substances and strict time limits, were incorporated in London (1990), Copenhagen (1992), Montreal (1997) and Beijing (1999).

The Montreal Protocol originally controlled just CFCs and halons. The London Amendment incorporated targets for carbon tetrachloride and methyl chloroform (1,1,1-trichloroethane). The Copenhagen Amendment added hydrochlorofluorocarbons (HCFCs), methyl bromide and hydrofluorocarbons (HFCs). While 191 countries have ratified the original Montreal Protocol, 179 have ratified the amendments of 1992, 159 in 1997 and 135 in 1999. Important issues on the agenda of the Meetings of the Parties in recent years have included the fund, ratification, compliance and trade with ozone-depleting substances. One controversial issue has been the regulation and exemption of methyl bromide 'for critical use', that is, in areas without workable technological and economic alternatives. Two extraordinary Meetings of the Parties were held in 2004 and 2005 to forge a settlement here.

The political process has been stimulated by effective decision-making procedures – rather unusually for international environmental cooperation at the time. Changes to the time limits are defined as 'adjustments'. Six months after adoption by the Parties, they automatically become binding on the signatories, thereby avoiding protracted ratification procedures within each country. These adjustments can also be adopted by majority vote, as in the EU. While unanimity is pursued in practice, the opportunity to resort to majority voting puts pressure on the Parties with the lowest ambitions since no country wants to be outvoted. New substances and changes to the protocol's provisions are defined as 'changes' and undergo more cumbersome procedures. Here, changes must be approved by a two-thirds majority of the Parties before they can enter into force. There are several special arrangements in addition to these procedures. As we have seen, developing countries had a decade longer to meet the targets. But this legitimised the Montreal Protocol's principle of shared but differentiated obligations. Everyone has to help mitigate the problem, but can contribute in different ways (Næss 2004).

The Montreal Protocol integrated financial and technological support to developing countries to help them meet their commitments. As we have seen, the Parties created a temporary multilateral fund in 1990 for this purpose. The fund became permanent in 1992 and, in addition to providing direct economic aid, is used to disseminate relevant information and training. The organisation of the fund balances the influence of developed and developing countries. The contribution of developed countries is set by the UN formula and smaller sums can be transferred as direct bilateral support. Projects are approved by an executive committee whose membership comprises seven developed countries and seven developing countries. Decisions are usually taken by unanimous vote, but can be passed with the backing of two-thirds of each group. Several UN bodies and the World Bank bring the support into the field, where the elimination of the use of ozone-depleting substances is the target. The International Monetary Fund provides economic support to Central and Eastern European countries not covered by the definition of developing country in the Montreal Protocol. In the period 1991–93, 160 million USD plus an extra 80 million USD was allocated to China and India on approval of the Montreal Protocol. From 1994 to 1996, 510 million USD was disbursed. Up to 2008, around 2 billion USD was transferred to developing countries via the fund. Although the fund is considered essential to induce developing countries to join in the effort to save the ozone layer, there were problems with delayed disbursements, particularly in the early years.

The Montreal Protocol introduced various trade restrictions as well (OECD 1997). The first type seeks to control trade with countries that are not party to the protocol. At the centre is the ban on importing and exporting controlled substances. This ban extends moreover to products containing controlled substances. It has been widened over the years as more and more substances come under its purview as the work has progressed. The second type seeks to control trade with ozone-depleting substances between Parties to the agreement. Illegal trade in, for instance, CFC-based cooling plants, is prevalent in many countries. The volumes traded are estimated to reach between 7,000 and 14,000 tonnes annually, or 10–20 per cent of the legal trade. An arrangement commits the Parties to the introduction of a licensing system to get the trade under control. Another arrangement concerns an export ban on non-complying Parties with the time limits set in the Montreal Protocol on phasing out the use and production of controlled substances.

Several of the described mechanisms encourage compliance with the Montreal Protocol. The protocol also contains a system connected directly to compliance. The negotiating Parties sought to build a system which encouraged rather than punished countries struggling to meet their commitments. The carrot – in the form of aid – should stand out, not the stick in the form of sanctions. In this philosophy the root of the compliance problems lies in inadequate economic, technological and administrative capacity than in a lack of political will. The Parties were therefore encouraged to report non-compliance difficulties themselves. Other Parties and the secretariat may also do this.

The compliance mechanism consists of an executive committee which deals with the 'reports'. The committee is made up of representatives of the member countries from different regions. They consider the items on the agenda but have no decision-making authority on steps to be taken. It was apparently set up at the initiative of Trinidad and Tobago – which goes to show that influence isn't the prerogative of the bigger countries in international environmental cooperation if the ideas are good enough. The committee reports to the Meeting of the Parties, which has the authority to enact necessary measures on the advice of the committee. These measures tend to include various forms of financial and technological assistance, but there is an opportunity to caution and suspend countries if the carrot method doesn't produce the desired result. One problem has been non-compliance by countries with transitional economies in Central and Eastern Europe. In 1997, for instance, Latvia, Lithuania, the Czech Republic and Russia reported compliance problems. Russia has been particularly problematic because of the extent of its ozone-depleting substance industry. Recent years have seen other countries make it to the top of the 'black list'. At the 2006 Meeting of the Parties, for example, countries across several continents were censured for non-compliance: Armenia, Congo, Ecuador, Greece, Kenya, Pakistan, Serbia and Iran.

The different institutional arrangements show how the ozone cooperation works through normative, cognitive and regulatory mechanisms. It is the balance between them that has been important in the ozone cooperation – not the individual mechanism per se. The most important cognitive mechanism is the joint scientific undertaking which systematically mapped causes, effects and measures. Public authorities and the business community have responded to the challenges by adopting regulatory measures, the heart of which is the date set for phasing out use and production of an increasing number of ozone-depleting substances. An important normative principle is compensation for developing countries via various mechanisms to ensure high participation and compliance.

A solution to the problem?

According to the United Nations Environment Programme, the production and use of ozone-depleting substances has been gradually phased out in developed countries and the same is about to happen in developing countries. Altogether, more than 95 per cent of all production and use of chemicals controlled by the Montreal Protocol is phased out. Because the lifetime of ozone-depleting substances in the atmosphere is so long, it can take a long time before the ozone layer can be said to have recovered its health. Measurements around the globe have shown how the ozone layer has thinned since the 1980s. As we have seen, the reduction was particularly severe over the Antarctic, where the biggest 'ozone hole' was measured in 2006. That said, the latest measurements seem to indicate an improvement in the state of the ozone layer. If the emission cuts continue, the ozone layer will probably recover in 2050. It would then be in the condition it enjoyed before 1980. If all emissions of ozone-depleting substances had stopped immediately, the ozone layer would be fully recovered by 2035.

A full recovery requires first that the Montreal Protocol Parties continue to observe their commitments. The amount of certain substances, like halons and HCFCs, continues to rise in the atmosphere, but will fall if the Parties keep true to their commitments. HCFCs are used as substitutes for CFCs, but are far less noxious to the ozone layer. The manufacture and use of HCFCs have risen sharply in recent years despite the full phase-out of use by 2030. This target was moved forward from 2040 at the 2007 Montreal Meeting of the Parties. Second, progress will depend on other man-made and natural factors. Volcano eruptions, solar activity, changes in the composition of the atmosphere and, not least, climate change could affect progress. Although climate change and depletion of the ozone layer should be considered separate problems, they are woven together in a highly complex way which is still subject to uncertainty. While climate change warms the lower layers of the atmosphere, it causes the stratosphere to cool, especially over the Arctic and Antarctica. This could in turn accelerate the depletion of the ozone layer. At the same time, ozone is a greenhouse gas: that is, the depletion of the ozone layer could contribute to mitigate climate change. But the majority of ozone-depleting gases are also powerful greenhouse gases.

There is little doubt that the international undertaking under the Montreal Protocol has succeeded in lowering the amount of ozone-depleting substances by adopting a sophisticated organisation of the international cooperation. So far, it has successfully set ambitious targets for ozone-depleting substances, encouraged broad participation and facilitated high compliance. Most independent analyses of the cooperation also give the Montreal Protocol high marks for effectiveness – perhaps the most successful global environmental agreement currently in existence. Precisely how effective the cooperation has been is difficult to say, however. According to the United Nations Environment Programme, the amount of ozone-depleting gases in the stratosphere would have been five times greater today without the Montreal Protocol. But continued international work is still important to reach the goal. The most important challenges are to ensure continued compliance, elimination of illegal trading, phasing out of ozone-depleting substances in developing countries and dealing sensibly with the large amounts of ozone-depleting substances still in circulation in, for example, old refrigerators and freezers. In addition, it is important to coordinate different international agreements to prevent ozone-depleting substances in the process of being phased out being replaced by substances likely to exacerbate other problems, such as climate change, for example.

Conclusions

In this chapter we have seen how independent discoveries and wide-ranging international research programmes have gradually unlocked the causes of the depletion of the ozone layer and, not least, revealed what can be done to solve the problem. In contrast to what applies to many other global challenges, the authorities and business community worldwide have responded by putting in place effective mechanisms. Internationally, an innovative and sophisticated regime was established which ensured participation of developing countries, ever-tightening control of an ever-growing inventory of ozone-depleting substances and high levels of compliance. The result has been a sharp fall (95 per cent) in the use and production of ozone-depleting substances. Compared with other global challenges, the problem of the production and use of ozone-depleting substances is relatively easy to solve because the substances are not critical to other activities and substitutes proved relatively inexpensive to devise. In other words, a positive interplay between a relatively benign problem and effective cooperation has contributed to the good results.

Because ozone-depleting substances have a long lifetime, it may not be possible to give the ozone layer a clean bill of health before 2050. That depends first on the impact of other natural and man-made factors such as climate changes. Second, it depends on continued compliance by the Parties to the Montreal Protocol with their commitments. Other challenges remain, including illegal trading in ozone-depleting substances, manufacture of ozone-depleting substances in developing countries and responsible handling of large quantities of substances which are still in circulation.

Bibliography

Benedick, R. (1998) *Ozone Diplomacy: new directions in safeguarding the planet*, 2nd edn, London: Harvard University Press.

Næss, T. (2004) 'Ozone: a success story on all fronts?' in J.B. Skjærseth (ed.) *International Regimes and Norway's Environmental Policy: crossfire and coherence*, Aldershot: Ashgate.

OECD (1997) *Experience with the Use of Trade Measures in the Montreal Protocol on Substances that Deplete the Ozone Layer*, Paris: OECD.

Skjærseth, J.B. (1992) 'The successful ozone-layer negotiations – are there any lessons to be learned?', *Global Environmental Change*, 2: 292–301.

4   International climate cooperation

Clear recommendations, weak commitments

Steinar Andresen and Elin Lerum Boasson

Important years

1988   Toronto Conference
1988   UN Intergovernmental Panel on Climate Change (IPCC) created
1992   Climate Convention adopted
1995   Berlin hosts first Conference of the Parties to the Convention
1997   Kyoto Protocol adopted
2001   US withdraws from Kyoto negotiations
2001   Marrakesh Accords – detailed rules for implementing Kyoto Protocol
        adopted
2005   Kyoto Protocol enters into force
2007   Bali Roadmap
2009   Copenhagen Accord
2010   Cancun Agreement

More than fifty years have passed since scientists first pointed to human activity as a contributing cause of changes in the earth's climate. All the same, climate change did not become an issue of major political importance internationally until the late 1980s. Making up for lost time, it attracts more political attention nowadays than any other environmental problem. Since the early 1990s, climate change has been the subject of protracted and deepening international political conflicts both within the North as well as between the North and the South, amply demonstrated at COP 15 in Copenhagen, 2009.

We start out by explaining what this environmental problem is all about and will show that climate change is an incredibly complex and a typically 'malign' problem. Then follows a summary of the four main components of the climate regime, the Intergovernmental Panel on Climate Change (IPCC, 1988), the Climate Convention (1992), the Kyoto Protocol (1997) and the Copenhagen Accord (2009). The Cancun Agreement of 2010 imported the essential elements of the Accord into the Climate Convention. In the next section we review the political process of agenda-setting and negotiations before evaluating what has been achieved. In the concluding section we sum up our findings, briefly address how the process can be explained and discuss the future of the climate regime.

What is the problem?

The natural greenhouse effect keeps the earth's climate system in balance. It's been doing this for millions of years. Over time the global mean temperature has fluctuated slowly by a few degrees. Today, however, the climate is changing at an unprecedented rate. For many years scientists could not agree on the explanation. We know now, though, that rising concentrations of carbon dioxide in the atmosphere trap the sun's rays longer before they are reflected back into space. In 1990, the IPCC said there was a more than 50 per cent chance that human activity was the leading cause of the growth in atmospheric carbon dioxide; by 2007, the probability had grown to 90 per cent (Solomon *et al.* 2007). Climate change, they contended, had already begun.

Human activity produces emissions of carbon dioxide, methane, nitrous oxide and some fluor and sulphur compounds. More than 50 per cent of these emissions are carbon dioxide from fossil fuels with 20 per from deforestation and other sources. Before the Industrial Revolution the concentration of greenhouse gases in the atmosphere was 270 ppm (parts per million or millionths of the atmosphere). By 2005, the concentration was 319 ppm. There is no scientific consensus on the level at which carbon dioxide should be stabilised to avoid calamitous climate change, but it is probably 450 ppm or less. Even this is expected to increase global temperature by 2°C, which may be hazardous enough. In order to reach this goal, greenhouse gas emissions will have to be cut by 50–80 per cent as soon as possible

The impact on the global climate will be the same wherever the gases are emitted. Historically, the wealthy countries have been the main emitters, but developing countries now account for the majority of emissions and their share of total emissions will rise steeply (Røgeberg *et al.* 2010). At present, however, measured per person, emissions from the wealthy countries are four times higher.

Climate change will cause sea levels to rise, and change local weather patterns. It will have a negative effect on wildlife, biological diversity, health, food security, buildings, transport systems and economic activity. A worst-case scenario envisions natural disasters, famine, decimation of entire communities. A warmer climate can also have some positive consequences in some parts of the world, for example improving yields from agriculture in Northern Europe. The negative consequences can be offset by adaptation to climate change, by taking preparatory measures to meet the severe weather events and by incorporating climatic conditions in planning, for example by anticipating rising sea levels and higher temperatures in housing developments and road building plans. Until recently, it was commonly assumed that developed countries would manage to accommodate such changes. According to the IPCC, the poorest countries face by far the biggest challenges, but the wealthy countries will also run into difficulties as they seek to adapt (Parry *et al.* 2007).

The negative consequences for society of climate change can be mitigated, by cutting emissions and taking adaptive steps (Metz *et al.* 2007). Today, nearly 80 per cent of the energy consumed by the world comes from the burning of coal, oil and gas. These emissions could be reduced by going over to renewable energy or by carbon capture and storage. However, this is a slow and often also costly process, in particular because coal is cheap and abundant in major emitting countries like China and the US. Emissions of carbon dioxide from deforestation and much of the methane and nitrous oxide that is emitted can be traced back to the way humans use land, especially the deforestation of the rain forests (see Chapter 10). Emission reductions will necessitate changes in the farming industry, waste handling and nature management. Again this is a cumbersome, slow and difficult process but there are interesting developments under way in this regard. According to the IPCC there are expertise and technology readily available that may contribute to alleviating the problems associated with climate change without appreciably damaging the global economy. If this perception had been shared among the nations of the world, more action would have been taken to counter climate change. This has not happened. For the world to move in the direction of a low-carbon economy the behaviour of ordinary people as well as businesses and industry will need to change radically. In addition, questions of fairness and equity loom large between rich and poor countries, adding to the difficulty of the problem. There is no 'silver-bullet', a cheap technological 'fix' to this problem as is the case for the ozone regime (see Chapter 3).

The major components of the climate regime

In what follows we review the four components of the international climate regime, the IPCC, the Climate Convention (1992), the Kyoto Protocol (1997) and the Copenhagen Accord (2009). The text is based primarily on the official negotiation texts and the IPCC's assessment report from 2007.

The IPCC is a scientific forum consisting of three sub-groups. They work to formulate common conceptions of the causes of the climate problem, its consequences and ways of meeting it. Working Group I is responsible for atmosphere and meteorology; Working Group II looks at the effects of climate change and adaptation; and Working Group III focuses on emission cuts. They condense the current state of knowledge in their respective areas.

The IPCC published Assessment Reports in 1990, 1995, 2001 and 2007. The draft reports undergo two comprehensive reviews, first by experts, then by governments, illustrating the intergovernmental nature of the panel: it is not a purely scientific one. After the lead authors have incorporated comments from reviewers, the final draft reports are submitted for approval to a panel of experts and government delegates. The scientific reports themselves usually go through without much debate, though the summaries may be the object of hard political negotiations. The final text, the summary for policy-makers, while basically a scientific document, also bears the influence of the policy-makers. Until quite recently most observers expressed confidence in this meticulous procedure. Irrespective of the recent criticism, in the course of the more than twenty years since the IPCC came into existence, significant steps forward have been made in the underlying science.

The Climate Convention is the overall framework for intergovernmental efforts to tackle the challenges posed by climate change and is ratified by practically every country in the world. First, the Convention sets out an ultimate objective of the Parties. It is to achieve the

> stabilization of greenhouse gas concentrations in the atmosphere at a level that would prevent dangerous anthropogenic interference with the climate system. Such a level should be achieved within a time frame sufficient to allow ecosystems to adapt naturally to climate change.
>
> (Art. 2)

Second, responsibility for the current state of affairs is laid at the door of developed countries which should therefore bear the greater part of the burden of solving it, in accordance with the Parties' 'common but differentiated responsibilities' as well as respective capabilities. The Convention also encourages Parties to reduce emissions and take adaptive action. The wording on adaptation nonetheless urges the wealthy countries to help developing countries meet the costs of adaptation.

The Convention sets out certain formal regulations. It establishes the formal structure around international cooperation on the climate, obliges all Parties to compile detailed national inventories of greenhouse gas emissions and mandates the establishment of an international climate secretariat. However, the Climate Convention does not contain any legally binding emissions reductions, only a 'soft' call for the developed nations to stabilise their emissions by the year 2000 compared to 1990 levels.

Based on the Convention's normative foundation, the Kyoto Protocol sets out formal rules in more detail compared to the Climate Convention. These can be divided into the following broad categories: 1) emission commitment levels; 2) methodologies for estimating emissions; 3) commitments regarding emission reductions and climate change adaptation; 4) procedures for ensuring compliance with commitments and addressing non-compliance; and 5) transfer of resources from developed to developing countries.

The Kyoto Protocol sets an upper limit to the emission amounts assigned to each developed country (Annex I) in the period 2008–12, compared with 1990 levels. On average, these countries shall reduce their emissions by 5 per cent, but variation within the group is relatively wide. The European Union (EU) stands apart because the Union as such was assigned an overall emission level target, rather than every individual EU member state. According to the Protocol, all six greenhouse gases should be included in the audit (that is, four greenhouse gases and two groups of these gases: carbon monoxide, methane, nitrous oxide, sulphur hexafluoride, hydrofluorocarbons, perfluorocarbons). Shipping and aviation are not included in the agreement, leaving out some major emission sources from the common international effort.

Cost effectiveness and flexibility are keywords in the Protocol's rules on implementing emission cuts. Given certain conditions, a Party can credit emission cuts made in one or several other countries to its own climate audit. There are three flexible mechanisms by which this can be achieved: 1) purchase of climate allowances: emission allowances from a different country (emissions trading); 2) joint implementation: facilitating concrete climate measures in another country *with* climate commitments; or 3) use of the Clean Development Mechanism (CDM): facilitating concrete climate measures in another country *without* climate commitments. The two latter mechanisms may result in emission credits that are traded in emission trading markets, but in practice only CDM credits are traded. These mechanisms, it is important to emphasise, should be supplemental to domestic emission reduction measures. A country's emission reductions cannot be made entirely outside the country; governments are free, however, to decide how much of their commitment should be met abroad. Parties shall further prepare national programmes containing measures in the energy, transport and industry sectors, and in agriculture, forestry and waste management. These programmes shall contain measures to mitigate climate change and measures to facilitate adequate adaptation to climate change. Users of the CDM shall pay a fee to help fund climate adaptation in developing countries.

The Kyoto Protocol provides for the establishment of expert review teams that check the veracity of information submitted by the Parties. Parties emitting more than their assigned allowance will have their allowance reduced for the ensuing period by 30 per cent. The wealthy countries are required to transfer resources to poor countries to help them reduce emissions and adapt to climate change.

The Copenhagen Accord endorses the continuation of the Kyoto Protocol and emphasises the principle of common but differentiated responsibilities but it has no formal standing in the United Nations (UN) negotiations. This changed after the adoption of the Cancun agreement. The Accord recognises the scientific view that the increase in global temperatures should be below 2 degrees Celsius but it is not legally binding like the Kyoto Protocol. It strengthens the general tendency to emphasise adaptation more strongly, especially in the vulnerable least developed states. Annex I Parties would commit economy-wide emission targets for 2020 while developing nations (non-Annex I Parties) would implement mitigation actions (Nationally Appropriate Mitigation Actions) to slow growth in their carbon emissions. However, the targets are set individually by the Parties and goals and actions were to be submitted by 31 January

2010. The Accord also recognises the crucial role of reducing emissions from deforestation and forest degradation in developing countries (REDD +) and to establish a new mechanism to mobilise financial resources. The Parties further agreed that developed countries would raise funds of $30 billion from 2010 to 2012 and that the world should raise $100 billion per year by 2020 to help developing countries cut carbon emissions. Finally, a Copenhagen Green Climate Fund as an operating entity as well as a Technology Mechanism were established. As all Parties did not accept the Accord, it was not formally adopted, only 'taken note of', while the Cancun Agreement in the final end was formally adopted by all Parties and all the main elements of the Accord were integrated in the Agreement.

Stated simply, we can say that the IPCC helps shape the cognitive perception of the climate problem, the Convention gives it its normative orientation in the form of principles and ultimate goals, and the Protocol provides the formal rules for states' conduct. The mitigation targets pledged under the Accord are formally adopted into the Convention through the Cancun Agreement, marking the first time all major economies have pledged explicit action under the UN regime since negotiations launched some twenty years ago.

The making of the international climate regime

It was in the 1950s that systematic scientific research started on the earth's climate, marked not least by the 1957 International Geophysical Year (Andresen and Agrawala 2002). Several transnational scientific networks emerged in the 1960s and in the 1970s the political relevance of climate change was highlighted by the United Nations Environment Programme in pointing to the social impact of climate change. It was not until 1988, however, that it became an item on the international political agenda, helped by the Toronto Conference of the Atmosphere. This was also the year the World Meteorological Organization and United Nations Environment Programme together established the IPCC. By then, the green movement had entered the scene and was restating the findings of the scientific community in even starker terms. At an individual level, the Conference was a forceful combination of activist scientists, activist politicians and green non-governmental organisations, but it also coincided with an unusually hot summer in the US. NASA scientist James Hansen made headlines when he told Congress that he was 99 per cent certain that the high temperatures indicated real warming trends. In terms of politics, the stakes had suddenly increased. According to the declaration, developed countries should reduce their carbon dioxide emissions by 20 per cent by 2005. It is easy to see today how unrealistic and optimistic this target was; the complexity of the issue was simply not grasped at the time. Nevertheless, the declaration was very important in providing a template for subsequent negotiations on similar matters. First, it called for the developed countries to take the lead and second, it introduced the so-called target and time-table approach.

The next two years saw numerous international conferences on climate change convened by different governments with increasing numbers of participating countries. Given the public support for green issues in most of the Organisation for Economic Cooperation and Development region it quickly became something of a 'green beauty contest' among certain wealthy countries to adopt the most ambitious emission commitments. Gradually, however, the major players took over the process, primarily the US and EU, and ambitions were toned down. 'Activist states' and environmental organisations lost some of their influence while the EU emerged as a pusher, and the US took the role of laggard.

In 1989 the UN General Assembly decided a Climate Convention should be negotiated under the auspices of the UN and all countries of the world were thereby invited to attend. 1991 marked the start of the official UN negotiations. Six negotiation sessions were arranged prior to the adoption of the Climate Convention at the Rio Summit in 1992. Activist states and the environmental movement wanted the rich countries to adopt a legally binding target to stabilise emissions by the year 2000, but the US rejected this idea. The US was the most influential actor during the negotiations and the outcome was a 'soft' declaration of political intent to stabilise emissions by the year 2000 for the rich countries (Annex I) with no reduction targets for developing countries (Andresen and Agrawala 2002). As shown in the above, a number of principles were also adopted. Virtually every country in the world signed the final Convention text at the global summit in Rio in 1992 and the Convention came into force in 1994.

The first Conference of the Parties to the Convention (COP 1) was arranged in Berlin in 1995. This led to the Berlin Mandate which stressed the need to strengthen Annex I commitments beyond the year 2000. At the time, Al Gore was vice-president of the US. He had been campaigning since the early 1980s to raise climate awareness and the US therefore agreed with the EU to start talks on legally binding emission reductions. The next milestone was COP 3 in Kyoto, 1997. After protracted negotiations, agreement was finally reached on a protocol text. In the final stages of negotiations prior to the Kyoto Summit, traditional state bargaining proceeded more or less behind closed doors. 'One broad observation is that for all the academic speculations about the decline of the nation state in the era of economic globalisation, the Kyoto Protocol is very much an agreement stuck by governments' (Grubb *et al.* 1999: 112). The Kyoto Protocol was a genuine compromise. Developing countries succeeded in their bid to avoid legally binding targets. The EU successfully campaigned for legally binding emission reductions, while the US was the main architect behind the so-called flexible mechanisms. Nevertheless, the US was the most influential actor. The US provided most of the ideas contained in the final Protocol. Neither the EU nor the environmental organisations supported the flexible mechanisms which would basically let countries buy themselves free of their domestic commitments. While the US Administration was able to convince its international counterparts to accept the design of the Protocol, it failed to convince the US Senate of the need for such an agreement. In July 1997 the Senate unanimously adopted the Byrd-Hagel resolution which implied that an international agreement that did not include 'meaningful' developing country participation would not be ratified. The Kyoto Protocol was therefore never submitted to the Senate for ratification.

Moreover, it soon became apparent that the delegates to the Kyoto Conference had in fact failed to agree on a number of issues. The Protocol provided the overarching principles and emission targets, but many ambiguous formulations invited a diversity of interpretations. At the fourth Conference of the Parties, a two-year action plan was adopted whereby detailed rules of procedure would be drafted. At the start of the sixth Conference of the Parties at the Hague in 2000, positions were still some distance apart, however. There was particular contention over whether carbon dioxide absorption by forests should be included in the climate audits, the rules for the flexible mechanisms and sanction mechanisms. Again, the main adversaries were the US and EU. The US negotiators attempted to water down the Kyoto commitments in order to make them more acceptable to the US Senate. In contrast the EU wanted to ensure domestic action to restrict emissions trading and minimise the use of sinks as a climate measure. Developing countries were unhappy with the developed countries' lukewarm approach to cutting their own emissions.

The intensity of the differences caused for the first time a Conference of the Parties to collapse. One of the problems related to the impending presidential election in the US which had left the country without a clear negotiating mandate. At an extraordinary Meeting of the Parties in Bonn the following spring (2001), the process was eased back on track. By then, George W. Bush was president of the US and had decided to pull the country out of the negotiations on specifying the Kyoto Protocol. The EU first tried to persuade the US to rejoin the negotiations. When this failed, the EU grew even more determined to reach agreement on the specification of the Protocol. One would have expected negotiations to have been easier after the US exit, but US allies, the so-called 'Gang of Four', Australia, Russia, Japan and Canada, managed to steer the outcome closer to what the US had wanted all along. At the seventh conference, in Marrakesh, autumn 2001, the Parties finally agreed to a detailed, but diluted version of the Kyoto Protocol (Hovi *et al.* 2003). Thus, the EU accepted a weakened Protocol, but had it not been for the EU, the Kyoto Protocol might not have survived at all.

At COP 8 in New Delhi in 2002, the EU tried to initiate discussions on future commitments after the Protocol's expiry in 2012. This was de facto blocked by a powerful new 'alliance' of the developing countries and the

US. They had one common objective, to resist any kind of commitment. Little happened therefore at the next COPs as the Parties were waiting for the Protocol to come into force. For the Protocol to become legally effec- · tive, it had to be ratified by countries accounting for 55 per cent of the emissions of greenhouse gases as of 1990. Canada and Japan ratified the Protocol, but Australia decided to follow in the footsteps of the US. Ratification by Russia was therefore crucial to the Protocol's legal standing. Russia was – and is – an extremely unpredictable climate player. Russia had nothing to lose from ratifying because emissions were down by more than 30 per cent on 1990 figures, but was still reluctant. Thanks to some active lobbying by the EU, Russia ratified the agreement in the autumn of 2004, and the Protocol entered into force in February 2005 (Oberthur and Kelly 2008).

The eleventh Conference of the Parties was held in Montreal in 2005 and served also as the first Meeting of the Parties (MOP 1) to the Kyoto Protocol. Ad hoc talks were initiated with a view to completing a new agreement for the post-Kyoto period, but these were *not* formal negotiations, the US and G-77 prevented that. The EU headed the group of countries working for a continuation of the Protocol, only with tighter commitments. The US and developing countries were still not willing to discuss concrete commitments. The developing countries lashed out against the developed world for failing to reduce their own emissions or meeting their pledges to provide financial and technological aid. One might have expected the negotiations to move forward when the Protocol came into force, but the atmosphere was muted at the 2006 Conference of the Parties, and progress was slow. Indeed, the then UN Secretary-General, Kofi Annan, lamented a 'frightening lack of leadership' in the negotiations (Pew Center 2006). No doubt, the EU tried to take on the leadership role, but was not able to generate any followers, a necessary criterion to qualify as leadership (Skodvin and Andresen 2006).

In the light of the relative stalemate that had impeded negotiations for so many years, progress was made at last at COP 13 in Bali in 2007 (Røgeberg *et al.* 2010). Most importantly, agreement was reached on the so-called Bali Roadmap. For the first time all Parties accepted formal negotiations to frame a new agreement following the Kyoto Protocol. Two working groups were established, the Ad Hoc Working Group on Further Commitments for Annex I Parties under the Kyoto Protocol (AWG-KP) and the Ad Hoc Working Group on Long-term Cooperative Action under the Convention (AWG-LCA). The latter was most important since it included non-Kyoto members such as the US as well as major emerging economies in the South like China and India. Negotiations concentrated on four building blocks: mitigation, adaptation, finance and technology. Adoption of an Adaptation Fund was also seen as a major achievement of the Bali meeting. The progress at Bali could probably be seen as the result of increasing political awareness of climate change in large parts of the world, particularly after the launching of the third IPCC assessment report. After 2007 the negotiations intensified significantly in order to reach a new comprehensive climate agreement by COP 15 in 2009.

Bali proved the exception to the rule, however. By the time of the next COP, in Poznan, the 'Spirit of Bali' had been subdued. While the world economy was healthy during Bali, by December 2008 the world was in the grips of an economic recession. In addition two of the key players, the US and EU, were more or less absent from the negotiating table. The EU was preoccupied with internal negotiations over its climate and energy policy package while the US negotiators, representing the outgoing Republican Administration, lacked both the incentive and mandate to participate actively. COP 14 has therefore been characterised as 'one of those in-between COPs'.

The negotiators met five times prior to Copenhagen and initially there was some optimism, as the new US President Barack Obama had given clear signals that he wanted a more ambitious US climate policy (Skodvin and Andresen 2009). The interest of non-governmental organisations and the media was overwhelming and they showed up in unprecedented numbers at Copenhagen, which was billed to be another milestone in the history of climate change negotiations. Climate politics had truly become 'high politics' in the sense of most countries understanding it as one of their core inter-national interests. This did not ease the negotiations, rather the opposite. When the policy-makers arrived towards the end of the negotiations there was no agreed common document, and delegates were feeling extremely anxious. Towards the very end, a small group of emerging economies, China, India, South Africa, Brazil together with the US, was able to hammer out the final deal, the Copenhagen Accord. It was a document of two and a half pages, reminding us of the fable of the mountain that gave birth to a mouse. Although many blamed the US, specifically the US Senate, for the rather bleak outcome, the most powerful vetoing power was probably China, stripping the document for all emission targets (Guardian 2010). The 'G-2' (China and the US) knew that any agreement without their consent would be worthless and acted accordingly. Many countries were frustrated because they were completely left out of the end game. Although many had little sympathy with the final outcome, they accepted it as the only feasible option; it was the best agreement in the circumstances. A handful of developing countries did not accept the Accord.

Expectations were extremely low before COP 16 in Cancun December 2010. Against this background the outcome was deemed rather positive. According to the Climate Convention Executive Secretary: 'The beacon of hope has been reignited and faith in the multilateral climate change pro-cess has been restored' (Earth Negotiations Bulletin 2010: 28). However, there were more significant changes in process rather than outcome. The Mexican government worked hard to keep the process of negotiations transparent and inclusive, avoiding the exclusive negotiations that had characterised the Copenhagen meeting. In the end, only Bolivia was against the agreement adopted. The process was also made easier as the Parties agreed to set aside issues that had stalemated the negotiations for years such as the prolongation of the Kyoto Protocol. China and the US were also able to avoid any open sparring. In terms of substance the negotiators agreed to anchor pledges made in the Accord and taking initial steps to strengthen such aspects as transparency and finance.

The significance of the international climate regime

In this section we evaluate the impact of the different components of the climate regime, starting with the Climate Panel. In general, the Climate Panel's reports have consolidated scientific consensus and brought scientific findings to a far wider audience than the scientific community. Although many other powerful players influence the scientific agenda in this field, there is little doubt that the IPCC has been *the* crucial body in promoting and assembling scientific data (Skodvin 2000, Skodvin and Alfsen 2010).

Over the past twenty years perceptions of the climate problem have changed beyond recognition, especially in the Western world. No longer seen as a complex, vague and unreal proposition, climatic variation and weather events are now commonly interpreted as an effect of climate change. Climate considerations are also increasingly seen as relevant in decision-making. The environment has attracted a fresh wave of interest in the period from 2005 to the financial crisis in the autumn of 2008, with the climate question attracting by far the most attention. Interest was highest in the wealthy countries, but developing countries like China are also increasingly concerned with the political issues raised by climate change. There is good reason to believe the Climate Panel's work was instrumental in this development. The IPCC was long dominated by Western scientists, a situation which undermined its legitimacy in developing countries, but the Panel now has a much broader membership, and is enjoying wider legitimacy as a result.

The Climate Panel's active use of the media created unprecedented interest in the last 2007 report. The message of the IPCC was reinforced by other players. The environmental movement called for concrete action while amplifying and simplifying the scientific message, often necessary to reach the public at large. In this period the media was also busy dramatising climate change with images of polar bears looking for ice, melting glaciers, tropical storms and natural disasters like droughts. Underlining the high credibility as well as the visibility of the Panel, the Norwegian Nobel Committee awarded the Nobel Peace Prize to the IPCC (together with Al Gore) in 2007. Hollywood celebrities and some of the world's biggest financial investors also threw themselves into the climate debate in this period characterised by an optimistic 'climate hype'.

This changed with the economic crisis of 2008, giving policy-makers a new problem to consider and the media to report on. True, a large cache of money had been allocated through various 'green' measures in the vast 'stimulus packages' adopted by most nations, but the state of the economy soon became the new name of the game, not the environment. In the run-up to the Copenhagen Conference over 1000 e-mails from and to researchers at the Climate Research Unit, University of East Anglia, appeared on the internet. Renowned climate scientists had apparently sought to minimise the influence of views they disagreed with while failing to document their own arguments. This so-called 'climate gate' contributed to undermining the validity of the IPCC conclusions and dampened enthusiasm for forceful climate measures. At about the same time the 2007 IPCC Report's prediction that the Himalayas could lose all their glaciers in twenty-five years, was shown to be wrong. These events prompted several reviews of the procedures as well as the substance of the work at the IPCC, the most authoritative being that of the Shapiro Committee, whose report was published in August 2010 (InterAcademy Council 2010). This report, as well as the others, endorses the main conclusions of the IPCC. That is, none of the reports weakens the case for acting to limit carbon emissions. However, in terms of process and organisation it is claimed that the IPCC does not live up to calls for transparency and accountability characterising the recent 'governance revolution' (Economist 2010). No doubt part of the explanation for the IPCC's loss of standing is the aggressive political campaign fought by forces which, for various reasons, are against climate action. Nevertheless, distrust of the IPCC and the economic crisis have both led to reduced public interest in the issue in most Western countries and also increased doubt about whether it is as serious a problem as has been made out (see for example the BBC Climate Change Polls 2010).

Of the different pillars of the international climate regime, the Climate Convention tends to attract least attention. This is not surprising. Lacking a binding target, it has generally been seen as a rather weak instrument. Nevertheless, this is where the strongest normative message is to be found. In principle it commits nearly every country, including the world's two largest emitters, China and the US, to work to stabilise the concentration of greenhouse gases in the atmosphere. How this commitment should be interpreted in practice, however, is far from clear. The more ambitious wealthy countries, led by the EU, tried giving the framework a more practical 'translation': the global mean temperature should not exceed 2°C. As we have seen this has later been endorsed by the IPCC as well as the Copenhagen Accord. However, for many it still represents a potentially dangerous increase in temperature, not least for the small, low-lying island states of the Pacific. Even if the target is generally agreed, the real indicator of how serious the Parties take the norms laid down in the Convention is their willingness and ability to reach the goal. If the goal is to be reached, global emission growth needs to be reversed as early as 2015. At present there are no indications that this will be possible (Røgeberg *et al.* 2010).

The principle of common but differentiated responsibilities has helped the developing countries avoid the imposition of emission cut commitments. Since the wealthy countries are mainly to blame for the problem, and are in a much better position to reduce their own emissions, it is only reasonable that they take the lead and reduce their emissions most significantly. This approach has, however, given succour to uncompromising ideological rifts between North and South. By not differentiating between the developing countries themselves, artificial divisions are created. While the Pacific islands and many populous areas in Asia and Africa are poor and extremely vulnerable, emerging economies like China and Brazil are far better equipped to meet climate change. There are wide dissimilarities in developing countries' contribution to climate change and some of the more wealthy developing OPEC countries even have higher per capita emissions than some of the Annex I countries. The two broad categories of the Convention have made it easier for the wealthiest and most affluent developing countries to hide behind ideological arguments.

Turning to the Kyoto Protocol, its emission commitments are far weaker than the normative principles of the Convention sanction mechanisms. As the content and approach of the new commitment period are still highly uncertain, the provision to cut emissions by an extra 30 per cent may lose most of its force.

Nevertheless, the Protocol represents a clear strengthening of the international pressure on wealthy countries because it is more specific and binding than the Convention. Following the negotiations on the Protocol, organisations, rules, procedures and other arrangements designed to mitigate the problem have sprung up like mushrooms, both nationally and internationally. Most developed Protocol members have created various climate policy measures and incentives. Support schemes designed to encourage the development of renewable energy, support for public transport expansion and requirements to use biofuel are among the commonest. Activity has been highest in Europe, but a lot has happened in countries without emission commitments, including Brazil, China and the US.

The establishment of detailed frameworks for emission trading has enabled the buying and selling of emission rights across national borders. Recalling that the EU was against emissions trading, somewhat paradoxically the EU system is by far the most advanced and comprehensive and has become considerably more stringent over time (Skjærseth and Wettestad 2008). It shares many of the features of the trading regime under the Kyoto Protocol, but there are significant differences as well. While Kyoto includes all greenhouse gases, the EU system is limited to carbon dioxide. And only energy production and certain types of energy-intensive industry are included under the EU system. Moreover, the Kyoto Protocol deals with trade between countries, the EU system with trade between companies. Emissions trading is also in the process of being introduced in other developed states as well as at the state level in the US.

The clean development mechanism has got off to a rather slow start, but the number of approved projects is rising quickly. China is the biggest recipient of projects and accounts today for more than half of the total emission reductions under this mechanism while the poorest developing countries lack the capacity to attract projects. Carbon capture and storage may well be able to diffuse low-carbon technology, but this may come in addition to carbon-emitting technology, not as a replacement. The effect of this mechanism on reducing emissions remains therefore an open question.

The Protocol has had a major influence on the development of regulatory mechanisms internationally and nationally. At the end of the day, what counts is the effect on the level of emissions. What have these three components of the climate regime produced in terms of results? The global emission figures are not encouraging. The growth rate has been approximately constant since 1980. Hence no reduction was detected after the introduction of the climate regime (Solomon *et al.* 2007). Is this because of deficiencies inherent in the climate regime? First, because Kyoto commitments are fairly weak and binding on so few countries, the effect of even full compliance on emission growth would only be marginal. This situation is exacerbated by the changing balance between the developed and developing world, where the former accounts for an ever decreasing share of total greenhouse gas emissions. Today, most greenhouse gas emissions come from countries without commitments, and the percentage is rising fast (Røgeberg *et al.* 2010). The significance of the Protocol diminishes even further insofar as many countries will probably fail to meet their emission targets, for example Australia, Canada and Japan. The 'top performer', that is, the EU, will probably achieve its 8 per cent reduction commitment largely thanks to major cuts by Germany and the UK, but unrelated to climate politics. Nevertheless, the EU is clearly a directional leader and good example, although it has not been able to generate the critical mass of followers during the process of negotiations.

Emissions trading among the wealthy countries is now in place, and while clean development programmes have been rolled out in developing countries, joint implementation has not really been utilised. The increase in emissions bears witness to the lack of success of the flexible mechanisms. Indeed, some are questioning whether emissions trading and clean development mechanisms can actually bring about net emission cuts at all. That said, the two mechanisms have only been in play for a few years, so it may be too early to draw conclusions. The EU has strengthened its system, and more countries may follow, although the US will not be one of them, at least not in the short term (Boasson and Wettestad 2010). Since developing countries are free to increase emissions in places where a clean development project is not in place, it is extremely difficult to estimate the effect of these projects. Even if the impact has been limited up to now, these projects transfer practical and institutional climate capacity to developing countries. The projects will likely improve as those involved gain in experience.

Will the Copenhagen Accord as later formalised in the Cancun Agreement promote climate action on the ground? So far, 138 nations representing close to 90 per cent of global emissions, have associated themselves with the Accord and more than 80 have entered specific mitigation pledges. Analysts agree that the pledges made are not sufficient to meet the 2 degree target, and these pledges were not changed as a result of the Cancun Agreement. The bottom-up 'pledge and review' approach, largely consonant with US wishes, is also adopted in the Cancun Agreement. Overall, the Cancun Agreement does not represent any fundamental changes compared to the Copenhagen Accord, although 'some more flesh has been added to the bones' (*Earth Negotiations Bulletin* 2010: 29). However, the Agreement is far less controversial than the Accord as it has now been brought formally into the UN system.

At the time of writing (autumn 2010) it is far too early to evaluate the practical significance – or the outcome – of the Copenhagen Accord and the ensuing Cancun Agreement given that 'the proof of the pudding lies in the eating'. The Cancun Agreement may represent an improvement to the Accord in the sense that it has a higher score in terms of legitimacy, but it represents a very small step in terms of reducing global emissions. In normative terms the Agreement is quite strong as it endorses the 2 degree goal, and its weakening of the recent artificial border between developed and developing countries is probably beneficial. In cognitive terms it creates confusion, though, since it remains unclear whether the mechanisms of the Kyoto Protocol will be prolonged or not. Overall it strengthens the tendency to emphasise adaptation more and has also spurred the debate and possible action on halting forests reduction and degradation through the REDD + mechanism. In contrast to the Kyoto Protocol it also conveys a much stronger message about the obligations of the rich world to facilitate more effective climate measures in poor countries. However, it remains to be seen whether the ambitious goals will be followed up. Lastly, the lack of a binding regulatory framework represents a major pitfall as it was no development on this issue in Cancun.

Conclusions

It took a long time from the scientific discovery of the climate problem for it to be translated into political action on the international stage. Early political ambitions were also on a much grander scale than the political will to realise them later on. Progress, nonetheless, was made with the political and scientific institutionalisation of the process in the early 1990s. The IPCC, Climate Convention, the Kyoto Protocol and the Copenhagen Accord seek progress through cognitive, normative and regulatory mechanisms. The scientific process under the aegis of the IPCC has had a significant cognitive impact. It has become better known and more visible over the years, and its main substantive conclusions stand firm irrespective of the more recent controversies, mainly dealing with how the process is organised. The normative effect of the Climate Convention has been less convincing. It gave expression to the Parties' willingness to undertake radical action to deal with the problem, but there has not been much practical follow-up. Also, distinguishing sharply between rich and poor countries may have been reasonable at the time, but is clearly less applicable today. The norm was fleshed out in the Protocol, but weakened somewhat in the Accord and the Cancun Agreement. Turning to the main regulatory instrument, the Kyoto Protocol, it has had a significant effect in terms of spurring action, programmes and institutions to combat climate change internationally and nationally, not the least through the construction of emissions trading and the CDM. They were both highly controversial when adopted, but have gained increasing support. Still, although they may be quite innovative these mechanisms need to be expanded and improved to produce the reductions necessary to solve the climate change problem. The same goes for the recent emphasis on REDD +. It may well be another relatively cost-effective step to deal with the problem, but it only represents a start – if it materialises. As noted above, the jury is still out on the regulative effect of the 'bottom-up', 'pledge and review' approach of the Accord, later endorsed in the Cancun Agreement.

Turning to the outcome indicator, for all the political and institutional energy poured into the problem and all the initiatives taken, global emissions continue to grow at a startling pace. International collaboration has first and foremost transformed the climate challenge into a major challenge for all humanity. Theoretical understanding is still waiting to be comprehensively translated into practice. Because of this crevice between talk and action, there is still a long way to go before the climate problem gets anywhere near a solution.

Why has there been so little progress? The main reason is the 'malign' nature of the problem of climate change compared to most other international environmental issues. The climate problem is simply much more than an environmental problem. It affects countries' economies and development in a major way, along with energy politics and trade. Strong vested interests within and between countries make necessary political action very difficult. The problem-solving ability of the climate regime has also been hampered by fundamental disagreement on how to approach the problem, not the least within the US and EU. The EU tried leading the process, but ended up spending most of its time and resources on internal policy development rather than on creating international alliances. The US has probably been the most influential actor, but is generally seen as a laggard. But even if the North were able to make real emissions reductions in the future, it would not be of much help. The real challenge lies in the South, which accounts for a rapidly increasing share of global emissions. One could have excepted negotiations to speed up when climate change became 'high level politics', but in practice the system was unable to deal with the tension this created.

There is general agreement that if a real long-term solution to the problem is to be found, technology is the key. According to the IPCC much of the necessary technology is present and cutting emissions substantially would not cost the world. From an impartial expert perspective this may have something going for it. The problem is that domestic and international politics is neither impartial, rational nor logical. So far the main emitting countries discount the long-term threat of global climate change and put more emphasis on other short-term economic and political priorities and interests. Moreover, the failure of global multilateral diplomacy to deliver on the issue may reduce the appeal of this approach, although some faith was restored in this approach at the Cancun meeting. Other arenas like the Major Economies Forum on Energy and Climate (MEF) and the Asia Pacific Partnership on Clean Energy and Development (APP) where all the major emitters are represented may still grow in importance. If this happens it is important that links and collaborative relations are forged between participants in order to stimulate synergies rather than differences among the various approaches.

Bibliography

Andresen, S. and Agrawala, S. (2002) 'Leaders, pushers and laggards in the making of the climate regime', *Global Environmental Change*, 12: 41–51.

BBC Climate Change Polls (2010) 'BBC poll on climate change' published by BBC on 4 February 2010. Available at: www.populus.co.uk/bbc-bbc-poll-on-climate-change-040210.html (accessed 7 February 2011).

Boasson, E.L. and Wettestad, J. (2010) *Understanding the Differing Governance of EU Emissions Trading and Renewables: feedback mechanisms and policy entrepreneurs*, FNI Report 2/2010. Lysaker: Fridtjof Nansen Institute.

Earth Negotiations Bulletin (2010) 'A brief analysis of the climate change conference', *Earth Negotiations Bulletin*, 12(498): 1–30.

The Economist (2010) 'Climate change assessment must try harder', 4 September: 78–79.

Grubb, M., Vrolijk, C. and Brack, D. (1999) *The Kyoto Protocol: a guide and an assessment*, London: Royal Institute of International Affairs.

The Guardian (2010) 'Global deal on climate change in 2010 "all but impossible"', 1 February. Available at: www.guardian.co.uk/environment/2010/feb/01/climate-change-deal-impossible-2010 (accessed 10 March 2010).

Hovi, J., Skodvin, T. and Andresen, S. (2003) 'The persistence of the Kyoto Protocol: why other Annex 1 countries move on without the United States', *Global Environmental Politics*, 3: 1–23.

InterAcademy Council (2010) *Climate Change Assessments: review of the processes and procedures of the IPCC*, Amsterdam: InterAcademy Council. Available at: http://reviewipcc.interacademycouncil.net/report/Climate%20Change%20Assessments,%20Review%20of%20the%20Processes%20&%20Procedures%20of%20the%20IPCC.pdf (accessed 7 February 2011).

Metz, B., Davidson, O.R., Bosch, P.R., Dave, R. and Meyer, L.A. (eds) (2007) *Contribution of Working Group III to the Fourth Assessment Report of the*

Intergovernmental Panel on Climate Change, Cambridge, UK: Cambridge University Press.

Oberthur, S. and Kelly, C.R. (2008) 'EU leadership in international climate policy: achievements and challenges', *The International Spectator*, 43: 35–50.

Parry, M.L., Canziani, O.F., Palutikof, J.P., van der Linden, P.J. and Hanson, C.E. (eds) (2007) *Contribution of Working Group II to the Fourth Assessment Report of the Intergovernmental Panel on Climate Change*, Cambridge, UK: Cambridge University Press.

Pew Center (2006) *COP 12 Report*, Arlington, VA: Pew Center on Global Climate Change. Available at www.pewclimate.org/what_s_being_done/in_the_world/cop12/summary.cfm (accessed 10 February 2010).

Røgeberg, O., Andresen, S. and Holtsmark, B. (2010) 'International climate treaties: the case for pessimism', *Climate Law*, 1: 177–99.

Skjærseth, J.B. and Wettestad, J. (2008) *EU Emissions Trading: initiation, decision-making and implementation*, Aldershot, UK: Ashgate.

Skodvin, T. (2000) *Structure and Agent in the Scientific Diplomacy over Climate Change: an empirical case study of the science-policy interaction in the Intergovernmental Panel on Climate Change*, Dordrecht, The Netherlands: Kluwer Academic Publishers.

Skodvin, T. and Alfsen, K. (2010) *The Intergovernmental Panel of Climate Change (IPCC): an outline of an assessment*, Policy Note 2010:01, Oslo: CICERO

Skodvin, T. and Andresen, S. (2006) 'Leadership revisited', *Global Environmental Politics*, 6: 13–28.

——(2009) 'An agenda for change in US climate policies? Presidential ambitions and Congressional powers', *International Environmental Agreements: politics, law and economics*, 9: 263–80.

Solomon, S., Qin, D., Manning, M., Chen, Z., Marquis, M., Averyt, K.B., Tignor, M. and Miller, H.L. (eds) (2007) *Contribution of Working Group I to the Fourth Assessment Report of the Intergovernmental Panel on Climate Change*, Cambridge, UK: Cambridge University Press.

Part III

Ocean management

5 Law of the sea

Protection and preservation of the marine environment

Øystein Jensen

Important years

1948 International Maritime Organization (IMO) created
1958 The four Geneva Conventions on the Law of the Sea adopted
1967 Oil tanker Torrey Canyon runs aground off Cornwall, England
1972 London Convention on Dumping of Wastes adopted
1973 International Convention for the Prevention of Pollution from Ships adopted
1982 United Nations Convention on the Law of the Sea adopted
1994 United Nations Convention on the Law of the Sea entered into force

Throughout time, humans have been able to use the planet's vast expanses of ocean spaces to exploit its resources, for voyages of discovery and as trade routes. Until recently, however, the implications of our use of the sea for the marine environment have received scant attention. The oceans were impervious to harm, it was thought, with ships and coastal industries simply using many areas of the sea as a dumping ground. Whether transported to the sea by air, by river or by direct discharge along the coastline, pollution was beginning to affect fish stocks and ocean flora. Up to the end of the 1960s, however, there was little political will to do much about the ever increasing contamination of the marine environment. Only when Liberian oil tanker *Torrey Canyon* ran aground off the coast of Cornwall in the United Kingdom, did the international community begin taking the marine environment seriously. *Torrey Canyon* was an environmental catastrophe which revealed an urgent need to protect the sea from oil spills resulting from incidents at sea.

Not long after, in 1969, an agreement was signed – the so-called International Convention Relating to Intervention on the High Seas in Cases of Oil Pollution Casualties – entitling the coastal state to take measures on the high seas deemed necessary to protect its coasts and affected interests from pollution of the sea by oil. At about the same time other important environmental treaties were adopted with a bearing on pollution of the marine environment of which the most important were perhaps the 1972

London Convention on Prevention of Marine Pollution by Dumping of Wastes and Other Matter and the 1973 International Convention for the Prevention of Pollution from Ships (hereinafter MARPOL 73/78).

A global legal framework for the protection and preservation of the marine environment applicable to all sources of pollution would have to wait, however, until the end of the Third United Nations Conference on the Law of the Sea, which started in 1973 and ended in 1982. The result of that conference – the United Nations Convention on the Law of the Sea of 10 December 1982 (hereinafter the LOS Convention) – has done more than any other treaty to shape international environmental law and is today a cornerstone of the international law of the sea. Knowledge of the LOS Convention is thus essential for understanding the international rules that apply to some of the most pressing issues of our time, that is, the management of the oceans' enormous resources and protection and preservation of the marine environment.

First, this chapter very briefly outlines the modern history of the law of the sea and the negotiations leading to the adoption of the LOS Convention. We shall thereafter explore some key aspects of the LOS Convention concerning the protection of the marine environment: the duty of states to protect the marine environment from pollution; the rights of states to combat pollution from different sources; and global and regional cooperation.

Emergence of a new legal framework: the LOS Convention

The formulation of the law of the sea after the Second World War reflects the ability of states to technologically and economically exploit the resources of the sea and seabed to an ever greater extent. Today, this includes expanding catch capacities of the fishing industry and, not least, our ability to extract oil and gas on the continental shelf. Regulatory mechanisms have been called for accordingly, to specify the rights and duties of states under international law.

The period from 1945 to 1960 was a time of clarification, codification and – to some extent – progressive development in response to technological change. In particular, the work of the International Law Commission was reflected in the four Geneva Conventions produced by the First United Nations Conference on the Law of the Sea, held in Geneva in 1958: the Convention on the Territorial Sea and Contiguous Zone; the Convention on the High Seas; the Convention on Fishing and Conservation of Living Resources of the High Seas; and the Convention on the Continental Shelf.

Still, a number of issues remained unresolved, for example what to do about setting the limits of the territorial waters and coastal states' fishing zones. Rules on the protection and preservation of the marine environment were also wanting in several respects. The Convention on the High Seas did include a ban on pollution by operations on the continental shelf, but *pollution* as such was not defined, and apart from an obligation to take due account of others' use of the sea, a prevalent ban did not exist.

Nor were the states attending the Second United Nations Conference on the Law of the Sea, held in Geneva in 1960 able to clarify these questions. The six-week conference was important for the emerging state practice in relation to limits of territorial waters and fishing zones. Many coastal states proclaimed exclusive fishing zones outside their territorial waters for their own fishermen. This upset several other states, however. Actions like these could undermine the basic principles of the freedom of the seas, such as the freedom of navigation. More than ever, there was a growing need and desire among states for a clarification of international law.

The first step in that direction – and indeed towards the adoption of the LOS Convention – was taken in 1967. It was Malta's Ambassador, Arvid Pardo, who in a celebrated speech at the United Nations General Assembly urged the creation of a more effective international legal regime for the world's oceans and the areas of the sea floor beyond 'a clearly defined national jurisdiction' to be defined as the common heritage of mankind. A new convention was needed. It would have to address all aspects of the law of the sea and recognise the interconnected nature of the problems facing the marine environment – and the need to deal with them as such. A new period of the post-war history of the law of the sea commenced. However, it was not so much because the major maritime powers had campaigned for a radical reconsideration of the existing law of the sea. They were quite satisfied with the existing legal order. It was in fact the dissatisfaction of the Third World which forced global action (Brown 1992: 172).

The Third United Nations Conference on the Law of the Sea was launched in 1973, lasted nine years and hosted eleven sessions. It was attended by some 160 states, several special interest organisations, various international organisations, numerous non-governmental organisations and also eight national liberation movements. The Conference was run on the princi-. ple of consensus. Only after all other means of achieving consensus had been exhausted would voting take place. A prominent feature of the negotiating process was therefore the many package deals resulting from political bartering, all to ensure widest possible backing for the LOS Convention's final provisions. After years at the negotiating table, 130 states voted for the draft LOS Convention. Four were against (United States of America, Venezuela, Turkey and Israel), and there were eighteen abstentions (including the Soviet Union, Germany and the United Kingdom).

The LOS Convention entered into force in 1994 and is today ratified by 160 states (July 2010). It contains regulations which together cover all areas of the sea, the air space above them, the sea floor and the subsoil. It regulates the rights and duties of states in these areas and provides among other things for marine scientific research, management of living and non-living resources, as well as rules on dispute settlement mechanisms to ensure the peaceful resolution of inter-state conflicts.

In addition, the LOS Convention establishes for the first time a comprehensive global legal structure for the protection and preservation of the marine environment. The rules seek to balance the free use of the sea on the one hand and the needs of coastal states to prevent, reduce and control pollution of the marine environment on the other. Provisions are given on a number of polluting activities including dumping and shipping. There are general provisions on the protection and preservation of the marine environment and responsibilities and duties of states in this connection. The LOS Convention urges and expects the international community to work together to develop regional and global procedures for the protection of the marine environment, taking into account the need to balance between economic and environmental interests. In what follows, we shall take a closer look at some prominent aspects of the legal framework that is now in place.

Duty of states to protect the marine environment

Under traditional international law, there was no specific duty to protect the marine environment from pollution. The decision in the so-called *Trail Smelter* case had established in 1941 the illegality of causing damage outside one's own territory. In that case a Canadian smelter was ordered to pay compensation for damages in the United States resulting from its emissions. As the Arbitration Court said at the time, no state has a right to use or permit the use of its territory in such a way as to cause damage to the territory of *other* states. The *Trail Smelter* decision had limited application, however, if the pollution did not actually affect others or the property of others. Nor could a duty to protect the environment *per se* be derived from the decision. Thus, beyond the limits of national jurisdiction, parties only had to take due consideration of others' use of the sea.

An absolute ban against marine pollution won't be found in the LOS Convention either. The Convention imposes a general obligation on states, however, to *avoid* polluting the sea. According to article 192 of the LOS Convention, states shall 'protect and preserve the marine environment'. This provision is also presumed to give expression to customary law and is therefore in its substance also binding on states that have not acceded to the LOS Convention specifically. The term 'marine environment' is not defined, but the obligation should be read as comprehending all areas of the sea. All the same, article 192 is first and foremost a framework provision, and the degree to which it can be said to establish obligations of a more tangible nature will basically depend on what other rights and duties can be inferred from the LOS Convention's provisions.

Further, states have a general obligation to *prevent* pollution of the marine environment. It follows from article 194 of the LOS Convention that states, individually or jointly, shall take the necessary steps to prevent, reduce and control pollution of the marine environment by all sources and to the best of their ability, applying the best practicable means at their disposal. One important difference from earlier treaties is the LOS Convention's scope of application: it covers all sources of pollution. The LOS Convention distinguishes between pollution from vessels, dumping, land-based sources and activity on the continental shelf. States shall take whatever steps are necessary to ensure that activity under their control does not damage the environment of other states. This applies also to pollution of sea areas outside *any* state's jurisdiction, notably the high seas and continental shelf areas stretching beyond the maximum permitted limits as provided for under article 76 of the Convention. As we see, the LOS Convention goes further than the *Trail Smelter* decision by prohibiting harm to the environment itself (Birnie and Boyle 1992: 254–57).

The provisions shall also, according to article 194, apply to the protection and preservation of rare and fragile ecosystems. Worth noting in this regard is also that the LOS Convention allows on certain conditions coastal states to legislate and enforce stricter rules for areas where, for instance, oceanographic or ecological factors justify higher conservation status.

An important point of article 194 is the general duty of care (due diligence) impinging on states in respect of the marine environment. States shall take all necessary steps to prevent marine pollution and use only the 'the best practicable means at their disposal'. Pollution from sources on land is given special attention. Consideration shall here be given to the state's economic capacity, its need for economic growth and characteristic regional features. However, while states are obliged in principle to take necessary steps to prevent harm to the marine environment, the practical aspect of the obligation must be weighed against, for instance, the measures' purely economic costs.

Now, this seems at first sight to give states very wide latitude indeed to decide what measures to enact in a particular situation. The duty of care under article 194 of the LOS Convention needs all the same to be read in light of the provisions on each of the specified sources of pollution, such as those applying to sea-going vessels. Thus, the LOS Convention obliges states to give effect to 'generally accepted international rules or standards' (see for example article 211). What this wording actually means in practice cannot be inferred directly from any provision of the LOS Convention itself. It does mean, though, that states, by acceding to the LOS Convention, commit themselves to adopt rules that are internationally accepted. For shipping, such rules are set out, for example, in MARPOL 73/78. States Parties to the LOS Convention must therefore through national legislation give effect to rules at a level that at least corresponds to those found in MARPOL 73/78, even if they have not acceded to that convention specifically. So although the LOS Convention does not specify which rules states are obliged to incorporate on the domestic level, the duty of care can be said to demand a lower threshold of standardised minimum rules.

A more ambitious idea in this direction concerns the effect on the force of these rules by considering the duty of care as an expression of customary international law. In that case, it would be binding on all states. Against the background of the comprehensive acceptance and enactment of, for instance MARPOL 73/78, states that are not party to the LOS Convention could nevertheless substantially be bound by such 'generally accepted international rules or standards'.

The important thing to note here, all the same, is that states' duty of care is more tangible and wider in scope than what appears to follow from the rather vague terminology of article 194 (and, for that matter, other provisions of the LOS Convention on the specific sources of pollution). States enjoy some latitude in their choice of international rules and standards currently in force. On the other hand, national measures must meet certain minimum criteria.

The scope of state power to prevent, reduce and control marine pollution

The LOS Convention introduces wide-ranging and complex rules on the pollution of the sea from a variety of sources. It distinguishes primarily between different types of marine pollution and the rights and duties bearing on states in relation to each of them with a view to protecting and preserving the marine environment.

First, there is the pollution stemming from sources on land, including rivers, estuaries, pipelines and discharge plants. These sources of pollution account for about 80 per cent of all effluent flowing into the sea. Unlike other pollution source categories, article 207 of the LOS Convention does not require states to build on international minimum rules. All the same, they shall take international rules, standards and recommended procedures and approaches 'into account'. States shall also initiate other steps that are necessary to prevent and reduce pollution from land-based sources. They are generally free to decide on the cooperative level of these steps (global, regional or bilateral cooperation).

The body of rules under the LOS Convention that applies to land-based pollution sources is clearly the result of a compromise. It appears to have been difficult to persuade governments to make significant commitments on pollution stemming from their own land territory. The wording of the LOS Convention bears evidence of such trepidation and is formulated rather loosely. Negotiating governments chose instead to highlight and encourage international collaboration. Article 207, paragraph 3 is illustrative. States, it says, 'shall endeavour to harmonize their policies in this connection at the appropriate regional level'.

One of the most prominent regional treaties on this type of pollution is the Oslo–Paris Convention of 1992 (hereinafter OSPAR) (see Chapter 6). The purpose of OSPAR is to protect the marine environment of the North East Atlantic. The treaty replaced the earlier Oslo–Paris Conventions of 1972 and 1974. OSPAR is a good example of states promoting a regional approach to combating marine pollution from land-based sources. Since such cooperation has proved advantageous and benign as well, it is not strange that it has been difficult so far to agree on a global treaty on this specific topic beyond what currently follows from the framework of the LOS Convention.

Another source of marine pollution is dumping. Dumping is typically waste discharged into the sea by vessels, platforms and other constructed installations at sea. The reason for prohibiting dumping is to prevent a minority of states from spoiling the marine environment to the detriment of everyone else.

Pollution by dumping is regulated by article 210 of the LOS Convention. States shall adopt laws and regulations to prevent, reduce and control pollution of the marine environment by dumping. Acting especially through competent international organisations or diplomatic conferences, states shall endeavour to establish global and regional rules, standards and recommended practices and procedures to prevent, reduce and control such pollution. Such rules, standards and recommended practices and procedures shall be re-examined from time-to-time as necessary.

The development of an international regime for this type of pollution started already with the United Nations Conference on the Human Environment (also known as the Stockholm Conference) in 1972 and the ensuing Convention on the Prevention of Marine Pollution by Dumping of Wastes and Other Matter (commonly referred to as the London Convention). As of today, more than 80 states have acceded to the London Convention, and the rules on dumping – unlike those on land-based pollution – enjoy a particularly global scope. They set out minimum rules and different harmful substances are classified according to degree of environmental hazard. For the most dangerous, the ban is total. The London Convention has its own 'treaty body', tasked with supervising the implementation of and compliance with the constituent treaty. The London Convention is considered to be one of the major legal instruments in combating marine pollution and has successfully established restrictive rules on the basis of broad international agreement beyond the LOS Convention's framework.

Article 208 of the LOS Convention regulates pollution from activity on the seabed subject to national jurisdiction. For coastal states with a significant offshore activity, the provisions here are particularly pertinent. States are obliged to adopt rules to prevent and reduce marine pollution resulting from or connected with seabed activities. According to the LOS Convention, these rules shall not be less effective than international rules. Also, states shall endeavour to harmonise their policies at the appropriate regional level. Acting especially through competent international organisations or diplomatic conference, they shall also establish global and regional rules, standards and recommended practices and procedures. As for dumping, the rules shall be re-examined from time-to-time as necessary.

Shipping is another source of sea pollution. In principle, shipping is relatively benign environmentally speaking and an economic form of transport. The total volume of sea pollution from international shipping should thus not be overstated in relation to other sources. Nevertheless, illegal discharges of oil from ships represent a major threat to the marine environment (Trieschmann 2010: 213). Also, shipping comes with a substantial environmental risk. All too often we have been reminded of what incidents involving oil tankers can do to the marine environment. And given that shipping is a highly international activity, it has been necessary to set up globally applicable rules to achieve as harmonious a regime as possible.

Article 211 of the LOS Convention continues the traditional system insofar as responsibility for regulating and controlling pollution from shipping resides primarily with the 'flag state'. A vessel shall always fly a flag. In addition to advertising the ship's nationality, the flag indicates which state has regulatory control of the ship – flag state jurisdiction. The reason for the primacy of flag state jurisdiction is that this state is considered best equipped to exercise jurisdiction over its own vessels.

According to article 211 of the LOS Convention, laws and regulations adopted by states for the prevention, reduction and control of pollution of the marine environment from vessels flying their flag or of their registry shall at least have the same effect as that of generally accepted international rules and standards established 'through the competent international organization'. As is generally acknowledged, the competent international organisation referred to here is the International Maritime Organization (hereinafter IMO). IMO is the United Nations' specialist agency responsible for improving maritime safety and preventing pollution from ships. The organisation has today more than 160 member states which ensure a global development of international rules on pollution from shipping, and that the content of important conventions (for instance MARPOL 73/78) satisfies a substantial minimum. This differs markedly from what applies to other sources of pollution. As we have seen, rules are there also established at the regional level and by (several) competent international organisations.

One serious problem emerging at irregular intervals has been the misuse of the right of every state to sail ships under its own flag (Churchill and Lowe 1999: 260). Some states allow registration of ships in their registers, ships with absolutely no other connection to the state in question. Shipowners let their ships sail under such 'flags of convenience' for several reasons, not least tax benefits. Article 91 of the LOS Convention therefore requires 'a genuine link between the State and the ship' to entitle the latter to fly the former's flag. Although the meaning of 'genuine link' is not spelled out, the reason is clearly to make the flag state's jurisdiction and control of the ship as effective as possible. Now, non-compliance with article 91 of the LOS Convention will clearly represent a violation of the Convention, but would hardly result in the non-recognition of the flag state or to the ship being considered stateless. That would undermine the entire flag state principle. Worse from an environmental perspective, though, is the large number of states providing flags of convenience that have not acceded to important environmental treaties in the field of shipping. 'Flagging out' could therefore be a ready method of circumventing important environmental rules.

Jurisdiction over pollution stemming from shipping is not limited to the flag state. Article 211 of the LOS Convention also addresses the jurisdiction of the coastal state in the different maritime zones from the coast: internal waters and ports; territorial sea; and exclusive economic zone. When foreign ships enter one of these zones, the flag state no longer has exclusive jurisdiction over the ship. The ship will also be subject to coastal state jurisdiction (also in the contiguous zone, on the continental shelf and on the high seas, coastal states enjoy a certain degree of jurisdiction over ships).

The right of the coastal state to adopt, control and enforce rules depends on and varies with the position of the foreign vessel at any one time. In short, one can say that the coastal state enjoys ever decreasing jurisdiction the further from land the vessel happens to be. In internal waters (including ports) and the territorial sea (i.e. up to twelve nautical miles from the territorial waters' baseline), coastal states exercise sovereignty. This has three major consequences for marine pollution. First, the coastal state can prohibit any discharge into the sea. Second, it can decide to give certain sea areas special protective status. And third, in its territorial and internal waters the coastal state may establish special routes for vessels with a view to reducing the risk of accidents and the pollution likely to ensue. Part II of the LOS Convention sets out detailed rules.

An important exception from the coastal state's unlimited authority in the territorial waters follows from the right of foreign ships to so-called innocent passage (see Part II, Section 3 of the LOS Convention). The LOS Convention limits the expedients available to coastal states to act against ships that represent an environmental hazard, but nonetheless are passing innocently through the state's territorial waters. A ship carrying an environmentally toxic cargo while engaged in innocent passage would, for instance, not in itself constitute a violation of the clause that passage should be 'innocent'. In principle, therefore, the state has no legal grounds to bar the ship from its territorial waters. The furthest it can go is to take precautionary measures that minimise the risk by, for example, requiring the ship to keep to a prescribed sea lane.

Under the LOS Convention, the right to innocent passage can only be forfeited if an act of 'wilful and serious' pollution takes place (see article 19, paragraph 2). The 'wilful' requirement (an act performed consciously and intentionally) usually excludes accidents. And even though most regular discharges while en route meet the criterion on wilfulness, they are rarely particularly serious in themselves. In other words, it takes quite a lot for a ship to forfeit its right to innocent passage for reasons of pollution.

Another exception disbars the coastal state from establishing rules affecting the design, construction, manning or equipment of foreign ships beyond what follows from 'generally accepted international rules or standards' (see article 21, paragraph 2 of the LOS Convention). This is to keep states from preventing a ship from enjoying the right to sail through the territorial waters or international straits. If every state could pick and choose its own standards on, for example, ship construction, navigational freedom could easily be undermined. This doesn't mean that the state's rules on ship construction and the like don't apply to foreign vessels, only that they must harmonise with international standards and not effectively prevent navigation.

The most important difference from traditional law of the sea on pollution-related jurisdiction over vessels is the LOS Convention's provisions on the exclusive economic zone (see article 211, paragraph 5 of the LOS Convention). The coastal state exercises sovereign rights for certain purposes, including protecting the marine environment, in an area of sea not exceeding 200 nautical miles from the baselines from which the breadth of the territorial sea is measured. Basically, all states retain the freedoms of the high seas within the 200 nautical miles limit, unlike the more limited right to innocent passage through the territorial waters. The coastal state, however, is entitled to regulate pollution from various sources, but in the case of pollution from vessels, the coastal state may only adopt rules which harmonise with and give effect to, again, 'generally accepted international rules or standards'. Thus, states cannot enact or enforce national pollution rules on foreign vessels which diverge from those established by the IMO. The purpose, here as elsewhere, is to avoid obstructing as far as possible international shipping.

There are, nevertheless, certain exemptions. One is environmental regulation of ice-covered waters. The LOS Convention has a separate provision reflecting the realisation that the ecological sensitivity of the Polar Regions justifies the use of special measures to protect and preserve the marine environment. According to article 234 of the LOS Convention, coastal states have the right to adopt and enforce non-discriminatory laws and regulations for the prevention, reduction and control of marine pollution from vessels in ice-covered areas within the limits of the exclusive economic zone, where particularly severe climatic conditions and the presence of ice covering such areas for most of the year create obstructions or exceptional hazards to navigation, and pollution of the marine environment could cause major harm to or irreversible disturbance of the ecological balance. Article 234 further stipulates that such laws and regulations shall have due regard to navigation and the protection and preservation of the marine environment based on the best available scientific evidence.

Acting under the authority of article 234 of the LOS Convention, Canada and Russia have instituted stringent national environmental measures, specifically with regard to navigation through their Arctic waterways of the Northwest Passage and the Northern Sea Route, respectively (Molenaar 1998: 421–26). Also IMO has designed rules for the specific purpose of regulating maritime activity in the Arctic. Work started in the wake of the *Exxon Valdez* catastrophe off the coast of Alaska in 1989. The resulting oil spill had a devastating impact on the marine environment and was a reminder of the extreme sensitivity of the Arctic to pollution. IMO adopted in 2002 guidelines on Arctic shipping, hoping in time to improve security for crews, vessels and the environment (Jensen 2008: 107–44). The Guidelines have later been adjusted to also apply for the Antarctic region.

Also in cases in which international rules are inadequate to protect particularly sensitive marine biospheres, tighter regulations can be adopted within the exclusive economic zone. These regulations tend to cover both discharges and maritime practices. Regulatory initiatives shall nevertheless be submitted to the IMO for approval. Thus, the coastal states themselves cannot tighten regulations single-handedly; they need to be justified and approved (see article 211, paragraph 6 of the LOS Convention).

If pollution regulations are violated in the exclusive economic zone, the enforcing powers of the coastal state increase in step with the gravity of the offence and resulting damage. In the gravest cases the state can take legal action and impound the ship (see article 220 of the LOS Convention). The coastal state has also powers of enforcement over ships which are in its ports voluntarily and which caused pollution *outside* the exclusive economic zone. If there is sufficient evidence, legal action can be initiated against the ship under certain conditions for discharging waste on the high seas. The coastal state is also empowered to intervene in pollution accidents to protect its coastline and related interests. On this point, the LOS Convention enacts important principles of *jus necessitatis*, as enshrined under customary international law, but purely preventative measures to hinder harm to the marine environment.

Global and regional cooperation

As we all know, pollution doesn't bother about borders drawn on maps. Preventing pollution needs collaboration and regulations across national borders. Thus, more than any other international treaty concerning the environment, the LOS Convention flags international cooperation as essential to progress in the fight against pollution. States shall not conduct themselves as if they were alone. They are obliged to work together globally and regionally to combat pollution of the marine environment as efficiently and as sensibly as possible.

To this end, the LOS Convention requires States Parties to collaborate directly or through competent international organisations in formulating rules, standards and procedures for the protection and preservation of the marine environment (see article 197 of the LOS Convention). As seen above, the global alliance to combat pollution from shipping is particularly illustrative. For instance, the IMO has negotiated MARPOL 73/78 along with several other international treaties, guidelines and recommendations.

The LOS Convention also urges states to work together at the regional level in combating marine pollution. What 'regional' means is not clear from the terminology of the LOS Convention, but articles 122 and 123 dealing with collaboration between states bordering so-called 'enclosed or semi-enclosed sea[s]' give an indication. In these cases states should cooperate with one another in coordinating policy and management. It goes without saying that the environment is a typical issue area. One cannot drink from one side of a cup of tea, and pollute from the other.

There exists a number of regional agreements and mechanisms precisely in the area of marine pollution. One example is regional alliances on matters pertaining to the North Sea, the Mediterranean and the Baltic (Brownlie 2003: 282). At the political level, the North Sea Conferences (see Chapter 6) and the Arctic Council could also be mentioned as cooperative mechanisms. The latter is an important forum for states bordering the Arctic Ocean, in addition to Sweden, Finland and Iceland. The locomotive in the alliance is the collective challenge posed by climate change, resource exploitation and environment, alongside the desire to promote sustainable development. Of the five permanent working groups, one works specifically on pollution.

What can such regional mechanisms achieve in practice? First, special geographical or ecological reasons could favour regional collaboration. Perhaps the best example is the environmental regulation of ice-covered waters and the Arctic, as mentioned above. Another is the growing focus on the marine environment and pollution of European waters. Accidents involving oil tankers raised awareness initially of the problems of access to ports for ships in distress, but later of marine pollution problems as well. As part of the European Union's (EU's) work to protect the marine environment, the European Maritime Safety Agency was founded in 2002 with a view to providing the EU Commission and Member States with adequate technical and scientific input to ensure high environmental standards through the Union's harmonised rules. The EU's maritime strategy illustrates very well the development of an enhanced regional alliance for combating marine pollution and efforts to prevent loss of biological diversity.

Secondly, there are types of pollution problems that are most amenable to solution at the regional level. They include, for instance, pollution in connection with shipping accidents, the environmental impact of which can be very serious but may only affect a limited geographical area and a small number of states. The Bonn Agreement of 1992 is one example. It provides for an early warning system and multilateral response by countries bordering the North Sea and seeks to limit damage caused by pollution from oil and other dangerous substances. A counter-pollution plan has been prepared to enable immediate surveillance and response to major incidents and indicate counter-pollution strategies. The Copenhagen Agreement of 1971 (revised in 1993) applies similarly between Denmark,

Finland, Iceland, Norway and Sweden. The States Parties have agreed to cooperate on investigations, reporting and assistance to protect the marine environment from pollution by oil or other hazardous substances.

Finally, a regional approach can be particularly useful in monitoring the environment. Environmental surveillance is important not only in connection with the investigation and as evidence in the prosecution of criminal offences. It can also form the basis for prioritising between environmental measures and create a framework for developing and pursuing targets and mechanisms under environmental policy. Collaboration on surveillance of the marine environment has therefore been established for several areas of the sea, including the North Sea through the Bonn Agreement. Also, the EU's maritime strategy gives priority to the surveillance of the environment, especially insofar as it concerns oil spills from vessels. Every day, quantities of oil are routinely dumped into the sea. Most discharges are small, but together account for the biggest share of oil pollution from ships. Estimates performed by the European Commission's Joint Research Centre suggest that of total oil pollution, 25 per cent stems from accidents, while 75 per cent results from operational discharges (Vidas 2010: 30–31). There is a significant degree of uncertainty on the possible long-term effects of this pollution and its impact on marine biological diversity and ecosystems. The extent of these discharges, however, suggests that both the shipping industry and coastal states should take the problem seriously.

Conclusions

The purpose of this chapter has been to present an outline of the most important regulations under modern international law of the sea with regard to pollution of the marine environment. The LOS Convention is the key international legal framework under which most states are bound in these questions. It establishes for the first time a global legal framework for the protection and preservation of the marine environment. The most salient provisions in the LOS Convention are probably those setting out the comprehensive duties of the States Parties to adopt national rules and regulations to prevent and reduce marine pollution, and contribute to the establishment of regional and global regulations to the same purpose. Possibly the most important impact of the LOS Convention is that treaties dealing specifically with pollution sources, such as those found in MARPOL 73/78, have been 'accepted' under the Convention as minimum standards and further that states shall as far as possible pool their resources in combating marine pollution.

Whether the LOS Convention brings about a real reduction in marine pollution remains unclear, and will of course depend on the type of pollution involved, and the ability, capacity and willingness of states to enforce the regulations in an adequate way. Due to the LOS Convention's compromise solutions and vague provisions, regional regulatory mechanisms might be more effective and important in the long run. But this should not stand in the way of the LOS Convention's success – both in terms of its overarching objectives and material substance – in demonstrating virtually universal support for the fight against marine pollution. So far, the LOS Convention represents the most important step the international community has ever taken towards a global legal regime for a sustainable use of the world's oceans.

Bibliography

Birnie, P. and Boyle, A. (1992) *International Law and the Environment*, Oxford: Oxford University Press.

Brown, E.D. (1992) 'Law of the sea, history', in R. Bernhardt (ed.) *Encyclopedia of Public International Law* 3. Amsterdam: Elsevier Science Publishers.

Brownlie, I. (2003) *Principles of Public International Law*. Sixth edition. Oxford: Oxford University Press.

Churchill, R.R. and Lowe, A.V. (1999) *The Law of the Sea*. Third edition. Manchester: Manchester University Press.

Jensen, Ø. (2008) 'Arctic shipping guidelines: towards a legal regime for navigation safety and environmental protection?', *Polar Record*, 44: 107–14.

Molenaar, E. (1998) *Coastal State Jurisdiction over Vessel Source-Pollution*. The Hague: Kluwer Law International.

Trieschmann, O. (2010) 'Illegal oil spills from ships: monitoring by remote sensing' in D. Vidas (ed.) *Law, Technology and Science for Oceans in Globalisation: IUU fishing, oil pollution, bioprospecting, outer continental shelf.* Leiden and Boston: Martinus Nijhoff Publishers.

Vidas, D. (2010) 'Responsibility for the seas' in D. Vidas (ed.) *Law, Technology and Science for Oceans in Globalisation. IUU Fishing, Oil Pollution, Bioprospecting, Outer Continental Shelf.* Leiden-Boston: Martinus Nijhoff Publishers.

6   North Sea pollution control

One problem, different solutions

Jon Birger Skjærseth

Important years

1972   Oslo Convention adopted
1974   Paris Convention adopted
1984   First international North Sea Conference held
1987   Ambitious reduction targets adopted
1992   OSPAR Convention adopted
2000   EU Water Framework Directive adopted
2006   Last international North Sea Conference held
2008   EU Marine Strategy Framework Directive adopted

Between 1970 and the mid-1980s, the international effort to reduce pollution in the North Sea and the North East Atlantic was essentially marking time. Emissions were growing, as were suspicions that the state of the environment was worsening. The main problems were land-based discharges, dumping of toxic waste as well as emissions from the oil and gas industry and ships. At an international conference arranged in 1987 ministers of the environment from each of the eight North Sea states pledged action to reverse the trend. The North Sea Conference heralded several ambitious international commitments; their importance to international marine pollution control can be felt to this day.

This chapter explores the reasons behind the 1987 breakthrough and its significance for the international effort to cope with marine pollution in the North Sea. The chapter concentrates on two of the leading challenges: land-based discharges of hazardous substances and nutrients (phosphorous and nitrogen). We shall also examine how the North Sea states – that is, Norway, Denmark, Germany, Netherlands, Belgium, France, Sweden and the UK – managed to end the dumping of toxic waste. Thereafter follows an examination of the international cooperation under different, sometimes overlapping international institutions: North Sea conferences, the OSPAR Convention and the EU. Indeed, as we will be contended, the various institutions have fulfilled different functions all of which are needed to make international environmental cooperation effective.

North Sea pollution as a problem: uncertainty but 'better safe than sorry'

In July 1971 the cargo ship *Stella Maris* sailed from the port of Rotterdam heading for the northern reaches of the North Sea. The captain notified the port authorities of his intention to dump 650 tonnes of highly toxic waste off the Norwegian coast for which he had been hired by a chemical manufacturer. The operation prompted a strong protest from the Norwegian government, and pressure was brought to bear on the Dutch government to take action before it was too late. There was only one snag: there was no international law to prevent the captain from proceeding with his assignment. In theory, anyone could go and dump whatever and wherever they wanted. The skipper subsequently gave in to pressure and began to look for another likely spot where he could dump his cargo, this time between Iceland and Ireland. This triggered another round of protests from those two countries; the chemical company, wary of the negative publicity, finally capitulated. What the incident revealed was the lack of international rules that could prevent pollution of the marine environment; and it showed the potential strength of political and popular pressure (Skjærseth 2002a).

Great quantities of hazardous waste were dumped into the sea following the Second World War. Expanding economies created more and more waste; the North Sea countries looked for new, inexpensive ways of getting rid of it. By the late 1960s, companies specialising in collecting toxic waste and dumping it in the North Sea were appearing. Everything from old wartime ammunition to radioactive waste was dumped from ships. Industrial waste, which was so toxic that governments refused to dispose of it on land, was burned at sea in special incinerator ships. The incineration of waste released dioxins, which are among the most toxic substances known to man. Although dumping and incineration accounted for only a small proportion of discharges to the North Sea, one was sitting on a time bomb. The North Sea is one of the world's most lavish marine environments, providing many of the species of fish found on dinner tables throughout Europe.

Surrounded by densely populated areas, the North Sea is under constant pressure from human activity (Freestone and Ijlstra 1990). It is one of the busiest maritime areas in the world as well, and plays host to many of Europe's leading seaports. The discovery of enormous oil and gas deposits turned the North Sea into one of the leading centres of petroleum production. But unremitting contamination followed, not to mention the risk of oil accidents. Land-based effluent was transported by rivers and deposited directly into the sea via discharge outlets. That is where most of the pollution comes from. The most serious problem is the discharge of different types of hazardous substance and nutrients (Skjærseth 2004). Hazardous substances are toxic chemicals which are not readily degradable in nature.

They accumulate in living organisms through the food chain and can cause irrevocable harm to health and ecosystems. Hazardous substances are, in other words, a serious threat to public health, food supply and biological diversity. One of the important groups of hazardous substances is the heavy metals. Mercury, lead and cadmium are among the most problematic in terms of the environment. Another group is the organic hazardous substances, such as PCB and dioxins. The main sources of land-based hazardous substances are mining, waste treatment, manufacturing and households. Nutrients (phosphorous and nitrogen) are essential to a healthy ecosystem, but oversupply can result in eutrophication, that is, algae growth, toxic algal blooms and oxygen depletion. The main sources here are agriculture, sewage disposal, manufacturing and fish farms.

As mentioned already, by the mid-1980s there were strong indications that certain areas of the North Sea were seriously contaminated. But no one really knew which substances were being released, in what quantities, or how environmentally dangerous they were. Indeed, there were practically no reliable data on discharge trends even by the late 1980s. There was, however, one aspect of all this that had attracted suspicions since the 1970s: the prevailing North Sea current moves in an anti-clockwise direction. Pollution can therefore be carried northwards, from the UK via the continent and along the Norwegian coast. Some countries were exporting their waste, others were importing it. So the North Sea countries had different interests to address the problem. The main problem was that countries exporting their waste had scant interests in adopting stringent regulations. The scientific work was also affected by the varying interests. For instance, it took six years before a recommended mechanism was in place to monitor toxic titanium dioxide waste in dumping areas (Skjærseth 1992). Some countries, like the UK, wanted to see monitoring and research efforts restricted to observing tangible negative effects of even the most toxic substances in the marine environment, well aware of the difficulties involved. The majority were content with assessing, identifying and controlling the actual discharge of the most dangerous substances. In addition to various interests related to cost and benefit, consensus proved even more elusive because of the different national regulatory traditions (Skjærseth 2000).

The first report on the environmental status of the North Sea was presented in 1984. It said that because so little was known it was virtually impossible to verify any link between emissions, concentrations and harm to marine organisms. In this climate of uncertainty, governments could reject calls by environmental organisations to clean up the North Sea. A more comprehensive report came out in 1987. While uncertainty remained high, it said, there was quite a lot of information on the state of the environment. The North Sea was 'moderately polluted' in some areas, but the effect on plankton, fish, seabirds and marine mammals was probably quite serious. In light of these suspicions the study of the environment became an urgent priority. An international, 77-strong team of scientists was convened. It was asked to submit its report in 1993. The conclusions in this report, supported by the whole team, confirmed earlier conclusions, and highlighted again the level of uncertainty concerning the links between causes and effects. At the same time, the report painted a more pessimistic picture. The concentration of certain substances was too high in wide areas of the North Sea, and action was needed across several fronts. The transportation of pollution from country to country was also confirmed. The team's most important message was perhaps that it was futile to expect research and monitoring to provide scientific certainty on every cause and every effect. The North Sea is such a complex ecosystem; it would probably never be fully understood. Facing such uncertainty, a precautionary approach began gaining momentum as a platform for setting targets and taking action to reduce and prevent North Sea pollution.

The next and so far latest status report was published in 2000. It examined the entire North East Atlantic, dividing it into five regions. The North Sea (including the English Channel) was one. The report addressed the effects of climate change on the marine environment as well. As before, uncertainty remained high, although more was known about some of the discharges, concentrations and impacts. There were also positive developments, despite the many challenges ahead. As we shall see below, there are several reliable sets of data which show trends and changes over time. The report identified as the most urgent challenges hazardous substances, eutrophication and fisheries.

The political process: towards different cooperative institutions

The *Stella Maris* incident was one of the reasons behind the 1972 Oslo Convention. The Convention's aim was to control dumping from ships and aircraft and waste incineration in the North East Atlantic. As its name indicates, negotiations on the first comprehensive international environmental accord for these waters took place in Oslo, with Norwegian authorities playing a central role. Two years later, a similar agreement was signed in Paris. The Paris Convention addressed land-based pollution. A permanent secretariat was created, based in London, along with two collaborative bodies (Oslo and Paris Commissions), the members of which met annually to discuss measures under the framework of the international agreements. Different working groups were set up to monitor environmental conditions and assess possible measures and targets. In addition to the eight North Sea states and the European Union (EU), four other countries bordering the Atlantic took part: Portugal, Spain, Iceland and Ireland. The Oslo Convention included Finland as well. Although these conventions set down international rules, they were relatively lenient until 1987. While the Oslo Convention was a step in the right direction, it failed to solve the problem. Waste incineration at sea grew to the mid-1980s, and dumping continued as before, though in a more controlled environment.

One of the reasons for the lack of progress, apart from different interests, was the lack of transparency; because critical scrutiny was difficult, environmental non-governmental organisations and the media were less well placed to put pressure on the cooperation. The rules of the game were designed to let the parties work in peace (Skjærseth 1998). No documents should be made public without the consent of all concerned. In addition, it was difficult to fast-track modifications of the conventions in response to fresh scientific data. Change in the legal framework required a protracted ratification process in each of the member states – sometimes lasting years at a time.

With the benefit of hindsight it is easy to see how the cooperation took on the appearance of an exclusive club, based on shared conceptions and understandings, but at the expense of effective bargaining. The same delegates from the same countries' environmental ministries met year after year and developed strong personal ties (Skjærseth 2003). Everyone had to agree about everything, although the Paris Convention allowed in principle for qualified majority voting. Because the Conventions covered the North East Atlantic as a whole, the principle of consensus involved countries without borders with the North Sea in decision-making, such as Spain and Portugal, whatever their individual challenges and environmental policy ambition. Spain, for example, was mostly preoccupied with implementing the Barcelona Convention, which regulated pollution of the Mediterranean. But even if there was little progress during that first decade, the legal framework and close relations would bear fruit later on.

Exasperated by the lack of progress, Germany arranged a conference for the eight North Sea countries in Bremen in 1984. Germany showed leadership in launching the precautionary principle, and successfully had a formulation inserted into the Bremen Declaration expressing that a strong belief of harmful effects was sufficient to warrant action. The watershed event, however, was the next North Sea Conference, in London in 1987, where the precautionary principle was officially adopted. The 1987 North Sea Declaration is considered the first international environmental agreement to recognise the principle. As we shall see in the next section, the 1987 event can be explained by a combination of greater environmental interest in Europe and the creation of a new institutional framework for the North Sea countries.

While the Oslo and Paris collaborations had only succeeded in passing a small number of rather weak international commitments, the North Sea countries were now set on laying down ambitious targets based on the precautionary principle. As the links between emissions and environmental impact were still uncertain and difficult to identify, recognition of the precautionary principle has to be counted as a landmark decision in the negotiations. All countries agreed now that if it was known that discharged substances represented an environmental hazard, it would be sufficient grounds for taking action. With regard to dumping at sea, the precautionary principle implied that the polluters had to prove that the substances were not harmful. They failed to do so. Dumping and waste incineration at sea were banned, and the North Sea states agreed a schedule to halve land-based discharges of hazardous substances and nutrients in sensitive areas between 1985 and 1995. These were political decisions based on the precautionary principle. There was no scientific reason to set the target at 50 per cent rather than 48 or 53.

The next North Sea Conference, held at the Hague in 1990, went further, particularly in the area of hazardous substances (Skjærseth 2002b). The 1987 decision was specified, resulting in a list of 36 substances, the most dangerous of which were to be cut by 70 per cent. The next North Sea Conference, at Esbjerg in 1995, can stand as a symbol of the sweeping changes in the international objectives that were taking place at the time. In the mid-1980s the number of controlled hazardous substances was very small, and the controls not very stringent. By 1995 the North Sea countries were agreeing to reduce the concentration of the most dangerous hazardous substances to the background levels of naturally occurring substances, that is, the concentrations one would have had without human activity, and to practically zero for man-made compounds by 2020. Interpreted strictly, the targets would mean stopping the discharge of these substances altogether. By this point, the North Sea Conference process had in many ways made itself redundant as a major source of new principles and ambitious international objectives. The 2002 Bergen North Sea Conference made only small advances and ministers admitted at the Gothenburg Conference in 2006 that work on most of the issue areas had been taken over by other cooperative bodies and organisations (see below). And despite the stated commitment to work together on the challenges facing the North Sea, no invitations to a new North Sea Conference have been despatched. The North Sea Conference process seems therefore to have come to an end, twenty-two years after the first meeting in Bremen (Skjærseth 2010).

In 1992, the Oslo and Paris conventions were merged into a single document, the OSPAR Convention, with Switzerland and Luxembourg as new members in addition to the original membership. OSPAR came into effect in 1998, and the Parties have concentrated on six core areas, each of which is supervised by its own committee. The areas are: assessment and monitoring; eutrophication; biological diversity and ecosystems; hazardous substances; offshore oil and gas industry; and radioactive substances. Measures in each of these areas are adopted mainly as binding decisions or recommendations.

Between 1977 and 2005, the OSPAR Parties adopted ninety-six decisions and recommendations, and several agreements, mainly on guidelines on monitoring practices. Although the Parties are empowered to withhold assent, they seldom do. The UK has made most reservations, five altogether, followed by France, Finland and Spain with three apiece. On the one hand the reservation right promotes decision-making effectiveness because one avoids having individual countries impeding progress for the rest. On the other, it is the countries with the highest activity levels in a particular area that tend to make reservations, and that does make it difficult to achieve an effective solution of the problem. Collaboration under the OSPAR framework has also benefited transparency and scrutiny. In 1993, for example, a decision was made to place all documents in the public domain unless otherwise decided. Thirty-three voluntary and private organisations, mostly within the private and environmental non-governmental sectors, enjoy observation status today.

The EU has played an increasingly important role in the North Sea cooperation, both as a member of various bodies in its own right and by its participation together with European Economic Area member states in OSPAR and the North Sea conferences. Before the latest eastward expansion of the EU, resulting in twelve new member states, nearly all EU members were parties to OSPAR. Change in the EU decision-making procedures in the environmental sphere from unanimity to qualified majority helped engineer a comprehensive, ambitious regulatory regime to combat marine pollution. As under OSPAR, discharges of hazardous substances are regulated from point sources, such as manufacturing plants, mainly by means of requiring the use of the 'best available technology' and by setting emission targets. Discharges from diffuse sources, such as cultivated land, are controlled by means of 'best environmental practices', marketing and use of products (Skjærseth 2010).

An important EU directive is the 1996 IPPC – Integrated Pollution Prevention and Control – Directive. It seeks to gather regulations on all hazardous emissions to air, water and soil from a single enterprise under a single emission permit issued by a single authority. It has led to legislative and administrative reorganisation in several European countries. Another is the EU Water Framework Directive from 2000. It seeks to achieve an integrated system of water management in the individual countries. Waterways, groundwater and coastal waters are covered by the directive, along with measures to improve water quality. One innovation in this directive is management by river basin – the natural unit – instead of administrative or political boundaries. This ecosystem approach aims to improve coordination between authorities and sectors. For nutrients, the Urban Waste Water Directive of 1991 and Nitrates Directive are both important. The Waste Water Directive imposes stringent conditions on sewage treatment facilities. The Nitrates Directive complements the Waste Water Directive in regulating nitrogen emissions from the farming industry (Skjærseth 2010).

The EU has also adopted a new Marine Strategy Directive. It seeks to ensure a healthy environment by 2020 by means of the ecosystem-based management in different regions and sub-regions, such as the North East Atlantic and North Sea. While the Marine Strategy Directive complements the Water Framework Directive and ensures a coherent system of management across the hydrological (or water) cycle, it overlaps OSPAR and North Sea declarations. To what extent the different international regimes will prove to complement or work against each other in practice remains to be seen.

Mutually complementary institutions

So far, synergy rather than conflict has characterised the work of the different international environmental institutions (Skjærseth 2006a, 2006b). The key to understanding how the North Sea cooperation works is to examine the division of competences between the various international institutions. As we have seen, dumping and the land-based discharge of nutrients and hazardous substances are regulated (to different degrees) by three international institutions, that is, the North Sea conferences, OSPAR and EU: a recipe for duplication, muddle and inefficiency one might think. Within the North Sea cooperation, however, all three institutions have acted to complement one another by fulfilling different functions, facilitating overall effectiveness.

First, the political 'soft law' North Sea conferences have speeded up decision-making within OSPAR and the EU. The non-binding North Sea Declarations risked the same fate as the empty electoral pledge: easy come, easy go. This was avoided, however, because the Declarations were later adopted by OSPAR and the EU. The ambitious North Sea Declarations were thus made binding on the Parties under international and EU law. Their adoption also led to the expansion of the sea areas covered under the North Sea Declarations, that is, the North Sea, with the inclusion of wider areas covered by OSPAR and the EU. One of the main mechanisms of translating declarations adopted at the North Sea conferences into OSPAR and EU legislation lay partly in the overlapping memberships of the three institutions.

Why did the breakthrough occur at the North Sea conferences rather than OSPAR or the EU? Although the so-called algal invasions of 1988 and 1989 and increasing awareness of environmental issues in the late 1980s made a difference, the North Sea conferences led to a significant re-organisation of the international cooperation. Countries not bordering the North Sea were decoupled from the work under the North Sea conferences. This led in practice to the exclusion of some of the 'laggards', like Spain and Portugal, leaving the UK alone with its unenviable environmental reputation as the 'dirty man' of Europe (Skjærseth 2000).

It was not enough to isolate the UK, however, because British environmental authorities still had the powers to oppose ambitious proposals. But the conference process allowed for greater transparency and attracted wide publicity. The North Sea conferences proceeded at the political level; decisions could take effect immediately; and environmental organisations were allowed to participate. The conferences benefited from a public opinion that was increasingly geared towards an ambitious environmental policy. Dumping and waste incineration were, moreover, ideal targets for Greenpeace campaigns because they were so visible. Reports of toxic substance being dumped overboard didn't look good when shown on TV or in the newspapers. Unlike the Oslo and Paris Commissions, the North Sea conference also initiated a systematic process of monitoring state compliance, with information on which countries were doing what being made public. All these changes added to the pressure on the UK from the environmental organisations and some of the other North Sea countries. The result was that the political cost to the UK came to out-weigh the economic benefits of, for instance, dumping industrial waste into the sea. Political pressure mounted after the first North Sea conference, culminating in August 1993 when Norway's environment minister Torbjørn Berntsen – known in Norway as 'Mr Lip' – regaled his British government counterpart John Gummer using a phrase translated by the English papers as 'shit bag'. The remark fell in a quarrel over acid rain and discharges from the nuclear fuel reprocessing plant at Sellafield into the Irish Sea.

The second effect is that OSPAR and the EU have facilitated domestic implementation of the North Sea declarations by higher authoritativeness and enforcement competence. The direct link here is the reference in the North Sea Declarations to OSPAR and the EU on implementing activities. The significance of OSPAR lay in decisions that are binding under international law, even though the Parties lack the means to enforce compliance. Further, the long history of working together since the early 1970s has helped establish new norms. Indeed, the very act of dumping waste into the sea was gradually perceived as inherently wrong, irrespective of the impact on the environment (Skjærseth 2000). OSPAR was particularly important with regard to dumping of toxic waste and waste incineration because the EU had limited competence in those areas.

Dumping of industrial waste is an example of how important it was to translate the North Sea Declarations into binding commitments. Although the 1987 North Sea Declaration set 1990 as the deadline to end dumping, the UK issued permits allowing 50,000 tonnes of hazardous waste to be dumped in 1989. The other North Sea countries were horrified by the plans and protested vigorously. They argued that the dumping permits violated binding commitments under the scope of the Oslo Commission. Greenpeace got wind of the plans and alerted the media. It led to an extraordinary meeting of the Oslo Commission. A panel of experts from each of the North Sea countries looked at the new permits and reiterated the original objections. One of the major chemical companies involved withdrew its application because it had 'suddenly' found an alternative site on land for its waste. The whole episode was beginning to be embarrassing for the environmental authorities, and in 1990 John Gummer decided to stop the UK's dumping of industrial waste, including sewage sludge containing hazardous substances.

Table 6.1 Permits and actual dumping of liquid industrial waste in the sea from the UK 1988–93

Year	Licenses issued	Licensed quantity (tons)	Tonnage deposited
1988	19	311,411	249,744
1989	16	292,968	248,454
1990	5	228,000	209,961
1991	2	205,000	191,945
1992	2	75,604	180,725
1993	0	0	0

Source: Skjærseth (2002a).

But the norms were also undergoing a less conspicuous transformation in the UK as well. The unit in the British Department of the Environment responsible for issuing dumping permits began to regard dumping as the 'last option', though they maintained their stance on dumping as an innocuous activity as far as the environment was concerned (Skjærseth 2000).

OSPAR's powers are wider than those of the North Sea conferences and those of the EU wider than OSPAR's because EU member states have transferred national sovereignty to the EU. The EU can act with greater force because the directives are directly binding on member states. The EU has its own court as well, which can issue penalties in the form of fines and other measures to countries for non-compliance with environmental legislation. The court has taken steps in respect of many directives of relevance to marine pollution. It threatened the UK, for instance, with heavy day fines for failing to meet EU bathing water standards, and is one of the reasons why the UK is currently in compliance with the regulations.

Many EU directives have important implications for marine pollution, but we shall restrict ourselves here to one example showing the importance of EU enforcement capacity. The North Sea Declaration's aim to reduce nitrogen emissions by 50 per cent in 'sensitive areas' by 1995 had little, if any, effect on the farming sector, the most important source of nitrogen emissions in the North Sea states and the EU (Skjærseth 2006a). The low impact was mainly due to a combination of strong farming lobbying and different interests between the environmental and farming authorities. According to the UK authorities, there were no 'sensitive areas' in the UK and accordingly no need to take any action at all. Although the 1991 EU Nitrates Directive is an extremely poor example of 'effective' EU implementation, it nicely illustrates that the EU has more powerful tools at its disposal than OSPAR and the North Sea conferences when states do not comply. In 1997, thirteen of the then fifteen EU member states were threatened with legal action if they failed to improve implementation of the Nitrates Directive. In 1998, representatives of the EU parliament were 'shocked' by the lack of progress. Member states were hauled before the

EU court for breaching their obligation to set up adequate monitoring procedures; for not defining 'nitrogen sensitive' areas; and for failing to adopt action plans as required under the directive. The UK, which believed it had no sensitive areas, was sentenced in 2000 for defining 'sensitive area' too narrowly. Following the verdict, the areas defined as sensitive multiplied several times over.

A report issued by the EU Commission on the implementation of the Nitrates Directive between 2000 and 2003 finds progress in most areas. All countries have now defined 'nitrogen sensitive areas' and all have adopted action plans, though of varying quality (Ireland as late as 2006, fifteen years after the directive entered into force). Monitoring has improved; there is less use of fertiliser; and there are indications of declining or stable concentrations of nitrogen in surface water. We shall see below how this helped reduce eutrophication of the North Sea from land-based sources.

Positive results, but high uncertainty and great challenges

As far as dumping and waste incineration are concerned, a clear relationship is found between international collaboration and success at solving the problems. Cooperation under the Oslo Commission led to the introduction of legislation in member states banning dumping in the sea without a permit issued by the environmental authorities. The authorities in each country gradually got a good idea of what was being dumped, by whom, where and how much. When the international commitment was adopted by the different countries to stop the dumping practice, it was easy to implement because the authorities could simply stop issuing permits. Belgium, Germany, France and the Netherlands reduced waste dumping from 2.3 million tonnes to zero in 1989. The Netherlands stopped certain manufacturing operations until the companies had developed other ways of reducing waste quantities. Waste incineration at sea ended as well (Skjærseth 2002a).

For land-based emissions, the picture is more complicated. There is less information and emissions are affected by many different factors. New hazardous substances are also being introduced, some as substitutes for controlled substances. The most reliable data we have so far cover the period 1990–2002, and were obtained by scientific working groups affiliated to OSPAR. With regard to reducing river- and land-based discharges of heavy metals such as cadmium, mercury and lead, there has been considerable success. For the North Sea, cadmium input fell by 49 per cent, lead by 33 per cent and mercury by 73 per cent. According to the European Environment Agency, progress in the area of organic environmental pollutants lindane and PCB has been good as well. Measurements of marine concentrations of other organic environmental pollutants indicate some improvement, but concentrations are still too high relative to background values of both natural and man-made environmental pollutants. Work to achieve the 2020 target on hazardous substances is thus far from over. For emissions of nutrients to the North Sea, progress has also been good. Input of nitrogen in the North Sea has fallen by 12 per cent and direct discharges of phosphorous by 33 per cent. (Data on input from rivers are uncertain due to flood variations.)

Discharges into the sea are also affected by other international environmental agreements, including the Stockholm Convention on Persistent Organic Pollutants. Input to the sea from the atmosphere is regulated by the Convention on Long-range Transboundary Air Pollution (see Chapter 2), and emissions to air and water from ships by the International Maritime Organization (see Chapter 5). Other factors, such as technological progress, economic activity and flooding affect the trends as well. All the same, there is little doubt that the North Sea Declarations, OSPAR and the EU have been instrumental in the progress witnessed.

Conclusions

In this chapter we have looked at the background to the landmark decision of the 1987 North Sea Conference and its implications for the international effort to reduce and prevent marine pollution. The work acquired a radically new direction in response to the poor performance and results of the international marine pollution cooperation under the Oslo and Paris Conventions. Emissions grew, and there were strong indications of declining environmental quality. But little was known about actual causes and effects, or about the wider ramifications. Germany therefore acted independently and launched a North Sea Conference process based on the precautionary principle to kick-start work in the area. It led to sweeping international decisions to cut emissions of hazardous substances and nutrients dramatically and prohibit dumping and waste incineration in the North Sea and the North East Atlantic.

There are two basic reasons why the breakthrough happened at the North Sea conferences. First, Oslo and Paris Convention countries without borders with the North Sea were decoupled from the North Sea conferences, isolating the UK as the principal laggard of the North Sea states. Second, public concern for the environment was growing, and the conferences led to several changes in the ways the parties worked together, which increased the political pressure on the UK. In the end the UK redefined its policies and has since played a more constructive role in the cooperation. The 'soft law' North Sea Declarations were also incorporated into international law through OSPAR decisions and several EU directives. This was important to strengthen the implementation of action necessary to achieve the international North Sea Declaration targets. The EU in particular has an ability to enforce compliance when implementation has slowed down.

Dumping and waste incineration at sea of extremely toxic substances are things of the past thanks to this concerted effort. Land-based discharges of a range of controlled hazardous substances and nutrients have also fallen significantly. The reasons are complicated, but the North Sea Declarations, OSPAR and the EU have made substantial contributions. These international institutions have tended to act in complementary fashion, while at the same time regulating the same activities. The political 'soft law' North Sea Declarations have speeded up decision-making within OSPAR and the EU whereas OSPAR and the EU have facilitated implementation of the Declarations in different areas.

The combined problem-solving capacity provided by the North Sea Declarations, OSPAR and the EU, are important to understand the increasing effectiveness in dealing with North Sea pollution. To understand why significantly more progress has been achieved on dumping and incineration than land-based discharges, we have to look at different problem-types. Even though these problems share some basic similarities, such as asymmetrical interests between the states, the order of magnitude was different. Land-based emissions account for approximately 70 per cent of contaminated inputs to the sea. Consequently, the size of externalities is much greater. Moreover, the costs of dealing with land-based effluents are much higher as compared to dumping. Land-based inputs originate from a wide range of sectors ranging from industry to agriculture and regulation would have a larger potential to distort competition. The dumping and incineration problems were also highly visible compared to diffuse land-based emissions. Since the *Stella Maris* incident, dumping at sea has attracted high media attention, public concern and attention from the green movement. Especially Greenpeace has been active in pushing for a ban on dumping since the 1970s. Dumping and incineration vessels served, as noted, as perfect targets for campaigns and these problems were also framed in terms of values and symbols.

Bibliography

Freestone, D. and Ijlstra, T. (eds) (1990) *The North Sea: perspectives on regional environmental co-operation*, Special Issue of the International Journal of Estuarine and Coastal Law, London: Graham & Trotman.

Skjærseth, J.B. (1992) 'Towards the end of dumping in the North Sea – an example of effective problem-solving?', *Marine Policy*, 16: 130–40.

——(1998) 'The making and implementation of North Sea commitments: the politics of environmental participation', in Victor, D.G, K. Raustiala and E.B. Skolnikoff (eds) *The Implementation and Effectiveness of International Environmental Commitments*, Cambridge: MIT Press and Laxenburg: International Institute for Applied Systems Analysis.

——(2000) *North Sea Cooperation: linking international and domestic pollution control*, Manchester: Manchester University Press.

——(2002a) 'Towards the end of dumping in the North Sea', Chapter 3 in Ed. Miles, A. Underdal, S. Andresen, J. Wettestad, J.B. Skjærseth and E. Carlin, *Regime Effectiveness: confronting theory with evidence*, Cambridge: MIT Press.

——(2002b) 'Cleaning up the North Sea: the case of land-based pollution control', Chapter 7 in Ed. Miles, A. Underdal, S. Andresen, J. Wettestad, J.B. Skjærseth and E. Carlin, *Regime Effectiveness: confronting theory with evidence*, Cambridge: MIT Press.

——(2003) 'Managing North Sea pollution effectively: linking international and domestic institutions', *International Environmental Agreements: politics, law and economics,* 3: 167–90.

——(2004) 'Marine pollution: international ambition, domestic resistance', in Skjærseth, J.B. (ed.) *International Regimes and Norway's Environmental Policy: crossfire and coherence,* Aldershot: Ashgate.

——(2006a) 'Protecting the North-East Atlantic: enhancing synergies by institutional interplay', *Marine Policy,* 30: 157–66.

——(2006b) 'Protecting the North East Atlantic: one problem, three institutions', in S. Oberthür and Gehring, T. (eds) *Institutional Interaction in Global Environmental Governance,* Cambridge: MIT Press.

——(2010) 'Exploring the consequences of soft law and hard law: implementing international nutrient commitments in Norwegian agriculture', *International Environmental Agreements: Politics, Law and Economics,* 10: 1–14.

7 International fisheries politics

From sustainability to precaution

Olav Schram Stokke

Important years

1609 Publication of Grotius' *Mare liberum*
1882 North Sea Fisheries Convention
1902 International Council for the Exploration of the Sea
1948 Agreement for the Establishment of the Asia-Pacific Fisheries Commission (originally Indo-Pacific Fisheries Commission); several other regional or species-based commissions established in subsequent years
1958 Four Geneva Conventions on the Law of the Sea
1977 Exclusive economic zones recognised as customary international law
1982 United Nations Convention on the Law of the Sea
1995 United Nations Fish Stocks Agreement (on straddling or highly migratory stocks)
2009 FAO Agreement on Port State Measures to Prevent, Deter and Eliminate Illegal, Unreported and Unregulated Fishing

A man may fish with the worm that hath eat of a king, and eat of the fish that hath fed of that worm

> (Shakespeare, *Hamlet,* Act IV, sc. iii)

The idea that marine fisheries may require active conservation to remain sustainable is little more than a century old. Measures constraining harvesting effort in rivers and lakes date back thousands of years – but, for ocean resources, most scientists and decision-makers well into the 1900s tended to view the conservation challenge in much the same way as today's climate sceptics see global warming: they acknowledged great fluctuations in the availability of fish, but considered the human contribution to this as miniscule. The Second World War proved a turning point in this regard. Fishing had been greatly constrained by naval operations, and remarkably rich post-war catches indicated that the war years of lighter pressure had caused the stocks to thrive. Conservation is a relative newcomer in international fisheries politics, which originally focused on utilisation and distribution – primarily access to fishing grounds and constraints on gears that might benefit one state or one sector at the expense of others.

The problem facing international fisheries regimes is how to balance utilisation and conservation of a scarce resource while distributing the benefits among the states involved. Overcapacity results in fierce competition among and within states, rendering this problem malign, or politically difficult. The global regime for sustainably managing fisheries resources is codified in the 1982 United Nations (UN) Convention on the Law of the Sea: it defines the rights and roles of coastal states, flag states and port states in the making and enforcement of fisheries regulations. Stocks that are shared among states or that occur on the high seas are usually managed under regional fisheries regimes. These institutions provide means for cooperative research and joint regulation, and sometimes even procedures for verifying rule compliance and responding to violations. However, their effectiveness in solving the problem of resource management varies greatly across cases. One aim of this chapter is to identify institutional features and other factors that can explain such variation in the performance of international fisheries regimes.

The first section elaborates on the underlying problem that international fishery management regimes seek to solve. Then follows a brief history of the global fisheries regime and the political struggles that shaped its allocation of competences among states and regional management regimes. How these regimes work, and their effectiveness and performance, are in focus in ensuing sections, while the final section summarises the argument and draws some implications for international fisheries politics.

The problem: too many vessels chasing too few fish

Overcapacity may be the most visible challenge facing international fisheries politics, but the fundamental issue is that fish stocks are common-property resources. Harvesting capacity grew rapidly after the Second World War, partly due to improved technologies developed for military purposes. Submarine warfare, for instance, generated better echo sounding and sonar technologies, making it easier to locate and retrieve the fish. Other important advances include the development of the power block, which increased the efficiency of purse seining several-fold, synthetic netting, improved refrigeration and wider use of freezer and factory trawlers. World capture fisheries production doubled from 1950 to 1960: it then continued to grow steadily for another thirty years until levelling off around 90 million tonnes (FAO 2009a: 6). Regional variation is considerable: the production per fisher is almost ten times higher in Europe and North America than in Asia and Africa, where nearly 95 percent of the world's thirty-five million fishers reside. While the number of industrialised vessels has remained stable during the past decades – around 23,000 out of an estimated 2.1 million engine-powered fishing vessels (FAO 2009a: 28) – their harvesting efficiency is growing. In developing countries, relatively low productivity in the traditional sector is more than counterbalanced by a steady rise in the number of fishers, up by nearly fifty per cent since 1990. Overall, harvesting capacity is growing in all parts of the world.

Rising capacity would not pose a problem if fish were abundant – but today, hyper-modern and traditional fisheries alike face a shrinking resource base. More than a quarter of the world's recorded fish stocks are overfished or have collapsed, while half are fully exploited, including the most commercially important (FAO 2009a: 30). A recent study indicates that large and valuable predatory species like tuna and swordfish were ten times more abundant before they became subject to industrialised exploitation (Myers and Worm 2003). To some extent, fishers have been forced to follow the food chain downwards, towards smaller predators and plankton eaters (Pauly *et al.* 2002: 691). The world's total marine fish capture has remained relatively stable in recent decades, but many previously important stocks are decimated.

The mismatch between harvesting capacity and fish abundance results from the common-property nature of most fish stocks – meaning that they are open to exploitation by a large number of users. An often-cited example known as the 'tragedy of the commons' (Hardin 1968) illustrates the problem. On a commonly owned piece of grazing land, the rational move for each herdsman is to add steadily more of his own animals, since the benefits of grazing are his to keep fully, whereas the costs of over-grazing will be divided among the users. Since none of the herdsmen can prevent the others from doing the same, however, they risk exhausting the carrying capacity of the land, thereby bringing ruin to them all. The same logic applies to a fish stock under an open-access regime. To the individual fisherman, restraint on his part will only leave more for the others to catch, so it would appear that the sensible option is to take as much as he can.

In the terms set out in Chapter 1 of this volume, international fisheries management is a relatively malign problem, with common interests in restraining the harvesting pressure, competing interests in distributing it and clear incentives to violate agreements on restraint and distribution (Underdal 2002). For more than a century, breaking the common-property link between individual rationality and collective ruin is precisely what international fisheries institutions have sought to achieve.

History: nationalisation of the oceans

The present division of competence to manage fisheries among coastal states and others, centred on 200-mile exclusive economic zones (EEZs), has emerged through processes of commercial and political rivalry, legal arguments backed by power capabilities, and deliberate use of resource crises to legitimise changes of existing rules. In 1351, England and Castile entered into the first known international fisheries agreement (for details see Fulton 1911: 67). This treaty and similar ones in the centuries that followed largely concerned access to fishing grounds near the coast, but the extent of coastal state jurisdiction was hotly contested. Valuable fisheries were sources of tax incomes and community wealth, and thus worthy of military protection if necessary. In an excellent piece of early contract research, Hugo Grotius defended Dutch maritime interests in his 1609 *Mare liberum*. His contractors challenged Portuguese monopoly claimants to shipping routes to the Far East (Churchill and Lowe 1999: 4), but fishing by the Dutch off the English coast formed part of the backdrop. In Grotius' view, fish were inexhaustibly abundant and should therefore, under natural law, be free for exploitation by the enterprising. Englishman John Selden responded quickly with *Mare clausum* and the argument that a monarch could claim portions of the sea as readily as he could claim land. With the emergence of EEZs three and a half centuries later, the world largely came around to Selden's view. In the meantime, the universally applicable international fisheries regime was one of open access, except for narrow strips along the coastlines that could be effectively controlled from the land – today called the 'territorial' sea.

In the high seas beyond territorial waters, international attempts to regulate fisheries first appeared in a region where rapid technological advances merged with dense populations and relatively limited fish resources. The 1882 North Sea Fisheries Convention aimed to prevent clashes between trawlers and drift-netters and to establish common rules of conduct, but did not include specific conservation measures (Sen 1997: 87). Since 1902, the International Council for the Exploration of the Sea (ICES) has helped to coordinate scientific investigations in the North Atlantic and, from the late 1920s, has supported the development and operation of numerous regional conservation regimes (Halliday and Pinhorn 1996: 9). After the Second World War, a range of permanent fisheries commissions emerged targeting either certain regions or specific stocks – the Asia-Pacific Fisheries Commission (1948), the International Commission for the Northwest Atlantic Fisheries (1949), the Inter-American Tropical Tuna Commission (1949) and the North East Atlantic Fisheries Commission (NEAFC 1959), among others. These various treaties anticipated the current distinction in international environmental diplomacy between a framework agreement and subsequent protocols containing substantive regulations. The post-war wave of international regimes for cooperative fisheries management emerged in a bottom-up fashion, with membership and regulations shaped by regional needs and circumstances.

Alongside the emergence of regional fisheries regimes, governments met under the auspices of the United Nations to codify and strengthen global rules on resource exploitation and other uses of the oceans. This development, which produced four 1958 Geneva Conventions and the comprehensive 1982 Law of the Sea Convention, is presented in Chapter 5: suffice it here to highlight a few points. Upon adoption, the Law of the Sea Convention provisions on the 200-mile EEZs had already become customary law (Burke 1994), implying coastal-state sovereign rights to regulate the use of some nine-tenths of the world's marine living resources. Since then, global commitments to cooperate on fisheries management in the remaining high-seas areas have been sharpened. The most important instrument is the 1995 UN Agreement Relating to the Conservation and Management of Straddling Fish Stocks and Highly Migratory Fish Stocks (the Fish Stocks Agreement; see Stokke 2001). Parties to that treaty may not legally allow their fishers to operate in an area regulated by a regional regime without joining or cooperating with it. The traditional freedom to fish on the high seas is accompanied by an increasingly elaborated duty to cooperate on conservation and management through regional fisheries regimes.

While global negotiations tend to attract most interest in many areas of environmental protection, international fisheries politics occurs mostly at the regional level. Especially after the extension of coastal-state jurisdiction, the stocks and ecosystems requiring multilateral engagement typically involve fishers from a limited number of states. Around twenty regional fisheries management bodies regulate harvesting activities in international waters today and another twenty-odd bodies have advisory mandates (FAO 2009b); in addition there are numerous bilateral agreements concerning shared stocks. The next section examines how states and others operate these regional regimes to improve the management of marine living resources.

International fisheries regimes at work

International attempts to constrain overcapacity or prevent it from yielding excessive pressure on fish stocks depend crucially on national management systems that vary considerably in structure and effectiveness. Within states, such management arrangements are sometimes developed and operated informally among fishers in local communities (Ostrom 1990), but usually governments orchestrate them through corporative networks involving industry associations, scientists, and, more recently, civil society groups as well (Mikalsen and Jentoft 2008). Four types of regulatory instruments are employed to balance utilisation and conservation while attending to distribution. Technical measures like minimum mesh-size rules or time closure of fishing grounds predominated early on, and have remained important. Input controls, such as requiring a permit before a vessel may participate in a given fishery, emerged to regulate highly effective gear like trawls or especially valuable species. For decades, output controls in the form of catch quotas were the main instrument of the International Whaling Commission, operative since 1948, and have marked management under international fisheries regimes since the 1970s. Economic measures like tax exemption rules and subsidies are a fourth category; they have generally had the effect of stimulating capacity to the detriment of long-term conservation. Deciding on the dosage and mix of these regulatory instruments is difficult enough within states because of the need to balance economic, social and ecological concerns. It is even more demanding when several governments, with different industry structures and administrative traditions and capacities, need to agree on common measures.

In order to deal with the challenges of international resource management, regional fisheries regimes typically comprise a scientific advisory committee, a political decision-making body and a small secretariat. Since rule enforcement often proves to be the weak link in international environmental governance, many of these institutions also create a special body to monitor and sometimes review national implementation and propose measures for improving compliance. These distinctions between knowledge building, regulation and compliance enhancement neatly sum up the basic tasks of resource management, and structure this review of how states operate international fisheries regimes.

Scientific advice: synergy and legitimacy

Most international fisheries treaties acknowledge the need for scientific input to management decisions, and encourage parties to cooperate on fisheries research. Coordinating the compilation and analysis of biological and other data, including by harmonising methods, has obvious resource-pooling benefits and can also make scientific input more persuasive. Broad international involvement tends to enhance the legitimacy of scientific inputs among fishing industries and governments (see Mitchell *et al.* 2006). In the Northeast Atlantic, many fisheries commissions take their advice from the ICES; otherwise, most regional fisheries regimes worldwide create their own scientific advisory bodies. Such bodies usually do not organise data collection and analysis themselves. Their main tasks are to give the national research programmes of their members a multinational setting, to provide opportunities for coordination, to monitor the quality of relevant information on stocks in an area, and to provide, as requested, advice on various conservation and management measures.

A pressing challenge facing scientific advisory bodies concerns inadequate or unreliable data. The main sources of information are the fishers themselves, but scientific surveys are also important. While surveys are costly, they also allow scientists to use standardised gear over time and thus control for the continuous advances in fishing technologies. International fisheries regimes typically request governments to report on the amounts taken of the different species and on input factors for each vessel, such as number of trawl hauls or fishing days. Declining catches per unit effort could be an indication of a stock at risk, while information about size composition indicates the proportion of spawning fish and hence the prospects for stock replenishment. After the introduction of national catch limits, operators have had greater incentives than before to underreport catches and to discard small fish or less valuable species. Since discarded fish usually die, such high-grading is not only wasteful but can also lead scientists to underestimate figures for total fish removal. Accurate stock assessment requires reliable catch reports and regular scientific surveys: these are difficult or costly to obtain, and are often in short supply.

In short, those providing scientific advice on fisheries conservation and management base their input on catch reports that are never complete and are often unreliable; on scientific surveys that cover only parts of a stock's migratory area and for only parts of the year; and on inadequate knowledge about stock interactions and other environmental conditions. Working under these difficult circumstances, scientific advisory bodies contribute by reaping synergies in data gathering and analysis, by levelling the factual ground for debate over conservation measures and by supporting the perception among governments and target groups that scientific inputs are impartial and reflect the best available knowledge.

Regulation: competing interests, new principles

The political body of an international fisheries regime, usually called a commission, is responsible for adopting adequate conservation and management measures and for overseeing their implementation. Each member state has a seat in such a commission. Decision-making rules vary but usually give members an opportunity to veto, or at least reserve assent and opt out of, contentious obligations. Thus, while the principle of knowledge-based management is often cited in international fisheries governance, the principle of sovereignty tends to precede it and compounds the problem of balancing utilisation, conservation and distribution.

Setting a total allowable catch is the most prominent regulatory device applied by international fisheries commissions. The principles guiding it have changed over time. For many years, *maximum sustainable yield* was the main standard underlying scientific recommendations on fisheries management; it is even written into the Law of the Sea Convention. This term denotes the highest long-term average catch that can be taken from a stock each year under the given pattern of exploitation (that is, given the age composition of the catch) (ICES 1990: 56). Underlying this standard were frequent empirical observations of a bell-curved relationship between the pressure on a stock and the catch per unit effort, indicating that intensive exploitation might jeopardise future use. The 1995 Fish Stocks Agreement was important in codifying the *precautionary approach* to fisheries, which entails greater safety margins than does the maximum sustainable yield. At the core of the precautionary approach are pre-defined biological reference points for each stock and political commitment to act forcefully if the spawning stock should fall below certain levels (Hewison 1996). Another increasingly weighty principle is *ecosystem-based management:* governments are expected to manage stocks under a comprehensive plan covering the larger food webs that link micro-organisms and complex predator–prey relationships in a given area of sea. Putting the precautionary and the ecosystem-based approaches into practice are among the main challenges for regional fisheries management regimes today.

One impediment to ambitious international regulation is that conservation measures differ in their distributive effects among the users of a stock. At the end of the Second World War, for instance, Britain proposed a freeze on the size of the global fishing fleet (Døhlie 2007: 26). Many other governments opposed the idea because such a rule would favour countries that, like Britain at the time, already had modern and efficient vessels. More recently, the Norwegian–Soviet Joint Fisheries Commission failed throughout most of the 1980s to adopt scientifically recommended mesh size and quota requirements, in part because both measures would affect Norwegian and Russian operators asymmetrically. Smaller mesh size in trawl bags would hit the Russians more severely because the main stock, cod, tends to be smaller off their coasts and because their industry, unlike Norway's, is largely made up of trawlers. Conversely, drastic quota cuts would hit the Norwegians harder because their smaller coastal vessels have a shorter range and fewer alternative employments. Predictably enough, the compromise was for the Russians to have their way on mesh size, while the Norwegians won out on the catch limits. Unfortunately, these examples are rather typical of how conservation suffers when states fail to cut through the tangle of distributive challenges.

Among the advantages of centring international fisheries management on catch quotas is to allow governments to deal simultaneously with questions of conservation and distribution. Some organisations, like the Commission for the Conservation of Antarctic Marine Living Resources and certain tuna management commissions, do not allocate the total quota among their member states. While such an 'Olympic fishery' arrangement can be convenient for governments, by side-stepping the need to agree on a distribution formula, the potential costs are also severe. Regimes allowing everyone to keep on fishing until the total quota has been taken favour highly efficient vessels, and thus counter efforts to scale back the global fishing capacity. Numerous criteria have been proposed for guiding the allocation of international fishing quotas among states, but two stand out in practice (Stokke 2001). One is historical catches, meaning that past is prologue in international fisheries diplomacy; some regimes even use fixed division keys for the various species. The second main criterion is zonal attachment, which refers to the average proportion of a stock that occurs over the year in a state's EEZ. While historical catches and zonal attachment can be persuasive arguments, the outcomes of annual quota negotiations often reflect the relative bargaining strength of the parties – including their ability to cope without an agreement (Harsanyi 1969).

Thus, national interests, power relations and sometimes competing legal principles are major ingredients when states agree on regulatory measures for balancing use, conservation and distribution of fish resources. Over the past two decades, the convergence around a precautionary and an ecosystem-based approach to management are the most striking developments in this regard.

Compliance: undermining the flag-state monopoly

Fisheries regulations are not worth much if governments fail to implement them or fishers do not comply, yet international fisheries regimes have traditionally played modest roles in this aspect of resource management. By the late 1960s, systems of mutual inspection were established in some regional commissions, but legal prosecution of violators remained the prerogative of the flag state, and the effect was miniscule. Awareness that systems of enforcement were inadequate on the high seas was one of several reasons for extended coastal-state jurisdiction: within the EEZs, coastal states enjoy sovereign rights of enforcement over their own vessels as well as foreign ones. They can require detailed catch reports, inspect vessels whenever they like, request on-board observers and oblige vessels to sail to specific checkpoints or to install satellite-based Vessel Monitoring System devices. Moreover, vessel operators must accept that legal action can be taken whenever rule violations are revealed. The legal basis for taking effective measures to enhance compliance with international regulations is thus much firmer when the fishery occurs in an EEZ rather than on the high seas.

In many national zones, an active enforcement capacity is indeed in place. Cross-checking catch data in the logbooks against landing declarations is a primary means of control. The cost of physically inspecting a vessel at sea or land is very high, so even wealthy states must be satisfied with spot checks. Unsurprisingly, fishery surveillance and control is usually far less ambitious off the coasts of developing countries where significant harvesting capacities are often employed. Leading fishing powers like Japan, the EU and Taiwan responded to the extension of coastal state jurisdiction by negotiating access and fishing rights in the zones of Third World countries. These deals offered a new source of income for these coastal states but in some cases also resulted in practically uncontrolled fishing and decimation of fish stocks, to the detriment of local fishermen. Among the tasks of the UN Food and Agriculture Organization (FAO) is to run or support development programmes aimed at strengthening fisheries administrative systems and enforcement capacities in developing countries (Hersoug *et al.* 2004). While an international legal basis for intrusive compliance measures exists within national zones, the resources available for employing them vary considerably.

On the high seas, the flag state still enjoys a near-monopoly as regards regulation and enforcement, but interesting changes are underway. Sustainable management requires that flag states take their responsibilities under international law seriously and ensure that vessels comply with national and international regulations when operating on the high seas. In many cases, the problem is that fishing vessels fly flags of convenience, which means that the states legally entitled to control their activities lack incentive and capacity to do so. Estimates are necessarily rough but indicate that up to twenty per cent of the vessels fishing on the high seas are registered under flags of convenience (DeSombre 2006: 92). The 1995 Fish Stocks Agreement was a landmark event in the gradual movement to change this situation by widening the scope for states other than the flag state to conduct non-courtesy inspections (that is, without the consent of the captain) on the high seas. The emergence of regional systems of port state control represents another important advance by mobilising the jurisdiction that port states have over vessels during voluntary calls. The flag state remains crucial to effective enforcement of high-seas fisheries regulations, but international agreements are gradually involving other states as well.

Whereas joint research and harmonised regulation have marked international fisheries regimes for more than a century, states have been more reluctant to engage in international compliance control. One reason is that activities like inspection, detention and legal prosecution are closer to the core of sovereignty and are thus guarded more jealously by the flag state. The extension of coastal state jurisdiction shrank the area where non-flag state enforcement competence is lacking. On the remaining high seas, more recent advances like clearer flag-state responsibilities and collaborative port-state controls serve to broaden the basis for verifying compliance and responding to violations. The impact of these various means for building knowledge, making rules and enhancing compliance on resource management is the subject of the next section.

Effectiveness and performance

An international institution is effective when it contributes significantly to solving or mitigating the problem it was set up to counter (Levy *et al.* 1995: 291). Since the problem of resource management is to balance concerns for utilisation with those for conservation and distribution, developments on those three dimensions are reasonable starting points for an assessment. The next step is to examine the causal contribution of the international fisheries regimes for diversity and change in management performance.

Advances in problem solving

Changes in production, trade and the harvest:capacity ratio are of interest for evaluating whether international fisheries management regimes succeed in making the utilisation of the world's fish resources more rational. Global fishery production has risen by some sixty per cent over the past twenty years to 140 million tonnes, easily outpacing population growth – but this development is mostly due to fish farming (FAO 2009a: 4). Marine catches have remained rather stable. Global trade in fish is constantly breaking new records. In real terms (adjusting for inflation), fish exports worldwide more than doubled from 1986 to 2006, reflecting the rising market power of large retail chains with global processing and distribution channels (FAO 2009a: 49–59). Net export of fish from developing countries has been growing much faster than the corresponding figures for agricultural produce. To some extent, therefore, ocean resources now serve as an economic dynamo in many developing countries – and indeed, that was among the goals of those pressing for extended coastal state jurisdiction (Juda 1979). Moreover, the share of the global fish catch that goes to feeding people rather than animals is growing, and currently accounts for three-quarters. By contrast, when it comes to the harvest:capacity ratio, the number of vessels and catch capacities continue to spiral upwards in many places, despite general consensus that such growth is wasteful, since many vessels are idle large parts of the year, and also adds incentives to overfish quotas or otherwise violate conservation measures. There is little evidence to indicate that states are acting forcefully on this challenge. One important driver of capacity, fisheries subsidies, is addressed by the World Trade Organization, but vague definitions and obscure exemption clauses have left ample political space for lobbyists in countries where the fishing and ship-building industries wield strong influence (Stokke and Coffey 2006). The number of vessels has fallen slightly in leading fishing nations like Russia, Britain, Japan and South Korea, but average vessel size is growing. Overall developments in rational utilisation of fish resources are mixed, with stable capture-fish production, rising trade and too small steps towards scaling down the present overcapacity.

In terms of conservation, the large picture is that expansion of coastal-state jurisdiction in the 1970s has failed to deliver significantly more sustainable management of marine resources. While production has grown in the most productive fishing areas, the Northwest Pacific and the Western Central Pacific, the global percentage of collapsed or overfished stocks is actually twice the level before the introduction of EEZs (FAO 2009a: 32–33). In some regions, like the Northwest and Southeast Atlantic, catches are significantly down on earlier numbers following the collapse of major stocks like Northern cod off Canada. Three developments go a long way in accounting for this partial failure. First, many coastal states have not taken seriously the duty to conserve resources that came with the right to manage them. For wealthy zone-expansion winners like the USA and Canada, heavy investments in domestic catch capacity soon allowed domestic industries to fish just as close to, or above, the sustainability threshold as the foreigners had. Second, many fish stocks found predominately in national zones straddle into the high seas and thus remain available to distant-water fishing fleets, which have been eager to exploit such opportunities after the gradual phase-out that has occurred from many national zones. In other cases, foreign fleets have been able to operate illegally inside the national zones of coastal states unable to patrol their zones properly. A third reason why extension of coastal state jurisdiction has not resulted in adequate resource management is the steady improvement of fish-finding and harvesting technologies which allows fishing in more remote areas and at greater depths. Fishing of deep-sea stocks in international waters has grown rapidly in recent years, but the prospects ahead are uncertain. Lucrative deepwater species like the Patagonian toothfish in the Antarctic are more sensitive to pressure than are coastal species, due to slow growth and low fecundity, and therefore depend more on effective management. Coastal states and distant-water fishing nations share the responsibility for inadequate conservation. The pressure they strive to contain stems from enterprising industries and continuous advances in fisheries technology.

Finally, distributive change has been substantial under the EEZ-based ocean regime, but with notable elements of continuity. The extension of national jurisdiction obviously entailed a radical redistribution of assets from major long-distance fishing nations to coastal states. Yet, as noted above, adaptive moves by transnational fishing fleet operators allowed many of them to continue more or less as before, with the willing support of their home governments. Under bilateral agreements, coastal states in Africa, South East Asia and elsewhere have swapped access rights to their EEZs for fees, development aid, or investment on land. Another element of continuity is that international regimes managing what remains of high-seas areas are generally conservative in their approach to distribution, since historical catches are a major criterion for allocation of national quotas. Most such regimes are open to new members only on certain conditions, including that existing members do not veto their admission. The UN Fish Stocks Agreement provides that regional regimes shall not exclude states with a 'real interest' in a fishery but fails to define that term (Balton 1996), so that in practice the extent of openness to newcomers varies across regional regimes depending on the political circumstances. Global and regional institutions are important for the distribution of ocean resources, but such outcomes also reflect the strategies and the power capabilities employed by companies and states set on utilising those resources.

The global division of competence to regulate and oversee harvesting activities and the institutional set-up of regional fisheries regimes can explain only parts of these developments in resource use, conservation and distribution. As the remainder of this section will show, other important factors include changes in the configuration of national interests, power capabilities and various forms of leadership.

Regime contributions

The role of international fisheries regimes in influencing these developments can be viewed through the prism provided in Chapter 1, which highlights impacts flowing from what sociologist Richard Scott (e.g. 2001) has called *the three pillars* of institutions. Impacts deriving from a regime's regulative pillar revolve around legally binding rules and systems for verification and enforcement. Impacts flowing from the normative pillar concern the compellingness of regime norms, their ability to shape what actors consider appropriate or morally justified behaviour. The cognitive pillar, finally, comprises those parts of a regime that impinge on how states and other actors perceive the problem, including its severity compared to other challenges and the costs and benefits of alternative measures. So how can we link the developments above regarding utilisation, conservation and distribution to each of these pillars of global and regional fisheries regimes?

Some very significant fisheries-regime impacts are regulative in nature. Foremost among them is the extension of coastal-state jurisdiction, which renders the problem of international fisheries management less malign in several respects. First, many commercial stocks which used to require multilateral cooperation could now be managed unilaterally or bilaterally, which greatly facilitated the adoption of international regulations. Northeast Arctic cod, for instance, today the world's biggest cod stock, used to be managed jointly by nine states members of NEAFC, but since 1976 it falls under the ambit of the Joint Norwegian–Russian Fisheries Commission (Stokke 2001). The treaties underlying the old multilateral commissions were renegotiated to reflect narrower scopes in spatial and usually in stock terms. Also new regional regimes were created, especially in waters adjacent to developing countries and frequently involving advice and support from the FAO. A second way in which extended coastal-state jurisdiction influenced the international fisheries management problem was to reduce fears that other states might take undue advantage of the cooperation by implementing agreed restraints leniently on their own fishers. The EEZs dramatically increased the spatial scope of coastal state competence to monitor the compliance of foreign vessels with international regulations and to punish violations. The international fisheries management problem became less malign with the spatial expansion of national regulation.

Expectations that another division of competence between coastal states and flag state would be conducive to resource conservation strengthened the case of those pressing for change. The EEZ concept managed to gain broad acceptance during the third round of the UN Conference on the Law of the Sea mostly because it balances coastal-state demands for natural-resource control and maritime-state requests for unrestricted navigation (Burke 1994). Moreover, the two superpowers, the USA and the Soviet Union, were among those who stood to gain the most from its adoption; and some persistent coastal states, like Iceland, had already established fisheries zones unilaterally and were deploying military forces to defend them. Demands by developing countries for a New International Economic Order in the late 1960s and onwards also concerned the use of ocean resources

(Juda 1979). International institutions may influence the malignancy of the problem they address, but they themselves reflect the accommodation of conflicting interests, leadership of various sorts and the power relationships that underlie accepted state practice.

Yet another significant regulative effect of international fisheries institutions is the strengthening of collaborative port-state measures to improve compliance with international regulation of high-seas fisheries. Regional regimes for managing the tuna fisheries in the southern Atlantic and Pacific have shown the way (Palmer *et al.* 2006), and similar arrangements are now in place in many regions. A vessel unable to verify that its cargo has been caught by legal means, or that is on a black list issued by the relevant fisheries commission, can be denied access to land or tranship its catch. The 2009 FAO Agreement on Port State Measures to Prevent, Deter and Eliminate Illegal, Unreported and Unregulated Fishing provides a joint framework building on the most advanced regional commissions (Lobach 2010). Common ingredients in such compliance systems, which could not operate without the collaborative vehicle that regional fisheries regimes provide, are satellite-based monitoring of fishing and transport vessels; requirements that foreign landings or transhipments occur in designated ports with inspection capacities and following prior notice; and documents verifying compatibility between fishing rights and the cargo. Under some regimes the flag state must confirm in each case that the fish were caught legally. The International Commission for the Conservation of Atlantic Tunas has gone even further and can decide to ban the import of seafood from any vessel flagged by states that fail to take strong measures to prevent unregulated fishing. Like extended coastal-state jurisdiction, these various port-state measures underscore the significance of the regulative pillar of international fisheries regimes in strengthening the basis for verification of compliance and response to rule violation.

The normative pillar of institutions leans on the regulative pillar insofar as specific rules and stronger compliance measures confirm that members of international regimes are sincere in their commitments to the underlying norms; otherwise they would prefer indeterminate provisions that are difficult to verify. Also other features of international environmental regimes aim to enhance their compliance pull (Franck 1990), like the extensive use of scientific expertise in the preparation of rule-making and the involvement of industry and civil society organisations (Bodansky 1999; Mikalsen and Jentoft 2008). International fisheries regimes have moreover promoted and adapted certain substantive principles of environmental governance that support their legitimacy. They pioneered the principle of knowledge-based management by linking up to established international fisheries-research organisations or by creating their own bodies – although as noted scientific advice has frequently been overridden by other impulses. Other norms were originally hammered out in international environmental diplomacy but are now highly influential in the fisheries sector, especially precaution, transparency and ecosystem-based management. Just like the precautionary approach, norms in support of transparency of documents and meetings achieved prominence in international fisheries management during the UN Conference on Environment and Development in 1992, and their inclusion in the 1995 FAO Code of Conduct for Responsible Fisheries and the UN Fish Stocks Agreement triggered far-reaching changes in regional fisheries regimes (Aqorau 2001; Stokke 2001). In the Common Fisheries Policy of the European Union and other regional arrangements, the precautionary approach has encouraged the development of multi-year management plans that imply a more predictable regulatory environment for the industry while seeking to keep catches within reasonably safe biological limits. The ecosystem approach to fisheries management has a somewhat longer history (Tarlock 2009). While implementing it fully requires more knowledge about the structure and mechanisms of these ecosystems than scientists have today, practical results abound and include successful efforts under some tuna commissions to drastically reduce bycatch of dolphins, for instance by allocating shrinking bycatch quotas among the vessels engaged in the fisheries (Hall *et al.* 2000). Decision-making procedures and substantive environmental principles support the normative pillar of an international fisheries regime and reinforce their compliance pull on states, fishers and others engaged in the implementation of conservation and management measures.

The cognitive contributions of international fisheries regimes are perhaps most evident in the advice that scientific bodies provide regularly concerning total allowable catch or technical regulations, which typically forms the point of departure for international negotiations. International collaboration enhances the credibility and the legitimacy of these inputs by supporting the perception among decision-makers that scientific advice reflects the best available, impartial knowledge of the problem in question (Mitchell *et al.* 2006: 316). Nevertheless, the independence of these scientific bodies versus industry and government varies among international regimes. In principle, scientific advice is not supposed to be prejudiced by national interests – but it is governments that designate the members of such expert bodies, and relations between leading research institutions and national bureaucracies are often quite close. On occasion, such relations can form the basis for pressure of various sorts towards advice that is more compatible with certain political priorities. For instance, the polarised debate in the International Whaling Commission over the highly contentious moratorium on commercial whaling, operative since 1986, was compounded by the relatively close links of some leading scientists with environmental and animal rights organisations or pro-whaling states (Andresen 2000: 50). Peer review of recommendations and their basis is the most important means for protecting the scientific advisory process from political pressure, sometimes reinforced by additional procedures. For instance, the ICES Advisory Committee follows the practice of inviting scientists from countries other than those engaged in a given fishery, to review the advice. Scientific input typically forms a starting point for negotiation of international measures, and insulating the advisory process from biases of various sorts helps to strengthen the cognitive pillar of international fisheries regimes.

Accordingly, the observation that in many cases international fisheries arrangements fail to balance utilisation and conservation does not imply that these institutions are ineffective. The global rules and the regional regimes examined in this chapter have clearly enhanced decision-makers' knowledge concerning the trade-offs between present and future use and the interconnectedness of ecosystem components. Such cognitive effects are reinforced by the greater normative pull that results from increasingly specific commitments assumed voluntarily, reflecting principles applicable also in other fields of environmental governance. One important regulative effect of global and regional fisheries institutions has been to reduce the number of states that must agree for international rules to be conducive and to facilitate their enforcement. These cognitive, normative and regulative regime consequences derive from institutional features that were once controversial – like steadily new restrictions on the high-seas freedom to fish, the EEZs, independent scientific advice and port-state enforcement procedures. Global divisions of competence and the institutional set-up of regional regimes impinge on the conservation and management of the world's marine living resources. They have been achieved only after political struggles involving intellectual leadership, unilateral action and multilateral diplomacy.

Conclusions

We are now in a position to offer answers to the five questions that run through this volume and concern the nature of the problem, the history of international cooperation, regime operations, their effectiveness and the factors accounting for diversity in performance (see Chapter 1).

The general problem addressed by international fisheries regimes is resource management, which means balancing use, conservation and distribution. Under open-access conditions, a fish stock is a scarce common property resource: that complicates international negotiations and entails incentives to cheat on agreed commitments. Such malignancy is tempered by the shared interest that states have in keeping the overall pressure on fish stocks at a level that allows for replenishment. At the international level, from the 1970s resource management became somewhat less difficult with the extension of coastal-state jurisdiction, because the annual negotiations now tend to involve a smaller number of states and because by far most of the world's marine living resources are found inside the 200-mile EEZs where coastal states may employ the full range of enforcement measures. On the other hand, substantial overcapacity in world fisheries ensures a continuous pressure on decision-makers, so that the problem of resource management remains relatively malign.

In the decades following the Second World War, advances in technology and sustained investment in the fishing fleets in many places led to over-fishing and lower catch rates, spurring in turn the establishment of new regional management institutions and the strengthening of existing ones. The long-term trend in international fisheries management is towards greater influence of coastal states, and more recently of port states, at the expense of traditional high-seas freedoms. While flag states retain a near-monopoly on regulation and enforcement action outside the EEZs, governments have gradually established the principle that the right to utilise marine resources is not unrestricted. It comes with a duty to conserve the resources – and in many cases that requires cooperation through international fisheries commissions. About twenty multilateral regional fisheries bodies and numerous bilateral arrangements provide the main vehicles for research cooperation, generation of scientific advice, and negotiation and adoption of international fisheries regulations.

Within regional fisheries regimes, the setting of a total allowable catch for each stock is now the foremost conservation and management measure, but technical regulations like mesh-size limits are also important. Coastal-state control over EEZ resources gives such states prominent positions in regional regimes for managing stocks that occur both in national zones and on the high seas. In the best of cases, such regimes involve all states engaged in regional harvesting, but a frequent challenge is the presence of vessels registered in states that have failed to join·and that therefore remain unbound by international regulations.

The overall effectiveness of international fisheries regimes varies considerably, but some progress is discernible with respect to both regulation and enforcement. Despite extended coastal-state jurisdiction, no less than a quarter of the world's commercially exploited fish stocks have collapsed or are suffering from overfishing. International fisheries institutions build common knowledge as well as normative obligation among their members, but too often regulation is obstructed by consensual decision-making rules, opting-out procedures and the fact that alternative conservation measures may affect states differently. The emergence of precautionary and ecosystem-based approaches to fisheries management is in the process of improving this situation somewhat. Scientific advice to regulatory commissions used to reflect the researchers' estimate of the maximum sustainable yield for each stock. The precautionary approach requires recommendations with greater safety margins than before, as well as political commitment to quickly rebuild a stock should it fall below certain predefined biological reference points. A closely related trend is the development of multi-year management plans. Along with rising attention to ecosystem effects of bycatches and discards, these developments promise to render international regulation of fisheries more adequate. Responding to the pervasive challenges of illegal, unreported or unregulated fishing, regional fisheries regimes have recently developed a range of measures aimed at making such activities less lucrative – including such port-state controls as denial of landing or transhipment of cargo that cannot be documented as originating from harvesting operations compatible with international regulations. Despite such advances, and more specific flag-state responsibilities to regulate and monitor the activities of fishing vessels, compliance control remains a weak point in international fisheries management compared to the building of scientific knowledge and the adoption of binding regulations.

Variation in the management performance of regional fisheries regimes derives in part from distinctive institutional features like the impartiality of scientific advisory bodies, majority or consensual decision-making, substantive principles of management, the stringency of conservation measures, and the structures for collaborative surveillance and enforcement. Just like the global rules dividing the competence to fisheries regulation and enforcement among categories of states, such institutional features reflect political struggles whose outcomes depend on the interest configurations, the leadership mobilisation and the power relationships in each case. Global institutions like the FAO help to facilitate the diffusion of the most progressive features and practices under regional fisheries management regimes. In the years ahead, international fisheries politics seem likely to revolve around the implementation of the precautionary and the ecosystem-based approaches to fisheries management and the strengthening of compliance control.

Bibliography

Andresen, S. (2000) 'The whaling regime', in S. Andresen, T. Skodvin, A. Underdal and J. Wettestad, *Science and Politics in International Environmental Regimes: between integrity and involvement*, Manchester: Manchester University Press.

Aqorau, T. (2001) 'Tuna fisheries management in the Western and Central Pacific Ocean: a critical analysis of the Convention for the Conservation and Management of Highly Migratory Fish Stocks in the Western and Central Pacific Ocean and its implications for the Pacific Island States', *International Journal of Marine and Coastal Law*, 16: 379–431.

Balton, D.A. (1996) 'Strengthening the law of the sea: the new agreement on straddling fish stocks and highly migratory fish stocks', *Ocean Development and International Law*, 27: 125–52.

Bodansky, D. (1999) 'The legitimacy of international governance: a coming challenge for international environmental law?' *American Journal of International Law*, 93: 596–624.

Burke, W.T. (1994) *The New International Law of Fisheries: UNCLOS 1982 and beyond*, Oxford: Clarendon Press.

Churchill, R.R. and Lowe, A.V. (1999) *The Law of the Sea*, Manchester: Manchester University Press.

DeSombre, E. (2006) *Global Environmental Institutions*, London: Routledge.

Døhlie, K.H. (2007) 'Ressursar under press: Norges rolle i det nordaustatlantiske fiskerisamarbeidet 1946 – 1977', unpublished Master thesis, Department of Archeology, History, Cultural Studies and Religion, University of Bergen.

FAO (2009a) *The State of World Fisheries and Aquaculture 2008*, Rome: Food and Agriculture Organization.

——(2009b) 'What are Regional Fishery Bodies?' *FAO Fisheries and Aquaculture Department*, Rome: Food and Agriculture Organization. Online. www.fao.org/fishery/topic/16800/en (accessed 8 September 2010).

Franck, T.M. (1990) *The Power of Legitimacy Among Nations*, New York: Oxford University Press.

Fulton, T.W. (1911) *The Sovereignty of the Sea*, Edinburgh: William Blackwood and Sons.

Hall, M.A., Alverson, D.L. and Metuzals, K.I. (2000) 'By-Catch: problems and solutions', *Marine Pollution Bulletin*, 41: 204–19.

Halliday, R.G. and Pinhorn, A.T. (1996) 'North Atlantic fishery management systems: a comparison of management methods and resource trends', a special issue of *Journal of Northwest Atlantic Fishery Science*, 20: 3–135.

Hardin, G. (1968) 'The tragedy of the commons', *Science*, 162: 1243–48.

Harsanyi, J.C. (1969) 'Game theory and the analysis of international conflict', in J.N. Rosenau (ed.) *International Politics and Foreign Policy*, New York: Free Press.

Hersoug, B., Jentoft, S. and Degnbol, P. (2004) *Fisheries Development: the institutional challenge*, Delft: Eburon.

Hewison, G. J. (1996) 'The precautionary approach to fisheries management: an environmental perspective', *International Journal of Marine and Coastal Law*, 11: 301–32.

ICES (1990) 'Report of the Seventh Dialogue Meeting', *Cooperative Research Report*, Copenhagen: International Council for the Exploration of the Sea.

Juda, L. (1979) 'UNCLOS III and the new international economic order', *Ocean Development and International Law*, 7: 221–55.

Levy, M.A., Young, O.R. and Zürn, M. (1995) 'The study of international regimes', *European Journal of International Relations*, 1: 267–330.

Lobach, T. (2010) 'Combating IUU fishing: interaction of global and regional initiatives', in D. Vidas (ed.) *Law, Technology and Science for Oceans in Globalisation*, Boston: Martinus Nijhoff.

Mikalsen, K.H. and Jentoft, S. (2008) 'Participatory practices in fisheries across Europe: making stakeholders more responsible', *Marine Policy*, 32: 169–77.

Mitchell, R.B., Clark, W.C., Cash, D.W. and Dickson, N.M. (eds) (2006) *Global Environmental Assessments: information and influence*, Cambridge, MA: MIT Press.

Myers, R.A. and Worm, B. (2003) 'Rapid worldwide depletion of predatory fish communities', *Nature*, 423: 280–83.

Ostrom, E. (1990) *Governing the Commons: the evolution of institutions for collective action*, Cambridge: Cambridge University Press.

Palmer, A., Chaytor, B. and Werksman, J. (2006) 'Interactions between the World Trade Organization and international environmental regimes', in S. Oberthür and T. Gehring (eds) *Institutional Interaction in Global Environmental Governance: synergy and conflict among international and EU policies*, Cambridge, MA: MIT Press.

Pauly, D., Christensen, V., Guénette, S., Pitcher, T.J., Sumaila, U.R., Walters, C.J., Watson, R. and Zeller, D. (2002) 'Towards sustainability in world fisheries', *Nature*, 418: 689–95.

Scott, W. R. (2001) *Institutions and Organizations*, Thousand Oaks, CA: SAGE.

Sen, S. (1997) 'The evolution of high-seas fisheries management in the North-East Atlantic', *Ocean Development and International Law*, 35: 85–100.

Stokke, O.S. (ed.) (2001) *Governing High Seas Fisheries: the interplay of global and regional regimes*, Oxford: Oxford University Press.

Stokke, O.S. and Coffey, C. (2006) 'Institutional interplay and responsible fisheries: combating subsidies, developing precaution', in S. Oberthür and T. Gehring (eds) *Institutional Interaction in Global Environmental Governance: synergy and conflict among international and EU policies*, Cambridge, MA: MIT Press.

Tarlock, D. (2009) 'Ecosystems', in D. Bodansky, J. Brunnée and E. Hey (eds) *The Oxford Handbook of International Environmental Law*, Oxford: Oxford University Press.

Underdal, A. (2002) 'One question, two answers', in E.L. Miles, A. Underdal, S. Andresen, J. Wettestad, J.B. Skjærseth and E.M. Carlin, *Environmental Regime Effectiveness: confronting theory with evidence*, Cambridge, MA: MIT Press.

Part IV

Nature protection and biodiversity

8 Convention on biological diversity

From national conservation to global responsibility

Kristin Rosendal and Peter Johan Schei

Important years

1971 Ramsar Convention on Wetlands of International Importance adopted
1973 Washington Convention on International Trade in Endangered Species of Wild Fauna and Flora: CITES, adopted
1979 Bonn Convention on the Conservation of Migratory Species of Wild Animals adopted
1992 Convention on Biological Diversity adopted
1994 Agreement on Trade-related Aspects of Intellectual Property Rights adopted as part of the World Trade Organization
2000 Cartagena Protocol on Biosafety adopted
2001 International Treaty on Plant Genetic Resources for Food and Agriculture adopted
2010 Nagoya Protocol on Access to Genetic Resources and the Fair and Equitable Sharing of Benefits Arising from Their Utilization adopted

Biological diversity is declining today 100–1,000 times faster than if natural attrition had proceeded without human interference (Heywood 1995: 232). Estimates put the number of species on earth at somewhere between 7 and 100 million: only 1.9 million of them are known and described scientifically (Wilson 1988). In effect, then many of the species that are disappearing are simply unknown to us. *Biological diversity* – or *biodiversity* – is not a very old term. It was coined during the 1980s to denote variation among all living organisms, *between* species and genetic variation *within* species. Later, it has also been taken to mean variation between ecosystems.

The fact that human activity can cause loss of species and that we need to target action to restore ecosystems and species, is not a recent discovery. Measures have been taken to protect different species and national reserves established to preserve spectacular areas of wilderness for over a century now. This chapter recounts how the international focus on conservation grew from a concern for individual cases and ecosystems to biological diversity as a common responsibility of us all. We shall also discuss how this outlook has affected wildlife conservation in different parts in the world.

In the first section of the chapter we ask how the loss of biological diversity became perceived as a problem. We review developments in the international effort, focusing here in particular on the most comprehensive agreement, the Convention on Biological Diversity. The third section discusses the effectiveness of this convention.

Loss of biological diversity

'Biological diversity' means for the purpose of the Biodiversity Convention the diversity of ecosystems and species, as well as variation in genetic material within species. In any ecosystem, a wood for example, or a lake, species exist in dynamic interaction. Some systems are simple, hosting a small number of species. Typical examples are certain types of northern tundras. Others contain vast numbers of different species, like tropical rain forests. Climatic variation, differences in top soil and historic events such as ice ages, continental drift and evolutionary processes have produced a wide variety of habitats and ecosystems around the globe. Each of these worlds contains unique biological resources giving us medicines, food and many other natural provisions essential to our survival. When the genetic variation in a given species declines, its resilience to disease and ability to fight off attacks from harmful organisms also declines. The species will lose its capacity to adapt to changes in the immediate environment, such as those caused by climate change for instance.

Biological diversity at all three levels (ecosystem, species and genetic) is therefore highly important for human flourishing and survival. Natural processes, that is, climatic, geological and biological, make ecosystems and species change over time. That some species disappear is natural, but the extinction rate today is 100–1,000 times greater than when human beings set out on the path to global dominance. Population growth, industrialisation, urbanisation, overexploitation and diffusion of alien species are reducing diversity and accelerating biological change. As the Millennium Ecosystem Assessment, a United Nations (UN)-headed group of 1,360 scientists from every continent on earth, concluded in 2005, ecosystems are being damaged and biological diversity lost at an increasing rate (MA 2005). And the situation is the same all over the world. The only ecosystems enjoying territorial growth are agricultural and plantation forestry areas.

For the rural poor, access to a balanced natural environment and natural resources means they can survive even without money. For urban and richer communities, biological diversity is a source of basic natural services. Nature can be viewed as a provider of some of the services humans need to flourish. Ecosystems or natural services can be divided into four categories: supply services; regulatory services; cultural services; and support services. Supply services are the production of food, fibre, medicines, clean water and the like. Regulatory services comprise flood regulation, pollination, climate regulation, erosion protection and pollution mitigation, etc. Cultural services are the possibilities afforded by nature for recreation, aesthetic pleasure, spiritual fulfilment and preservation of culture. Supporting services operate within such fundamental natural processes as photosynthesis, decomposition of organic material and recycling of essential nutrients. According to the Millennium Assessment's estimate, the loss of diversity translates into an annual loss of ecosystem services worth about 250 billion USD (MA 2005).

Neither agricultural production nor medical services would have been possible for most of the people on the planet without biological diversity. Selective animal and plant breeding to produce high yields and high resistance to disease and climate change requires access to a wide selection of genetic resources, not least in the form of seed (Kloppenburg 2004). In the age of biotechnology, genetic diversity is increasingly important medically and industrially. The food and pharmaceutical industries use genetic resources both in traditional and modern biotechnology. Traditional biotechnology means processes in which micro-organisms (such as yeast) act as catalysts in the production of consumables such as bread or beer. With modern biotechnology, or gene technology, genetic material is changed by moving genes between species or joining them in novel ways. Genetically modified organisms are what result from this procedure.

Bioprospecting means to investigate organisms, molecules and genes with a view to determining their medical and industrial value. These investigations can sometimes benefit from what is known locally about a plant's efficacy. Traditional knowledge has been found to increase the success ratio of bioprospecting by 400 per cent (Gehl Sampath 2005). Bioprospectors have discovered drugs for use in cancer therapy, transplantation medicine (cyclosporine from a mushroom first discovered growing on the Hardangervidda mountain plateau in Norway) and pain relief. Interesting bioprospecting programmes include, for instance, studying hibernating animals with a view to preventing osteoporosis (brittle bones), organisms living in the northern seas in case they can provide new drugs and studying spiders' webs to learn how to make stronger materials. As an illustration, less than 1 per cent of flowering plants, marine species and microbial diversity have been thoroughly investigated for their chemical composition (Aylward 1995:105; Sheldon and Balick 1995: 46). Diversity can be seen as nature's own life insurance policy. Genetic variation within a species is its survival ticket, and variation between species in an ecosystem is the system's performance and service guarantee. Moreover, biodiversity acts as an insurance policy for us, though we do not know what it contains exactly, or when we might need to redeem it. What is certain is that bioprospecting can make billions for the industry even if some of the projects fail.

The diversity of land-based species is highest in the tropical rain forests situated in less developed areas of the world (Heywood 1995). Many biotechnological products were discovered originally thanks to indigenous knowledge about food and medical plants in the southern hemisphere. The food and pharmaceutical industries are strongest in developed countries, however.

Driving the deterioration of biological diversity is a multitude of complex, intertwining forces. Land use change, land degradation and division threaten diversity at all three levels. Farming, plantation forestry, road building, industrial developments and deforestation represent the most serious threats to diversity. The introduction of alien species, pollution and chemicalisation of air, soil and water are other prominent factors. Industrial methods of capture and direct overexploitation can also cause problems. Climate change is an increasing danger for diversity, and is set to worsen moving forward. In the agro industry, high-yield, monocultural plant varieties are driving out local varieties adapted to local conditions. The result is an escalation in the loss of diversity.

The loss of biological diversity can in many cases be considered an unintended or unforeseen consequence of human activity. We know too little about how diversity is affected, and how it can be preserved in a sustainable development context. The value of diversity and the ecosystem services derived from it are not included in economic policy-making (EC 2008). Nor is diversity quantified well enough to be measurable in monetary terms. At the same time, we know that declining biological diversity will limit our ability to make diversity-based technological and industrial progress in the years ahead.

Establishment of the Biodiversity Convention

Loss of biological diversity is not a new phenomenon, but the pace of homogenisation has increased year on year. Collective international efforts to stem the tide are not new either. The 1970s saw the adoption of several international agreements aimed at protecting different species and areas. Examples are the Ramsar Convention (1971), which targets the preservation of wetlands; the Washington Convention on International Trade in Endangered Species of Wild Fauna and Flora – CITES (1973); and the Bonn Convention (1979) aimed at protecting migratory species that cross national borders. In contrast to these earlier agreements designed with particular species or groups of species in mind (like bats and small whales); activities (like trade in the CITES Convention); or protection of habitats (like wetlands of the Ramsar Convention); the Convention on Biological Diversity targets all three dimensions: ecosystems, species and genetic variety within species. As the negotiations proceeded on the Biodiversity Convention text, it became clear that focusing on protection and conservation would not be enough. New ways of utilising diversity sustainably and of sharing the benefits derived from the exploitation of the world's genetic resources would have to be conjured up. Around 1990, when the Biodiversity Convention negotiations began, the benefits likely to emerge from the use of these resources were assumed to be extremely valuable and were highly anticipated (Rosendal 2000). Rapid advances in biotechnology alerted politicians and industrial leaders to the economic potential of genetic resources. Modern biotechnology, or gene technology, emerged at the same time as the wider privatisation of plant breeding and medical research in the 1970s. Modern biotechnology also made it possible to fulfil the legal patent criteria for inventions involving biological material (Crespi 1988). It initiated a trend with companies taking out patents on naturally occurring organic material.

Private stakeholders in the developed world therefore used patenting more and more to secure sole rights to the use of important genetic resources; to the end product of plant variety breeding programmes; and to the results of biotech innovations based on materials, often sourced from developing countries. There were increasingly strong calls to strengthen and expand patent law to ensure rights to inventions and discoveries in the area of biological materials.

The countries supplying the genetic resources also wanted a fair share of the proceeds arising from their use. Patented material is often the result of applied indigenous knowledge and resources in local communities in poor countries. The plant material is also obtained freely – from gene banks, among other places, where seed material from developing countries is generally stocked (Kloppenburg 2004). Before the Biodiversity Convention, the biological resources of developing countries tended to be seen in terms of mankind's common heritage, that is, a resource freely available to all. While patenting in biotechnology was increasing, it has proved difficult to provide similar legal protection of the traditional knowledge about these resources. Patenting is also a costly affair, largely dominated by multinational corporations and hardly available to poor countries.

This provided the backdrop to a contentious debate between developing and developed countries on rights to genetic resources. Neither group is particularly homogeneous. Some of the developed countries, for example, including Australia, have a wide variety of indigenous and special species and ecosystems. Conversely, many developing countries seem relatively poor in terms of biological diversity even though the generic variation is as important as in other places because the species are adapted to the local habitats. Further, many of the countries known for the purpose of international negotiations as developing are highly developed technologically. They include India, Argentina and Brazil. Nonetheless, the developing countries joined forces in the 1980s to protest what they felt was unfair treatment inasmuch as their seed material was still considered to be part of mankind's common heritage – to which seed companies and the pharmaceutical industry enjoyed unfettered access – while they were obliged at times to pay dearly for the patented seeds and medicines. The situation gave developing countries a strong hand in the negotiations on the Biodiversity Convention. They had a strong normative argument given the obviously unfair distributive effects of the current ownership rights regime.

But because they would be hard pressed to regulate and control access to genetic resources or drum up the necessary legal expertise, their negotiating position was still relatively weak (Rosendal 2000; Schei 1997).

Leading developed countries and most developing countries came to the talks from widely different agendas to set up a convention on biodiversity, and with sometimes incompatible interests. Many developed countries, such as Germany, France and the US, wanted a straightforward deal to protect wildlife fauna, flora and habitats. Implicitly, they wanted the current arrangement to remain as it was, allowing them to enjoy free access to genetic resources in countries in the South. The developing countries, with the Nordic countries, wanted genetic material of wild and cultivated/agricultural species included in the Biodiversity Convention. They wanted to make sure that developing countries received a fair share of the proceeds from the use of the genetic resources. Many prosperous countries were put out because, they felt, focusing on genetic resources and their value politicised the talks. They wanted the traditional conservation strategy to continue, the cornerstones of which were the establishment of wildlife reserves and protection of endangered species. The US in particular was against pairing conservation with economic obligations in developed countries; nor were Americans interested in creating links between the use of genetic resources and benefit sharing, as this was against the wishes of the biotechnology sector. It is largely because the US was apprehensive that the wording of the Biodiversity Convention could harm the powerful domestic biotechnology sector that it is still among the tiny number of countries in the world not to have ratified the convention (Rosendal 2000).

In addition to the demand for a fair sharing of the benefits, the developing countries wanted compensation and incentives to preserve biological diversity, and avoid having to shoulder the greatest burden. How to parcel out the economic responsibility for preserving diversity has been one of the hardest topics at the negotiations. The Nordic countries acted as bridge-builders, urging a convention text which ensured that lack of resources and unfair, imbalanced division of proceeds would not impact adversely on developing countries' will and capacity to ensure the necessary management of the resource base (Schei 1997).

The Convention on Biological Diversity was agreed in Nairobi and signed at the UN Conference on the Environment and Development in Rio, in 1992. It entered into force at the end of December 1993. The Biodiversity Convention allowed for further talks to specify implementation procedures in protocols to the convention. In 2000, the Parties agreed a protocol on biosafety, the so-called Cartagena Protocol. It regulates international trade in genetically modified organisms. The Parties to the Biodiversity Convention also adopted a non-binding instrument, the so-called Bonn Guidelines (2002), concerning access to genetic resources and fair and equitable sharing of the benefits arising from their utilisation. Negotiations on developing and making the Bonn Guidelines legally binding continued under the Access and Benefit Sharing (ABS) talks, which concluded with a Protocol on ABS at the 10th Conference of the Parties in October 2010.

The Convention on Biological Diversity establishes special programmes for different ecosystem types, including a forestry programme (see Chapter 10). This is particularly important since up to 80 per cent of the planet's land-based species diversity is found in different types of forest, primarily tropical rain forests (Wilson 1988). Many wanted a separate protocol for biodiversity in connection with the agro industry, that is, agrodiversity. It was agreed, however, to delegate responsibility for negotiating a sepa-rate agreement on the protection of and access to plant genetic resources to the UN Food and Agriculture Organization (FAO). This is discussed in Chapter 9.

As the value of genetic diversity was being discussed in the process leading to the establishment of the Biodiversity Convention, patenting became a topic in the talks to establish the World Trade Organization (WTO) and a new set of rules for the organisation. The talks comprised what is known as the Uruguay round, 1989–94. A year following the entry into force of the Biodiversity Convention, developed countries gained acceptance for their position on the trade-related aspects of intellectual rights (the TRIPS Agreement). The goal of TRIPS is to strengthen and harmonise patent legislation in the WTO member countries, thereby stimulating innovation and protection of the results of all types of technological progress, including biotechnology and hence property rights to living organisms and material derived from them. The TRIPS Agreement's implementation mechanisms are much more robust than those of the Biodiversity Con-vention and have shaped convention negotiations significantly in recent years (Rosendal 2006a). We shall return later to the implications.

The main features of the Biodiversity Convention

The Biodiversity Convention is a relatively general and process-oriented text with a distinctive normative character. It has three main normative purposes: to ensure (i) the conservation and (ii) sustainable use of biolo-gical diversity and (iii) the equitable sharing of the benefits arising from the utilisation of genetic resources. The convention's wording on funding implies moreover an international recognition of the need to protect developing countries from having to bear the cost of preserving biological diversity alone. The three-dimensional objective reflects recognition that conservation, sustainable use and sharing of benefits from utilisation are mutually supportive conservation principles. This, along with the broad approach which embraces all three forms of biological diversity, shows that the Biodiversity Convention is effectively an agreement on sustainable development. The Parties agreed later to work for a more concretely for-mulated objective by 2010, whereby significant reductions in the loss of biological diversity should have been achieved – but this failed.

The Biodiversity Convention articulates many general standards. The precautionary principle, which can be seen as a normative paradigm, is of central importance, both for the Biodiversity Convention in general and more explicitly articulated in the Cartagena Protocol. Of prime importance here, the Biodiversity Convention adopts the view of biological diversity as the heritage of all mankind, to be protected by the international community working together. The convention text also contains one of the strongest international expressions of the responsibility of states towards indigenous people and local communities in connection with the conservation of biological diversity. The Biodiversity Convention introduces a compromise where property rights (intellectual property rights, including patents) are offset part of the way by affirming that countries have sovereign rights over their own biological resources. This compromise is intended to act as a guide to the management of and international transactions concerning genetic resources. One of the innovative aspects of the Biodiversity Convention is the separate article on integrating consideration of the conservation and sustainable use of biological resources into the responsibilities and policy-making procedures in all sectors. It is not, therefore, the sole responsibility of the environmental authorities to ensure compliance and implementation of the obligations. What this means in practice, however, is interpreted differently in different countries. The wording does not, for instance, expressly require horizontal or inter-sectoral collaboration, something which in retrospect has proven to be a weak point of the convention.

The ecosystem approach is an approach to conservation that was developed under the Biodiversity Convention in which all three leading objectives were seen interconnectedly and conservation was also seen in an economic context. The approach is articulated in the Malawi Principles, which were accepted by the 2000 Conference of the Parties to the Biodiversity Convention. They highlight the necessity to take into account the structure and function of the ecosystems and for decision makers to view ecosystem pressures comprehensively.

No scientific panel was set up by the Biodiversity Convention, despite the fact that many environmental agreements do so. It did get its own advisory body on technical and scientific matters, but there is a tendency for discussions to turn political. There has, however, been no independent scientific forum where the scientific basis can be explored, and help provided on how the convention's principles and wording should be construed in practice, or to encourage public interest in the issues. The Millennium Assessment finalised its analysis of the situation facing ecosystems around the globe in 2005. Here the status for and management of biological diversity were also thoroughly examined, though the convention Parties do have the same approach to the findings and recommendations of the Assessment team as, for example, the Parties to the Climate Convention to findings and recommendations of the UN Panel on Climate Change (see Chapter 4). Currently, the situation has changed by the establishment of the Intergovernmental Science-Policy Platform on Biodiversity and Ecosystem Services (IPBES, June 2010) but it is still early days to judge the implications of this panel.

In a regulatory perspective, the Biodiversity Convention obliges Parties to prepare national action plans where they identify where biological diversity is in need of protection and conservation. Developing countries have agreed to this proposal providing developed countries agree to transfer technology and financial resources, and share responsibility for the conservation effort. This is why the Global Environment Fund is partnering and acting as the Biodiversity Convention's financial implementation arm in developing countries and in Eastern Europe. As this chapter goes to press, the normative objective, that is, a fairer division of the benefits from the use of genetic resources, has just been grounded in a more detailed, legally binding set of commitments – the Nagoya Protocol on ABS. The Cartagena Protocol is also quite detailed and includes, among other things, a requirement to obtain the prior consent of the country importing the genetically modified organisms, prior notification by the exporting country or party, along with special risk assessment and labelling rules.

The Biodiversity Convention: how effective and why?

As of 2010, 193 states and the EU have ratified the Biodiversity Convention. The small number of exceptions are the US, Holy See and Andorra. How has this affected regulations and work to address the conservation of biological diversity around the world?

The decision at the 2002 Johannesburg environment summit to reduce the loss of biological diversity by a large margin by the year 2010 reinforced the objective developed under the Biodiversity Convention. At the same time, the convention's implementation was seen to be too slow. The rather unclear 2010 target was later enumerated by most European countries, which made commitments to reverse the loss of biodiversity by 2010. In 2006, the global 2010 target was incorporated into the UN's millennium target but otherwise there is little progress on this goal.

Most countries have now prepared strategies and plans for implementing the Biodiversity Convention. There has been a rapid rise in the establishment of conservation areas with high, although somewhat variable degrees of biodiversity protection. About 14 per cent of the global land mass is now protected in some form or another. Nevertheless, only about 1 per cent of the oceans have been protected so far. As mentioned previously, efforts to establish protected areas were well underway long before the introduction of this convention, and land conservation is also dealt with under several other international agreements, such as the Ramsar and Bern conventions.

Sectoral integration as a means of facilitating conservation of biodiversity was a new obligation under the Biodiversity Convention, but only a small number of states have so far fulfilled their obligations to a satisfactory degree. Sectors rarely work well together, and the sustainable use of diversity may therefore be a difficult target to achieve. It is particularly the primary industry sectors, those which manage forestry, fisheries and farming, which are important in the management of biological diversity. There are frequent disagreements between the environmental authorities on their respective powers and competencies, not to mention clashes between those working to conserve diversity and producers of food and fibre. Nor is there much harmonisation between general economic policy and the economic measures required to integrate biological diversity and the ecosystem services it sustains. The result is that some end up paying more than others to meet the cost of protecting biological diversity, and, at the national level, with some groups being affected disproportionately by implementation measures. This is a classic problem of environmental policy. The costs of the measure are concentrated and affect the few, while the benefits are spread to the enjoyment of all: clean, plentiful wildlife and fresh air.

The Biodiversity Convention is significantly lacking in specific, concrete implementation provisions necessary to turn the tide, and there is insufficient political and legal bite in the measures taken at the conferences of the parties, the agreement's highest body. One of the problems with the Biodiversity Convention is the lack of a formal, legal sanction capacity to invoke against countries that fail to fulfil their commitments. Since the convention's obligations are of the general kind, it is not always easy to identify whether governments are acting in compliance with them or not. Because the Biodiversity Convention largely leaves it to governments themselves to interpret how the different commitments should be pursued, the interpretations will vary correspondingly. At the same time, while the scientific community is urging the need of 'doing something', the parties have found it difficult to agree on which steps are necessary to implement the convention, what needs to be set aside in the form of resources, and how to give action sufficient political force.

The Biodiversity Convention has also been weakened by the lack of an independent scientific body. While the political and scientific communities have converged for some time in viewing the loss of biological diversity as one of the major environmental problems facing the planet, there remains a large measure of uncertainty and disagreement on the best way of getting to grips with the problems. It is not for want of acknowledging the unprecedented scale of rain forest depletion, forests which may hold as much as 80 per cent of the world's species diversity on land. But agreeing to divide the costs, to funding mechanisms and to taking the necessary action to protect biological diversity for the future remain elusive.

The Biodiversity Convention has facilitated the transfer of money and technology to developing countries. Much of the funding is managed by the Global Environment Fund. The money is aimed at global environmental problems and also intended to help build local capacity, but lack of adequate funding means that little has been achieved in this area (Andresen and Rosendal, 2011). A key issue is whether the scale of bi- and multilateral funding is proportional to the need for measures to conserve and use biological diversity sustainably. There is evidence that the benefits of bilateral agreements on bioprospecting will probably not measure up to expectations of potential rewards. One often sees poor, but biologically rich countries as the weaker part in negotiations on bioprospecting deals. First, the control and negotiating power of the developing countries is weakened because economically attractive biological material is rarely limited to the geographical territory of the country in question. Gene resources are also much harder to control than other natural resources because their value lies in qualitative traits, not in the buying and selling of large quantities, as with minerals and oil for instance. Second, the governments' capacity to bring the laws into place and ensure compliance is also highly variable. A third and major problem is the lack of compatible and supportive legislation in the user countries in the North to ensure that companies really do something to share the benefits fairly (Rosendal 2006b).

At the tenth Conference of the Parties to the Biodiversity Convention in Japan, Parties adopted the Nagoya Protocol on Access to Genetic Resources and the Fair and Equitable Sharing of Benefits Arising from Their Utilisation. It is still early days to judge the effects of this Protocol. It aims to balance access to genetic resources on the basis of prior informed consent and mutually agreed terms with the fair and equitable sharing of benefits while taking into account the important role of traditional knowledge. Progress towards a binding agreement in this area has been very slow and it may be argued that failure to reach agreement on the ABS Protocol might have been preferable to a weak instrument. Most importantly, the ABS negotiations are not happening in a vacuum. International agreements affect one another, so to understand the practical chances of success under this convention, we need to know something about the other, related agreements. In particular this is about future developments within the FAO, the WTO and the World Intellectual Property Organization, where parallel sets of international rules have been negotiated with a view to food security, plant breeding and technological development (Rosendal 2006b).

Both in the WTO and World Intellectual Property Organization, the US and Australia in particular have fronted efforts to secure and strengthen patent rights for industry, while the EU and the Nordic countries have tried to incorporate provisions enabling a fairer distribution of the benefits of genetic resources. Now the talks in the WTO have been at a standstill for several years, pressure is mounting insofar as a large number of bilateral free trade agreements have been established between developed and developing countries. It is the rich and political powerful countries that prevail in the international economic organisations, and what they cannot achieve here, can be achieved much more easily using the many bilateral free trade agreements. As a rule, the government of the developing country has to commit to strengthening patent protection laws at home on patents eventually licensed to the commercial enterprise for its products.

If we turn to explore the development of commonly recognised norms in international relations, however, we will come across a different trend. Many private companies have adopted the Biodiversity Convention's principles on the fair sharing of benefits accruing from the use of genetic resources so as to appear as a more legitimate partner in bioprospecting agreements (ten Kate and Laird 1999; Laird and Wynberg 2008). Support for these principles has grown inasmuch as similar treaties are being discussed in several other international fora, with an emphasis on equitable sharing and conservation of traditional knowledge. India and Brazil, for example, tabled an additional motion for the Agreement on Trade-related Aspects of Intellectual Property Rights to require patent applications to name where the genetic material stems from and the traditional knowledge on which it is based. The provision would ensure that informed consent had been obtained and the fair division of benefits had been decided before the genetic material is sourced out. The European countries have expressed some support for parts of this proposal – apart from those dealing with informed consent and equitable distribution. These questions, they suggest, should be treated under the Biodiversity Convention. The US and Australia are against the proposal altogether.

The Biodiversity Convention has prompted many countries to modify procedures and laws on access to, extraction of and equitable sharing of the benefits deriving from the use of genetic material. One example is Venezuela's reaction to President George W. Bush's 1992 refusal to sign the Biodiversity Convention. Venezuela gave notice that it would suspend all agreements on bioprospecting with US-based research institutions. Another is Australia, which has banned all extraction of plants and micro-organisms before a rigorous analysis of the material has been conducted by the authorities. More than fifty developing countries have formulated national laws regulating access to genetic resources and to secure a share of the benefits from their utilisation. Only three developed countries have introduced some type of access legislation: Denmark, Belgium and Norway. The most important barrier to effective ABS policies remains the lack of compatible legislation in developed countries.

Conclusions

The loss of biological diversity will undermine many of the ecosystem services on which we depend today, will slow biotechnological progress and compromise human well-being in many areas. The loss of biological diversity has been and still is a difficult problem to solve collectively or internationally. The Biodiversity Convention negotiations were brought to a successful conclusion in 1992 because, in many ways, it became a 'sustainable development convention'. The score is low, however, with regard to implementation effectiveness.

The Biodiversity Convention rests on three normative principles: the conservation of biological diversity; sustainable use of components of biological diversity; and equitable sharing of the benefits arising from the use of genetic resources. The convention's funding arrangement entails a commitment by the international community not to unload the whole cost of conserving biological diversity onto developing countries. The principle of equitable sharing is also important for achieving the overall objectives of the Biodiversity Convention. This normative sway of the Biodiversity Convention has slowly made it less legitimate to enter into transactions with genetic resources without concern for ABS. As this chapter goes to press, the Parties have just reached agreement on a legally binding system on ABS and challenges now concern how it can be enforced in transactions with genetic material. Several stumbling blocks remain both with regard to equity issues and conservation in general, but the Nagoya meeting showed that the parties were able to take a leap forward on biodiversity issues in spite of highly diverging interests.

Still, the Biodiversity Convention is general and so far lacks the specified, concrete implementation commitments that are necessary to reverse the negative trend in biodiversity loss. At the moment, there is not enough political or legal force behind the resolutions passed by the conferences of the parties. It remains to be seen whether the newly established scientific panel (IPBES) may affect this situation in a positive direction with a view to implementation.

Moreover, the issue of biodiversity loss is very hard to tackle, even harder than that of climate change. This is partly because the natural conditions vary widely from country to country, as do access to the necessary social, institutional and economic resources required by good environmental management. A further point is that biodiversity politics in general has no technological engine pulling it forward, unlike some policy areas where pollution is involved. There, the development of substitutes encourages the private sector to play alongside environmental organisations, something we have seen with regard to ozone problems (see Chapter 3). Simple technological solutions which ease the constant pressure on land use are harder to envisage.

Finally, the issue of biodiversity is riddled with conflicts at all levels. Wider protection of patents leaves developing countries with few incentives to conserve the rich diversity of species in their territories. The trends in patenting are also likely to undermine the ability of local communities and indigenous people to exercise their rights when faced with agreeing to bioprospecting deals. It will also reduce the economic value of the original genetic material (Correa 1999). Moreover, many are afraid that patenting will increase the cost of and limit the practice by farming communities of recycling seed, which gives them access to enhanced breeding material (seeds). Inasmuch as traditional knowledge and traditional cultivated plants and varieties do not enjoy comparable protection, several studies conclude that patents could run counter to the objectives of the Biodiversity Convention. The reaction in many developing countries is to regulate access to the genetic resources in law and try to secure a share of the benefits from their use. But without corresponding legislative changes in user countries in the North ensuring a fair distribution with provider countries in the South, these changes are to little avail (Tvedt 2006). At the same time, developing countries are criticised for adopting ABS laws because they allegedly obstruct access to genetic material, such as seed and for medicinal purposes. The tendency to take out ever wider patents and to increase access control is like a race with increasingly powerful means. The principles of access, equitable sharing, incentives to promote innovation and con-servation are difficult – but important – to harmonise in practical politics. These principles have all been recognised by the international community in various forums, but governments are not necessarily pulling in the same direction at the same time. Better understanding of conflict and synergy between international commitments and processes of cooperation is important to achieve a working balance between these objectives and principles.

The explanations for the slow pace of implementing the Biodiversity Convention include a lack of political will and deep-set political conflicts, incomplete legislation and an inadequate economic response. Neither economic nor legal instruments are sufficiently tailored today to achieve the level of stewardship aimed for by the Biodiversity Convention. As long as the value of biodiversity and ecosystem services are not integrated into the general economy, considerations of biological diversity will rarely be weighty enough to attract allies against more immediate, but tangible industrial and economic interests. A sensible policy of biological diversity stewardship will cost money. It is high time to start appreciating diversity by translating ecosystem services into economic values, as has been done in the case of most of the other resource accounts.

Bibliography

Aylward, B. (1995) 'The role of plant screening and plant supply in biodiversity conservation, drug development and health care', in T. Swanson (ed.) *Intellectual Property Rights and Biodiversity Conservation*, Cambridge: Cambridge University Press.

Correa, C. (1999) 'Access to plant genetic resources and intellectual property rights', Background Study Paper 8. Rome: FAO Commission on Genetic Resources for Food and Agriculture.

Crespi, S. (1988) *Patents: A Basic Guide to Patenting in Biotechnology*, Cambridge: Cambridge University Press.

EC (European Communities) (2008) *The Economics of Ecosystems and Biodiversity*, Wesseling: Welzel and Hardt.

Gehl Sampath, P. (2005) *Regulating Bioprospecting: institutions for drug research, access, and benefit-sharing*, Tokyo: United Nations University Press.

Heywood, V.H. (1995) *Global Biodiversity Assessment*, Cambridge: Cambridge University Press.

Kloppenburg, J. (2004) *First the Seed: the political economy of plant biotechnology*, Cambridge: Cambridge University Press.

Laird, S. and Wynberg, R. (2008) *Access and Benefit Sharing in Practice: trends in partnerships across sectors*, Convention on Biological Diversity Technical Series 38, Montreal: Secretariat to the Convention on Biological Diversity.

MA (Millennium Ecosystem Assessment) (2005) *Ecosystems and Human Well-Being: biodiversity synthesis*, Washington, DC: World Resources Institute.

Rosendal, G.K. (2000) *The Convention on Biological Diversity and Developing Countries*, Dordrecht: Kluwer Academic Publishers.

——(2006a) 'The Convention on Biological Diversity: tensions with the WTO TRIPS Agreement over access to genetic resources and the sharing of benefits', in S. Oberthür and T. Gehring (eds) *Institutional Interaction: enhancing cooperation and preventing conflicts between international and European environmental institutions*, Cambridge, MA: MIT Press.

——(2006b) 'Regulating the use of genetic resources – between international authorities', *European Environment*, 16: 265–77.

Rosendal, G. Kristin and Andresen, S. (2011) 'Institutional Design for Improved Forest Governance through REDD: Lessons from the Global Environment Facility', *Ecological Economics*, published online 27 April 2011.

Schei, P.J. (1997) 'Konvensjonen om biologisk mangfold', in W. Lafferty, O. Langhelle, P. Mugaas and M.H. Ruge (eds) *Rio + 5: Norges oppfølging av FN-konferansen om miljø og utvikling*, Oslo: Tano Aschehoug.

Sheldon, J. and Balick, M. (1995) 'Ethnobotany and the search for balance between use and conservation', in T. Swanson (ed.) *Intellectual Property Rights and Biodiversity Conservation*, Cambridge: Cambridge University Press.

ten Kate, K. and Laird, S. (1999) *The Commercial Use of Biodiversity: access to genetic resources and benefit-sharing*, London: Earthscan.

Tvedt, M.W. (2006) 'Elements for legislation in user countries to meet the fair and equitable benefit-sharing commitment', *Journal of World Intellectual Property*, 9: 189–212.

Wilson, E. (ed.) (1988) *Biodiversity*, Washington, DC: National Academy Press.

9 The plant treaty

Crop genetic diversity and food security

Regine Andersen

Important years

1983 International Undertaking on Plant Genetic Resources adopted
1992 Resolution on the need to pursue international negotiations on crop genetic diversity in agriculture adopted
1993 United Nations Food and Agriculture Organization resolves to begin negotiations on a binding international instrument for the management of crop genetic diversity
2001 International Treaty on Plant Genetic Resources for Food and Agriculture (Plant Treaty) adopted
2004 Plant Treaty enters into force
2006 Standard Material Transfer Agreement approved as a cornerstone of a Multilateral System of Access and Benefit Sharing under the Plant Treaty
2007 The Multilateral System of Access and Benefit Sharing under the Plant Treaty enters into force

The genetic diversity in plants is the foundation of all food production. Both professional breeders and traditional farmers depend on this variety. We find here the traits required to meet people's nutritional needs, produce adequate feed for domestic animals, protect crops from pests and disease, and, not least, adapt food production to shifting climatic conditions. Crop diversity is therefore the single most important environmental factor in agriculture today, precisely because it decides how far the production of food can be adapted to a changing environment. But crop diversity is declining at a precipitous rate, and new laws and regulations are making it increasingly difficult to gain access to these resources. This is putting food security at risk.

In a bid to reverse this situation the United Nations (UN) Food and Agriculture Organization (FAO) adopted in 2001 the International Treaty on Plant Genetic Resources for Food and Agriculture, which entered into force in 2004. This is the first legally binding agreement dedicated exclusively to plant genetic resources for food and agriculture, that is to say, genetic material of plant origin of actual or potential value for food and agriculture. Plant genetic resources for food and agriculture include species (like wheat and rice, apples and pears), varieties (such as the rice varieties Basmati and Jasmin), and genetic variation within varieties. They include agricultural plants as well as their relatives in the wild. For the sake of simplicity, though, we shall be talking about crop genetic diversity in this chapter, and the Treaty with the long-winded name we shall refer to as the Plant Treaty.

The purpose of the Plant Treaty is to ensure the conservation and sustainable use of crop genetic diversity and to make sure that the benefits arising from their utilisation are shared equitably – in harmony with the Biodiversity Convention (see Chapter 8). In this way, then, the Plant Treaty seeks to promote sustainable agriculture and facilitate food security in the world.

This chapter reviews the challenges facing the management of crop genetic diversity before presenting the story behind the establishment of the collaborative arrangement, and taking a closer look at the Plant Treaty itself. Although the Treaty is still young, we shall attempt to assess its achievements so far.

The problems the Plant Treaty sets out to solve

Conditions affecting the cultivation of crops, that is, plant diseases, pests and climate, are constantly changing. It is the job of plant breeders to meet these shifting conditions with the right crop varieties. To accomplish this, they need to be able to access a wide diversity of crops. In recent years, consumers in many western countries have grown increasingly aware of the nutritional qualities of crops, and of environmentally friendly production methods. As we learn more about healthy and unhealthy substances and how they affect the environment, this too will be a challenge for the crop breeding sector. Some crops, which only a few decades ago were neither popular nor considered particularly valuable, are today highly marketable commodities. One example is spelt (*triticum spelta*), a hardy crop which needs very little fertiliser and is therefore an environmentally friendly alternative to its relative, wheat. What's more, it is a godsend for some of the sufferers of wheat allergy.

History has numerous examples of the importance of crop diversity for food security (Fowler and Mooney 1990: 42–53). The most infamous is the Irish potato famine of the 1840s, which killed more than a million people and resulted in nearly two million more emigrating to the United States. A disease called potato blight was the cause, wiping out the potato crop on which most ordinary people depended. Potato varieties were limited back then, and it proved necessary to return to the cradle of potato cultivation in the Andes to find blight-resistant varieties. Only then was the crisis overcome.

For the roughly 1.4 billion poor farmers in developing countries who tend the land according to traditional methods, crop diversity is paramount (Andersen 2005b, 2008; United Nations 2009). To maintain production levels and nutritional value, as well as avoid plant diseases and pests, these farmers depend on genetic diversity in their fields, both within and between different plant varieties. They save the seed to sow in the next season, select the best plant material for the purpose, develop new varieties and exchange and sell seed and plant material among themselves, as they have been doing since the dawn of agriculture. These customary practices are the foundations on which the immense diversity of crops we have today rests.

About 7,000 different plant species have been cultivated or gathered for food (Wilson 1992: 275), and the diversity within these species has been enormous. Some old cultivars, like rice and wheat, have seen as many as several hundred thousand different varieties (FAO 1998). But this diversity is shrinking at a tremendous speed. Eighty per cent of the varieties of important cultivars like maize and wheat have disappeared within the span of a century from the regions in which they originated. And the loss of fruit and vegetable crops is simply astonishing, with the loss of some species like apples and tomatoes in some countries approaching 80–90 per cent over the last century.

One of the leading causes of this genetic erosion is the modernisation of agriculture and the so-called green revolution of the post-Second World War period. These farming methods are based on the use of genetically homogeneous, high-yield varieties, and an ever smaller number of seed and plant material suppliers. A small number of varieties is left to dominate immense areas, to the detriment of the old diversity. While production and yield rates are higher, thus contributing decisively to meeting the food demand of rapidly growing populations particularly in the cities, the cost to future generations in the form of lost genetic diversity is hard to comprehend. Some varieties are stored for safekeeping in gene banks, but gene banks too have been affected by technical and managerial problems in many places. In some cases, gene banks have been looted in countries ravaged by civil strife or damaged by natural disasters. So gene banks are not immune to significant genetic erosion. On top of this, access to crop diversity is increasingly fraught as different regulatory mechanisms are urged into being by the seed industry.

Seed corporations demand intellectual property rights (that is, time-limited exclusive rights to utilisation, use and marketing of an invention or information) as a means of protecting new plant varieties. These rights are progressively enacted in law around the globe. In addition, many governments are tightening existing laws so as to reinforce the rights of breeders. It is all meant to cover the cost of modern plant breeding and incentivise activity in the area. While farmers used to pay a one-off licence fee on protected varieties when they bought seed from the suppliers, in many countries today, particularly in Europe and North America, they also have to pay a fee when they gather seed from their own fields to sow in the next growing season. Governments are increasingly ready to ban the exchange of seed of protected varieties between farmers.

At the same time, governments in an increasing number of countries are tightening seed marketing legislation (Andersen 2009). Farmers are seeing their customary rights to exchange and sell seed evaporate. The new rules apply to all kinds of plant varieties, whether they are protected or not, including traditional cultivars, farmers' varieties and material from gene banks. The rules have been adopted to ensure plant health and seed quality in agriculture. Under these rules, only authorised seed shops can sell plants. In addition, only seed from plant varieties that have been approved for marketing can be sold, and for most plant varieties, only certified seed can be sold. Land races and farmers' varieties are normally characterised by genetic heterogeneity and tend therefore to fall short of approval and certification procedures: buying and selling them is therefore illegal. When it is also illegal for farmers to exchange or sell seeds and propagating material among themselves, it is just a matter of time before this plant heritage disappears. The rules are demolishing the traditions and customs which produced this enormous diversity in the first place, but which now is facing accelerating attrition. At some point it will simply be impossible for customs and diversity to survive on the farms due to regulations to ensure plant health. This is a tremendous paradox: we have the very diversity of varieties to thank for the genetic characteristics needed to maintain the health of plants, and future generations depend on this diversity to ensure the health of their food crops.

Responding to the patent systems being introduced in many western countries, many developing countries have adopted their own rules to regulate access to genetic resources after the pattern of the Biodiversity Convention in order to ensure benefit sharing. Anyone wanting access to the genetic resources must file an application and negotiate the terms of a contract. For plant breeders, bilateral agreements for each accession can make breeding a complicated exercise, as a high number of accessions are required to develop one single variety. It will often take time to negotiate each contract and the lists of specifications to fulfil tend to be long, all of which serve in effect to limit access to crop genetic diversity. Less access also means that less benefits will be generated, and thus that there will be less to share.

The way things stand today, many stakeholders can limit each other's access to crop genetic resources. This in itself constitutes a threat to crop genetic diversity since these resources mainly consist of cultivated plants which need – exactly – cultivation to survive. Although samples are kept in gene banks, they cannot permanently replace active cultivation of the varieties in their 'proper' environment and the living knowledge that goes with it. In many developing countries, it affects traditional farmers' ability to make a livelihood. Given that 75 per cent of the world's poorest 1.2 billion people live in rural areas, often on marginal land, and depend on these resources for their survival, genetic diversity is a crucial factor in the battle against poverty. In a report to the General Assembly of the UN from the UN Special Rapporteur on the Right to Food these issues were explored as a basis for recommendations on how seed policies could be designed so as to serve the right to food and ensure the rights of all to enjoy the benefits of scientific progress (United Nations 2009).

Now although there is wide scientific consensus on the causes of the problems in this area, doing something about them is not as easy as it sounds. Opposing interests is one reason. To feed a fast growing population, genetically homogeneous high-yield varieties need to be grown on the largest possible areas. This is the main idea behind agricultural production today. Critics of this argument believe it is possible to feed the world's population in an ecologically sustainable way, that is, in a way which does a better job of conserving crop genetic diversity. Agricultural research has been myopic, they say, and led us down the wrong path. Here, allegation stands against allegation. What is increasingly accepted is that small-holders in marginal areas are often unable to use genetically homogeneous high-yield varieties because they are unsuited to the climate and environment (IAASTD 2008). Here, crop genetic diversity and ecological sustainability are crucial elements of food security.

The problems are also difficult to solve because the international seed industry has massive investments to protect – not to mention the surge of privatisation which swept over the breeding industry. Within three to four decades, much of the public breeding capacity has been transferred to private businesses which in turn have been bought up by bigger firms. Market concentration is rising steadily. A precondition for private stakeholders to take over was that economic incentives would be favourable for plant breeding, that is, profit opportunities in the market. This explains the emergence of a regulatory environment in which seed corporations can make money, while at the same obstructing the sustainable use and conservation of crop genetic diversity.

As we see, genetic erosion resulting from modern farming methods works in tandem with regulations and policies to limit access to crop genetic diversity to threaten global food production for current and future generations. Behind the predicament we are facing today lie conflicting and powerful economic interests. The Plant Treaty is facing an uphill struggle.

The story behind the Plant Treaty

The origins of the Plant Treaty stretch back as far as 1948 – but we can pick up the story in 1971 when the Consultative Group on International Agricultural Research (CGIAR) was established on the initiative of the Ford Foundation and Rockefeller Foundation who wanted all privately funded international agricultural research institutes and their gene banks gathered under a single umbrella. In 1974, the International Board for Plant Genetic Resources (IBPGR) was founded under the auspices of the CGIAR (in 1991 it was renamed International Plant Genetic Resources Institute; after merging with the International Network for the Improvement of Banana and Plantain in 2006, it became Bioversity International). From then on, efforts grew to collect seeds and genetic material from plant varieties around the world, especially in developing countries. It was a battle against time in many cases, as the green revolution swept across continents with its homogeneous, high-yielding varieties causing widespread genetic erosion. The IBPGR had considerable power over the direction of conservation activities and was assumed to have the authority to designate certain gene banks for holding particular collections. Around 85 per cent was stored in the developed world and gene banks in the CGIAR system (Fowler 1994: 184). Gene banks in developing countries were few in number and in most cases allegedly not up to the mark technologically. Nor was there enough know-how on documentation and storage management. So while many varieties were saved from certain extinction, many developing countries lost control of their own genetic resources.

These circumstances prompted Pat Roy Mooney to write *Seeds of the Earth: Private or Public Resources?* which came out in 1979 (Mooney 1979). It sparked a debate and is reputedly an important factor behind the initiative that established the first agreement on crop genetic diversity (Fowler 1994: 180), that is, the 1983 International Undertaking on Plant Genetic Resources for Food and Agriculture (IU). The Mexican delegation to the FAO General Conference tabled a proposal in 1981 to draft the elements of a legal convention on the feasibility of establishing an international gene bank. The proposal was welcomed by developing countries, deeply concerned at the time by the loss of control over genetic resources caused by gene bank activities. Most developed countries were sceptical, concerned as they were about the likely politicisation of the issue and loss of control over the gene banks. That scepticism notwithstanding, in light of the ongoing rapid genetic erosion, a decision was taken to investigate the idea's feasibility.

The agreement that the Parties arrived at was the IU adopted at the Twenty-second Session of the FAO Conference, 1983 in Rome (Conference Resolution 8/83), the aims of which were to ensure that crop genetic resources would be explored, preserved, evaluated and made available for plant breeding and scientific purposes. Following its adoption in 1983, 113 countries added their signatures, while a number of western countries whose input had been vital to getting the agreement passed, abstained. Thus, the agreement proved weak and its results meagre. The most important outcome was the agreements with international agricultural research institutes of the CGIAR system to place their gene bank collections under the auspices of the FAO. This brought about 600,000 seed samples into the system under multilateral control, making them at the same time available for breeding on terms specified by the FAO (FAO 1998: 83). The arena function of the IU should also not be understated: it provided a platform for continued negotiations on central matters related to the management of crop genetic resources.

Since the biggest problem for the IU was the non-accession of major western countries, the discussion at the FAO centred on means to persuade them to re-assess their position (Andersen 2008: 94). If the rights of plant breeders (variety protection) were recognised as compatible with the agreement, these countries would climb on board as well, they claimed. Developing countries protested, and wanted rights for farmers as a counter-move: it was after all the farmers who had generated all this diversity which plant breeders could now work with, and it was the labour of farmers that had ensured the survival of genetic diversity *in situ* on-farm (i.e. the natural surroundings where genetic resources are maintained and where they develop their distinctive properties). Their rights to the use of these resources for the collective good should therefore not be limited. On the contrary, farmers should be compensated and rewarded for their contribution to the global gene pool and their efforts on behalf of the global community (Andersen 2005a). The outcome was the simultaneous adoption of two resolutions in 1989 (Conference Resolutions 4/89 and 5/89), recognising the rights of plant breeders and of farmers.

A later interpretation of the IU in 1991 concluded that the wording in the IU that crop genetic diversity is mankind's common heritage was subject to the sovereignty of the states over their plant genetic resources (Conference Resolution 3/91). Against this background, FAO members responded that the conditions for access to crop genetic resources required further clarification. The original purpose of the IU – to ensure unrestricted access to genetic resources – was no longer clear, nor was the principle of these resources as being the common heritage of mankind. New factors had been introduced, which complicated the follow-up and limited its prospects for implementation.

In this period, negotiations on the Biodiversity Convention were into the home straight. Along with the text of the Convention, a resolution was adopted in 1992 that stressed the importance of crop genetic resources, the need to develop complementarity between the Biodiversity Convention and the FAO in this regard, and called for solutions to outstanding matters: (1) how to regulate access to gene bank collections acquired prior to the entry into force of the Convention; and (2) the question of farmers' rights (Resolution 3 of the Nairobi Final Act).

In 1993, the FAO Conference duly requested the FAO Director General to provide a forum to negotiate how to harmonise the IU and Convention – this was the process that would lead to the Plant Treaty. The negotiations proved extremely difficult for various reasons. First, many delegates, particularly from developing countries, believed a new agreement should steer clear of intellectual property rights to crop genetic diversity. This was founded on a response to the Agreement on Trade-related Aspects of Intellectual Property Rights (TRIPS) under the World Trade Organization which were mentioned in Chapter 8. Second, many developing countries had already adopted laws and regulations along the pattern of the Biodiversity Convention, which implied bilateral agreements between providers and recipients of genetic resources of a rather impractical nature with a view to accessibility and utilisation of crop genetic resources. This was not a model the new regime should emulate since it was unsuitable for domesticated plants. There had to be another way of regulating access which addressed the need to ensure fair distribution of benefits, while at the same time allowing free, facilitated access to these resources to enable their utilisation for food and agriculture – but still within the letter of the Convention.

On top of this, the delegates had to agree about farmers' rights. But what rights exactly? How could these rights be ensured without infringing against already existing rights of plant breeders? And what sort of duties should be imposed on states? Disagreement was endemic, causing the talks to lurch from side to side.

Right up to the last bell, large sections of the text remained bracketed, a sign of continued divergence (Andersen 2008: 100). That the Parties managed to agree on a text and adopt the Plant Treaty in 2001 at all came as a surprise to many observers. As of June 2009, 123 countries have become party to the Plant Treaty.

The Plant Treaty has a long and chequered history. When it was negotiated, other international agreements with their overlapping issue areas were already established and in the process of implementation. This added to the challenges facing the delegates, and the Treaty's implementation has been no less thorny. But let us take a closer look at the substance of the Plant Treaty.

The contents of the Plant Treaty

The most important articles of the Plant Treaty can be divided into four main areas. There are articles on (1) ensuring the conservation and sustainable use of crop genetic diversity (articles 5 and 6); (2) protecting and promoting farmers' rights associated with crop genetic diversity (article 9); (3) facilitating access to crop genetic diversity for a number of defined species under a multilateral system (articles 10–12); and (4) ensuring the distribution of benefits arising from the use of these resources through the Multilateral System (article 13).

Ensuring conservation and sustainable use of plant genetic resources

The Parties to the Treaty pursue an integrated approach to the conservation and sustainable use of plant genetic resources – though subject to their own national legislation and in cooperation with other Parties whenever appropriate.

Central measures for conservation are mapping, recording and collect-ing seeds and samples of varieties in danger of extinction or of potential use. The measures also include promoting and supporting the efforts of farmers to conserve plant genetic diversity *in situ*. The Parties shall further work together to promote the development of a secure gene bank system laying particular emphasis on the need for good documentation and the regeneration of seeds. Last, but not least, the Parties shall strive where appropriate to minimise or, if possible, eliminate threats to plant genetic resources. The provisions leave space for a certain degree of interpretative discretion: implementation is to proceed under the framework of national legislation, that is, to the extent that it does not infringe against the laws of the implementing country.

Sustainable use of plant genetic resources shall be promoted by the Parties in developing and maintaining appropriate policy and legal measures. A number of measures are suggested. For instance, the Parties may promote diversified agricultural systems that strengthen the management of plant genetic resources among farmers. They may also incentivise research that encourages the wider use of plant genetic resources. In this connection, so-called participatory breeding is mentioned as a sensible approach. Here, farmers and plant breeders work together to develop varieties particularly adapted to the conditions in which the crops are cultivated, while attending to other breeding goals considered of importance by the farmers. In general, the recommendation is to ensure that more varieties are brought into use, and it is particularly important to promote the use of locally adapted varieties. The Parties also recognised that adapting their breeding strategies and adjusting their national laws and regulations concerning variety release and seed distribution could be a sensible move to ensure appropriate synchronisation with the articles and suggestions of the Plant Treaty.

There is an emphasis on cooperation in implementing the articles on conservation and sustainable use, particularly with a view to supporting developing countries and countries with economies in transition, including through bilateral or multilateral development cooperation.

Protecting and promoting farmers' rights to crop genetic resources

Farmers' rights constitute one of the cornerstones on which the Plant Treaty rests because farmers are custodians and developers of the genetic resources in the fields, and require certain rights if they are to continue so doing. They need to be able to use, exchange, develop and sell their seeds and propagating material, as they have always done. Without these rights, farmers would be unable to make their contribution to the global genetic pool. And anyway, it has been internationally recognised since 1989 that the farmers who do this work on behalf of present and future generations should be compensated and/or rewarded for their contributions. All the same, farmers' rights was one of the most hotly discussed issues in the negotiations. While everyone was conscious of the invaluable work of farmers to develop plant genetic diversity, and of the need for the Treaty to include articles on farmers' rights, delegates found it extremely difficult to agree on what the rights should comprise, and the types of provision the Treaty set forth in this area. Powerful economic interests were at stake, especially those of the multinational seed industry.

The compromise entailed recognition of the enormous contribution of farmers in developing plant genetic resources as the basis for food and agriculture the world over, and of the responsibility of governments in the different countries to ensure that farmers can enjoy their rights. The rights themselves were not specified, but every country is expected to take steps to protect and promote farmers' rights in compliance with their own needs, priorities and legislation, where appropriate, the Treaty says. These provisions have drawn frequent criticism for leaving too much to the discretion of the Parties (Andersen 2005b). Others deem them appropriate enough insofar as the conditions under which farmers work every day vary widely from country to country, and devising articles of equal merit to them all would be extremely difficult. One should rather devote one's energies to developing the substance of farmers' rights, and to their realisation in connection with the international implementation of the Plant Treaty, they suggest.

The article on farmers' rights also offers advice on what governments might do to protect and promote farmers' rights, in compliance with each government's priorities. They could protect traditional knowledge of relevance to plant genetic resources; ensure the right to equitably participate in sharing the benefits arising from the utilisation of plant genetic resources; and enable farmers to participate in relevant decision-making at the national level.

There is a further caveat in the Treaty: nothing shall be interpreted so as to limit farmers' rights to save, use, exchange and sell farm-saved seed/propagating material, subject to national law and as appropriate. It could hardly be put less rigorously. For the crux of the controversy is about farmers' rights to preserve, use and sell their own seed as they see fit. And because these rights have been removed in many countries, the delegates were unable to agree on ensuring such customary rights as farmers have enjoyed for the past ten thousand years. The only thing this article affirms is the existence of such rights in different places. It is an admission of sorts, if the weakest imaginable. In contrast, the preamble of the Treaty contains formulations highlighting the importance of these rights to the realisation of farmers' rights as such (see also www.farmersrights.org).

Facilitating access to plant genetic diversity through a multilateral system

Access to genetic resources is considered the prime benefit arising from the use of plant genetic resources because it is the foundation on which the generation of all subsequent benefits rely. The provisions dealing with this concern the Multilateral System of Access and Benefit Sharing. To keep things simple, we refer to it as the Multilateral System.

The Multilateral System is a central pillar of the Plant Treaty. Rather than obliging users of genetic resources to apply for access and negotiate the terms in every single case, as the Biodiversity Convention provides for (see Chapter 8), access is made much simpler here. The applicant contacts a gene bank or other depository of genetic resources, signs an internationally negotiated standard material transfer agreement, and receives the material. The FAO acts as a third party to the transaction and monitors compliance with the terms of the agreement. Recipients of genetic resources are obliged to pay a fixed percentage of the profits from sales if they take out a patent for a product developed on the basis of resources obtained from the Multilateral System. If they do not claim protection through intellectual property rights, they can still pay a fixed amount into the system voluntarily if they commercialise the product. They also commit themselves not to seek intellectual property rights for material obtained from the Multilateral System in the form it was received from the system. It is quite uncertain, however, how effective this provision will prove, as only minor alterations of the material might free the recipients from this obligation.

All the same, the Multilateral System does not cover all food plants. It covers the genetic resources of 35 food crop genera and 29 forage genera which are under the management and control of the Parties and publicly available. In practice it means mostly seed samples are found in national and international gene banks. Sixty-four plants does not sound all that much, but many of the world's most important plants are included, such as rice, wheat, maize, potatoes, beans and bananas. Nevertheless many plants fall short of the Multilateral System, such as soybeans, tomatoes, oil palm, cotton, sugarcane, cocoa and many vegetables, in addition to important tropical forage plants. This is because some countries had significant resources of certain food crops for which they claimed to be countries of origin, and, consequently, to have a chance of making a good profit. It would therefore benefit them more to manage access to the crops themselves rather than placing them under the stewardship of the Multilateral System, they reasoned. China, to take one example, wanted full control over its soybean genetic resources, hoping to generate higher profits from entering into bilateral agreements on access to these resources than, they believed, would probably come their way via the Multilateral System.

So we have a rather peculiar situation regarding the regulation of access to plant genetic diversity in the world. For the plants covered by the Multilateral System, the rules set out in the Plant Treaty for this system apply: access to seed and plant material from these plant varieties can be arranged quickly and with a minimum of red tape using the standard material transfer agreement. There are, however, no clauses in the Treaty to regulate access to the remaining genetic resources. In effect then, such access is regulated by the governments of the countries which have them, and terms of access must therefore be negotiated bilaterally. Depending on the system adopted by the country in question, access will be more or less complicated, as explained above. To complicate the picture further, the simplified process under the Treaty is also limited to genetic resources used for food and agriculture. If the main use of the material is something else, such as medicine or bio-ethanol, the Treaty does not apply.

Not all of the plants remaining outside the Multilateral System are covered by the Convention either. Plant material deposited in gene banks before the Convention came into force in 1993 is not covered by the Multilateral System, nor regulated by the Plant Treaty or Convention. These genetic resources are not governed by any international regime at all, and it is solely up to the discretion of the governments in each case whether they will share the resources with others, and on what terms. This is considered to be one of the gravest shortcomings of the Plant Treaty. Nonetheless, plant material deposited in the international gene banks before the Treaty and Convention came into force is accessible on more or less the same terms as provided for by the Multilateral System, but on the basis of specific agreements with the Treaty's Governing Body (see below).

As the situation stands today, every country is a net recipient of genetic resources (Palacios 1998). What each country receives from other countries far exceeds what it disseminates from its own genetic pool. Crucially then, countries depend on each other to share these resources. That so many plant genetic resources are still not covered by the Multilateral System is therefore a big problem. Countries seeking to obtain greater returns by holding resources back have not felt the impact of this yet. In the long run, the effect could be the opposite in that they lose the most important benefit, access to plant material from these species.

Some of the countries in the South have accused countries in the North of doing everything they can to get the Multilateral System up and running so as to gain access to the world's genetic resources, but without meeting their own commitments under the rest of the Plant Treaty, in particular commitments to make financial resources available to conserve crop genetic diversity *in situ*, promote sustainable use and establish the rights of farmers in developing countries. Their suspicions are not unfounded: so far, it has proved impossible to raise more than a fraction of the resources required to make the Plant Treaty work and support developing countries in implementing it. Limiting the number of species covered by the Multilateral System is perhaps the only bargaining chip available to developing countries to get an effective system of benefit sharing in place.

Ensuring the sharing of benefits arising from the use of these resources through the Multilateral System

The sharing of benefits arising from the use of genetic resources is a crucial component of the Multilateral System. The Treaty itself stresses access to genetic resources as the most important benefit. Also highlighted are information exchange, transfer of technology, capacity building and sharing. Information exchange, technology transfers and capacity building are general commitments and as such not linked to the regulation of access to certain resources under the Multilateral System. The sharing of monetary and other benefits from the commercial use of the resources is, however, linked directly to access to genetic resources under the standard material transfer agreement and any transfers materialising from it. Opinion is divided on the likely outcome of the system in terms of monetary benefits. Patents are not often applied in plant breeding, so mandatory payments are expected to be minimal. But in any case, patience is needed before the results appear, not least because it usually takes some years to develop a new variety, market it and earn money from it.

The benefits arising from the use of the Multilateral System – monetary as well as non-monetary benefits – shall be diverted to farmers in developing countries and in countries with economies in transition who conserve and sustainably use crop genetic diversity. While the Convention favours providers of genetic resources, under the Treaty, the people who conserve and sustainably use diversity are supposed to enjoy the benefits. This is irrespective of whether their particular seeds were accessed for particular breeding purposes. What matters is that their contribution to crop genetic diversity is being rewarded.

All Parties to the Treaty have a place on the Treaty's Governing Body. It is the Treaty's highest body and convenes every second year to oversee implementation of the Treaty. A secretariat based in Rome is in charge of putting the Governing Body's decisions into action.

With the Plant Treaty, the international community has an important instrument with the potential to reverse the negative trend plant genetic diversity is undergoing and which is threatening global food security. But will the effort succeed?

Implementation and impact so far

As of writing, the Plant Treaty has been in force for six years and held three Sessions of the Governing Body. As a regime it is still in its infancy, despite lengthy gestation, partly because it was not ratified until 2004, and partly because important instruments like the standard material transfer agreement were not in place until 2006. The funding strategy, adopted in 2006 (Resolution 1/2006), and further detailed in the subsequent sessions of the Governing Body, is still not generating the funds required for the Secretariat to implement decisions at a full scale, and important measures cannot be included in the working plan due to lack of funds. In particular, the capacity building coordination mechanism suffers under lack of funds, and measures to implement Governing Body decisions on conservation, sustainable use and farmers' rights are side-tracked for the same reason. Nevertheless, substantial progress has been achieved in some areas.

According to a survey carried out by the FAO, most countries do implement a variety of policies and legal measures on different aspects of conservation and sustainable use of crop genetic diversity (FAO 2010). However, most countries seem to lack an integrated and coordinated approach in this regard. Existing legislation often obstructs progress and incentive structures are more noticeable by their absence (Andersen 2008). Farmers' rights are being steadily eroded in most countries, in terms of legislation. India is an exception, where legislation gives farmers rights to the use, exchange and sale of seeds as long as the brands of commercial players are not used. Despite the largely negative trend regarding legislation, numerous initiatives have been taken at the local level, often by civil society organisations, to support farmers in their work to conserve and develop crop genetic diversity, thereby contributing to realising farmers' rights (Andersen and Winge 2008). Local gene banks are being set up, participatory plant breeding activities are under way, help to accessing markets is made available and the work is supported in other ways. In many cases, the farmers are enjoying better results and, in consequence, improved livelihoods, from the active conservation and use of crop genetic diversity through such support. All the same, these are small initiatives, and the question is whether and how the work can be scaled up to the national level.

When it comes to *ex situ* conservation (collections of genetic resources kept outside their natural habitats, and often in gene banks), great progress has been achieved since the entry into force of the Treaty. In 2004, the Global Crop Diversity Trust was established as a public–private partnership to raise funds from individual, corporate and government donors in order to establish an endowment fund to provide complete and continuous funding for key crop collections. The goal is to advance an efficient and sustainable global system of *ex situ* conservation by promoting the rescue, understanding, use and long-term conservation of valuable plant genetic resources. The Trust is an independent organisation closely interlinked with the Plant Treaty. During the first session of the Governing Body of the Plant Treaty in 2006, a relationship agreement between the Governing Body and the Trust was formally approved. The agreement recognises the Trust as an essential element of the funding strategy of the Treaty. It provides for the Governing Body to give policy guidance to the Trust and to appoint four members of the executive board. It also recognises the board's executive independence in managing the operations and activities of the Trust. As of April 2010, the total amount of money pledged to the Trust amounted to US$168,179,144, of which US$142,000,925 had been paid (Global Crop Diversity Trust (2010)). Thus, the Global Crop Diversity Trust has become a great success in channelling funds for *ex situ* conservation.

In another step forward, the Svalbard Global Seed Vault was opened in 2008 in the Arctic permafrost of Svalbard, Norway. It offers free-of-charge back-up for the seed collections that are held in seed banks around the world. The seed vault has the capacity to store 4.5 million different seed samples. Each sample contains on average 500 seeds. Thus 2.25 billion seeds can be stored in the seed vault. It will therefore have the capacity to hold all of the unique seed samples currently held by the approximately 1,400 gene banks that are found in more than 100 countries all over the world. The seed vault will also have the capacity to store many of the new seed samples to be collected in the future. If seeds are lost – for example, as a result of natural disasters, war, or simply a lack of resources – the seed collections can be re-established using seeds from Svalbard. Each country or institution owns and controls access to the seeds they have deposited. The seed vault facility was built and is owned by Norway, and its operation is managed in partnership between the government of Norway, the Global Crop Diversity Trust, and the Nordic Genetic Resource Centre (NordGen). As of December 2009, more than 430,000 unique seed samples had arrived at the seed vault from seed banks all over the world. The Svalbard Global Seed Vault provides insurance against the loss of plant genetic resources for food and agriculture from the gene banks of the world and is, as such, an important component in the global effort to stop genetic erosion. With these developments, much has been achieved with regard to *ex situ* conservation since the Plant Treaty entered into force. Although the challenges are still huge in many parts of the world with regard to *ex situ* conservation, the prospects for improvement are better than ever.

With regard to the Multilateral System, progress has been quite substantial, although there is uncertainty in some countries about how to include their collections in the system in practice and manage them in accordance with the international rules. In the first eight months of operations, nevertheless, almost 100,000 transfers of genetic material had taken place under the Multilateral System. Since that time, the number has been steadily increasing.

The benefit-sharing mechanism is still weak, however. Since it is uncertain how much benefit the mechanism will actually generate (see above), optional benefit sharing is being discussed, as set out in Articles 13.2.d and 13.6 of the Treaty, and to some extent already taking place. For example, Norway is providing an annual contribution that is equivalent to 0.1 per cent of the total sales of seeds in the country to the benefit-sharing mechanism. It urges other countries and multinational companies to do likewise, as it would substantially improve the capacity of the benefit-sharing mechanism. With this regular contribution, and ad hoc contributions from some other countries, the first disbursement of benefits from the Benefit Sharing Fund was announced at the third session of the Plant Treaty Governing Body in June 2009. Eleven projects in developing countries were selected from a large number of applications to receive support for their contributions to the conservation and sustainable use of plant genetic resources for food and agriculture. The total amount of money disbursed was approximately US $500,000.

Work to promote non-monetary benefit sharing has been slow. An international workshop in Bogor, Indonesia, in 2010 dealt with the issue, and developed recommendations to the Governing Body to be discussed at its Fourth Session in 2011.

Conclusions

Managing crop genetic diversity involves several policy fields. It touches on, among other things, food security, environment and intellectual property rights. These fields have different rationalities and ways of thinking, and are dominated by different interests. This alone makes it difficult to agree to solutions which satisfactorily address the requirements for the conservation and sustainable use of crop genetic diversity and the equitable sharing of benefits arising from its use. The long process that culminated in the Plant Treaty is illustrative in that sense. While progress has been excellent in some areas covered by the Treaty, a great deal still needs to be done, as addressed above. In particular, *in situ* on-farm conservation of crop genetic resources, farmers' rights, and ways and means to strengthen the benefit-sharing mechanism under the Multilateral System need more emphasis. The Treaty has everything it needs to reverse the negative trends with regard to the management of crop genetic diversity in the world – it only needs to be implemented according to its intentions. Whether the international community will make use of this unique opportunity depends on political will.

Bibliography

Andersen, R. (2005a) *The Farmers' Rights Project – Background Study 1: the history of farmers' rights: a guide to central documents and literature*, FNI Report 8/2005, Lysaker, Norway: Fridtjof Nansen Institute.

——(2005b) *The Farmers' Rights Project – Background Study 2: results from an international stakeholder survey on farmers' rights*, FNI Report 9/2005, Lysaker, Norway: Fridtjof Nansen Institute.

——(2008) *Governing Agrobiodiversity: plant genetics and developing countries*, Aldershot, UK: Ashgate.

——(2009) Information paper on farmers' rights submitted by the Fridtjof Nansen Institute, Norway, based on the Farmers' Rights Project, submitted to the Secretariat of ITPGRFA, 19 May 2009, Doc. IT/GB-3/09/Inf, 6, addendum 3.

Andersen, R. and Winge, T. (2008) *Success Stories from the Realization of Farmers' Rights Related to Plant Genetic Resources for Food and Agriculture*, FNI Report 4/2008, Lysaker, Norway: Fridtjof Nansen Institute.

FAO (1998) *State of the World's Plant Genetic Resources for Food and Agriculture*, Rome: Food and Agriculture Organization of the United Nations.

——(2010) *State of the World's Plant Genetic Resources for Food and Agriculture: second report*, Rome: Food and Agriculture Organization of the United Nations.

Fowler, C. (1994) *Unnatural Selection: technology, politics, and plant evolution*, Yverdon, Switzerland: Gordon and Breach.

Fowler, C. and Mooney, P. (1990) *Shattering: food, politics and the loss of genetic diversity*, Tucson, AZ: University of Arizona Press.

Global Crop Diversity Trust Pledges (2010) Updated list of funds pledged and raised, available at www.croptrust.org/main/funds.php (accessed 26 April 2010).

IAASTD (2008) *International Assessment of Agricultural Knowledge, Science and Technology for Development: synthesis report*, Johannesburg: IAASTD.

Mooney, P.R. (1979) *Seeds of the Earth: private or public resource?* Ottawa: Canadian Council for International Co-operation and the International Coalition for Development Action.

Palacios, X.F. (1998) 'Contribution to the estimation of countries' interdependence in the area of plant genetic resources', Background Study paper No. 7, Rev. 1, Rome: Commission on Genetic Resources for Food and Agriculture.

United Nations (2009) *Seed Policies and the Right to Food: enhancing agrobiodiversity and encouraging innovation*, interim report of the UN Special Rapporteur on the Right to Food, Olivier De Schutter, transmitted by the Secretary General to the members of the General Assembly of the UN for its sixty-fourth session, New York, NY: United Nations.

Wilson, E.O. (1992) *The Diversity of Life*, Cambridge, MA: Belknap Press of Harvard University Press.

10 International forest politics

Intergovernmental failure, non-governmental success?

Lars H. Gulbrandsen

Important years

1983   First International Tropical Timber Agreement (ITTA) adopted
1986   International Tropical Timber Organization (ITTO) established
1992   Forest Principles (Non-Legally Binding Authoritative Statement of Principles for a Global Consensus on the Management, Conservation and Sustainable Development of All Types of Forests) and Convention on Biological Diversity adopted
1993   Forest Stewardship Council (FSC) established
1994   Second ITTA agreed (entered into force on 1 January 1997, superseding the first ITTA)
1995   United Nations Intergovernmental Panel on Forests (IPF) established
1997   United Nations Intergovernmental Forum on Forests (IFF) established
1998   Biodiversity Convention adopted a programme of work on forest biodiversity, which was expanded in 2002
2000   United Nations Intergovernmental Forum on Forests (UNFF) established as a permanent organisation
2003   EU Action Plan for Forest Law Enforcement, Governance and Trade (FLEGT) launched
2006   Third ITTA agreed
2007   Non-Legally Binding Instrument on All Types of Forests adopted at UNFF

The political stance of the international community on forest policy is a story of failed attempts to settle a legally binding forest treaty, and of creative solutions to emerge in the wake of these defeats. Because where governments have failed to adopt binding regulatory instruments, market-based certification schemes have emerged to promote sustainable forest management. And although governments have been unable to secure a global forest convention, they have managed to agree on a number of forest policy principles and recommendations. Yet, there is a long way to go before the international community manages to solve the problems of deforestation and forest degradation.

In this chapter we shall look at deforestation and degradation of forests as environmental problems of local, national and global proportions before addressing the various international forums established to tackle the problems and their performance in practice.

Deforestation and forest degradation

Deforestation and forest degradation are local, national and global environmental problems. Forests provide local communities with a number of ecosystem services like fuel, timber, erosion protection (soil leaching) and local water and climate regulation. In addition to forests' local and national value, their diversity of species, habitats and ecosystems is of global importance as a gigantic repository of biological diversity and genetic resources. Most of the planet's terrestrial species live in forests; nowhere else is there such an abundance of species as in the tropical forests. Some of the ecosystem services of forests can therefore be counted among global public goods, that is, assets enjoyable by all and from which no one can be denied. Taking care of the planet's biological diversity is therefore also to care for every single individual on the planet.

At the same time, commercial timber and privately controlled forests are private goods, enjoyed by only a minority. Differences in private and public benefits may result in failure to provide ecosystem services such as biodiversity conservation and wildlife habitats; forest owners will tend to provide too little of ecosystem services when the benefits primarily go to the public. Although more than three-quarters of the world's forests are owned by central governments, companies with logging concessions, forest owners and farmers have few or no incentives in many countries to produce or take care of global public goods. Indeed, in many countries expansion of agriculture and more or less unrestricted industrial logging have been official governmental policies. Agricultural expansion, commercial logging, mining and other forms of exploitation have already wrought untold damage on the biological diversity of forests. According to the United Nations Environment Programme, human intervention has accelerated the extinction of species by anything between a hundred and thousand times the natural rate. The estimate is uncertain because only a tiny fraction of species have been recorded and described scientifically. Every year, vast swathes of tropical forest are lost forever. The Philippines, for example, which used to be covered by a thick carpet of forest fifty years ago, is today a net importer of tropical timber. Deforestation is particularly serious in Latin America, South-East Asia and Africa, but forest degradation and biodiversity loss are problems facing all forest-rich countries. Deforestation and forest degradation are among the biggest threats to preserving our common natural heritage and the earth's biological diversity.

Deforestation affects the global climate balance as well, because trees absorb and store CO_2. Emissions from deforestation in developing countries account for about 20 per cent of global greenhouse gas emissions: reducing the rate of deforestation will therefore help cut greenhouse gas emissions significantly. According to the IPCC, forest ecosystems bind more than 4,200 billion tons of CO_2, of which 70 per cent is bound in the forest floor. An estimate computed by the IPCC puts the annual emission of CO_2 resulting from global deforestation at 5.8 billion tons. These emissions are currently not regulated by the Climate Convention or the Kyoto Protocol, though a proposal has been tabled in the talks on a new climate agreement to establish a payment mechanism to reduce the scale of deforestation in developing countries. The role played by forests in regulating the climate can be considered part of mankind's heritage as such, like biological diversity.

The causes of deforestation are multiple and complex and vary from country to country (Geist and Lambin 2002). The conversion of forests to agricultural land both for commercial and subsistence use is ranked as one of the leading causes in all developing countries. Commercial logging companies' exploitation of forests in states with weak legislation, poor law enforcement and inadequate systems of governance is another problem, especially in Asia, but increasingly in Africa as well. The cattle industry and clearing of forests to make way for grazing land for livestock are two of the leading causes in Latin America, while the collection of wood for fuel in Africa is another important factor. The demand for biofuel and cooking oil underpins incentives to turn tropical forests into plantations.

Illegal logging is another cause of deforestation. Although there is no recognised international definition, illegal logging is generally understood as activities that violate national laws. What is illegal will therefore vary from place to place and time to time. During the 1980s, for example, settlers in Brazil and Ecuador could claim ownership to land if they had cleared it themselves, and with the blessing of the law. This activity is illegal in both countries today. Indeed, the logging of threatened tree varieties in protected areas or outside licensed logging areas, and logging more than the permitted quota is illegal under the laws of most countries. Illegal logging, according to a World Bank estimate, robs governments of developing countries of about 5 billion USD in annual revenue and results in the loss of forest resources equivalent to 10 billion USD every year (Humphreys 2006: 142). This is economic criminality. It deprives poor countries of urgently needed tax revenue and threatens the livelihoods of millions of people whose livelihoods depend on forest resources. Illegal logging is also environmental criminality because it destroys ecosystems and threatens the fauna and flora of vulnerable forests.

Deforestation is essentially a tropical country problem, even though it is not limited to the tropics. Siberia in Russia and British Colombia in Canada are regions with shrinking forests, for example. The loss of biological diversity and degradation of environmental values in forests are serious environmental problems in all forest-rich countries.

Intergovernmental forest policy

There is no international forest convention to promote sustainable management and protection of the planet's forests. In the absence of a convention,
a patchwork of intergovernmental processes, partnerships and alliances
have sprung up, under the auspices of a range of international organisations and regimes. Although by no means an exhaustive account of all the
intergovernmental processes and initiatives in existence, this review details
some of the achievements and limitations of intergovernmental policy
processes to date.

UN forest negotiations

Deforestation of tropical forests claimed a place on the international
agenda in the 1980s. Alarming scientific reports on the rate of deforestation and environmental activism, backed by the likes of rock musician
Sting and other celebrities, brought the urgency of the situation home
to the public. The idea to create a legally binding international convention to
protect the world's forests was conceived before the 1992 UN Conference
on Environment and Development in Rio de Janeiro (Humphreys 1996).
Several developed countries wanted to initiate talks on a global forest
convention to be adopted at the Rio conference, similar to the conventions
on biodiversity and climate change. Forest-rich developing countries, led
by Malaysia, campaigned against the idea of a forest convention; they
wanted to retain undiluted national sovereignty over their forest resources.
The right to exploit forest resources was considered essential to development and as such an inalienable principle. And one of the reasons forest-rich
developed countries were calling for a forest convention to reduce tropical
deforestation, they argued, was to shield their own timber industries. That
the attempt to reach a compromise on a forest convention was futile
became eminently clear during the preparations for the Rio Summit. At
the Summit, the attending nations produced instead the so-called Forest
Principles – short for the Non-Legally Binding Authoritative Statement of
Principles for a Global Consensus on the Management, Conservation and
Sustainable Development of All Types of Forest – a rather insipid
declaration without binding legal force.

The Forest Principles acknowledge the sovereign right of all nations to
exploit forest resources in accordance to their own needs, as the forest-rich
developing countries had demanded. They highlight the role of the forests
in maintaining ecological balance at the global level, and the many and
diverse ecological functions at the local level and the role of forests as a
supplier of, among other things, fuel and timber. The need for financial
support for institution-building purposes in developing countries and recognition of the rights of indigenous peoples are also emphasised. Altogether,
the Forest Principles are essentially an assortment of good intentions and

weak rules on management and sustainable use of forests. Unfortunately, no balance was struck between use and protection of forests, and the principles are far too amorphous to have any real effect on forest management. There was deep disappointment among campaigners for a legally binding instrument. The optimists among them, who saw a half full rather than half empty glass, called the Forest Principles simply the first step on the road to instruments with greater legal clout. But the following years would prove them wrong.

To clarify and expand on the Forest Principles, the third session of the UN Commission on Sustainable Development in 1995 established the Intergovernmental Panel on Forests (IPF). Its successor, the Intergovernmental Forum on Forests (IFF), was created in 1997. Four sessions of the IPF between 1995 and 1997 and four rounds of the IFF between 1997 and 2000 produced a number of forest policy recommendations. Governments were, *inter alia*, encouraged to develop national forest programmes that promoted sustainable forestry. The policy recommendations suggested how such programmes could be organised in terms of participation, detail, oversight and implementation. The key question of whether to prepare a forest treaty, however, was put on hold in an amusing formulation which quickly earned the sobriquet 'the Monty Python Paragraph'. The IFF Proposals for Action (2000), endorsed by the UN, urged governments, within five years, 'to consider with a view to recommending the parameters of a mandate for developing a legal framework on all types of forests'. Joking apart, the wording was sufficiently woolly as to obtain the support of both advocates and opponents of a legally binding forest convention.

The provisional Forum on Forests was succeeded by a permanent one in 2000. Unlike its predecessors, the UN Forum on Forests (UNFF), as it was called, has universal membership and reports directly to the UN Economic and Social Council. It has continued to issue recommendations on forest policy, but the most divisive issue has remained whether to start talks on negotiating a forest treaty. The fifth session of the UNFF (2005) was much anticipated and expected to be a milestone event, because the meeting was tasked with evaluating the Forum's achievements and agreeing a strengthened arrangement on forests, possibly recommending a global forest treaty. However, states did not agree on the need for negotiations on a forest convention, and the session was widely regarded as a failure. Two years later, at UNFF-7 in 2007, states adopted a Non-Legally Binding Instrument on All Types of Forests. It provides a framework for national action and international cooperation on forest policy, but it reiterates existing political commitments and it is regarded as a rather weak political agreement. Delegates have decided to review the effectiveness of this agreement in 2015 and consider the option of a forest convention, along with other options, at that time. At UNFF-7, states also adopted a multi-year programme of work (2007–15) and agreed to convene biannually rather than annually.

Countries in favour of a global forest treaty include Canada, Finland, France, Norway, Russia, South Africa and most Eastern European and Central American countries. The US pushed harder than most for a forest convention at the Rio conference, but has since revised its policy and advocates instead other instruments and mechanisms. Other opponents include Australia, Brazil, China, Japan, New Zealand, the UK and many developing countries.

What explains this division? Obviously, national economic interests affect attitudes towards a forest treaty. Canada and other developed countries with substantial forest industries have lobbied for years for a forest convention that gave their own forest industries a competitive edge over developing countries with less robust environmental regulations. On the other side we find Brazil and many other developing countries. They fear the possible adverse consequences of a forest convention for their own forest industries. Some of the divisions are not as unequivocal, however, and have evolved over time. While some developing countries want the convention to include mechanisms for funding and technology transfers to improve the environmental record of their forest industries, others see the convention as likely to weaken their economy. Some of the countries in favour want to formulate rules with sufficient bite to protect the forests. Some would prefer a flexible regime which gave them a wide action radius. For some, a weak convention would be worse than no convention at all, because weak rules could be marshalled to legitimise individual countries' exploitation of their forest resources. Environmental organisations share these misgivings. While the environmental organisations were divided at the Rio Summit on the forest convention question, most are against the idea today. They fear that a weak forest convention could give the go-ahead for continued commercial exploitation and degradation of the forests.

Changes in governments' positions at the international level are affected by changes in domestic politics. Malaysia was one of the most entrenched opponents of a forest convention at the Rio conference, but argued for a convention at one of the UN Forest Forum meetings. This could be explained by the Malaysian forest industry's expansion into South-East Asia since the Rio conference. The interests of the industry would possibly be better served by a convention (Humphreys 2006: 45). Policy in the US went in the opposite direction. While the Clinton administration campaigned for a forest convention at the Rio Summit, when Clinton's second administration took office, the US was campaigning against. The domestic timber industry had been pressuring the government to oppose the idea, backed in part by members of Congress where the Republicans had regained the majority. The Canadian timber industry is more export-oriented and favoured a forest convention. It could help them capture market shares in a highly competitive marketplace.

In conclusion, a body of soft law on forests has emerged over the last 20 years. This body comprises several political agreements and policy recommendations, including the 1992 Forest Principles, the IPF proposals for action (1997), the IFF proposals for action (2000), UNFF resolutions, and the 2007 Non-Legally Binding Instrument on All Types of Forests. The UNFF remains the primary international forum for 'stand-alone' forest negotiations. It has produced a number of forest policy recommendations, but most of them are weaker than the IPF/IFF proposals agreed earlier (Humphreys 2006: 115). According to one analyst, the UNFF's failures are not accidental, as states opposing strong forest policies created a weak institution deliberately designed to *pre-empt* rather than provide governance (Dimitrov 2005). Against this it can be argued that the UNFF, as noted above, has a higher profile in the UN system than either of its predecessors and that states have simply failed to agree on difficult questions regarding forest conservation and governance. In any case, the UNFF has clearly failed to provide leadership and direction on global forest policy.

The Convention on Biological Diversity

Because most of the world's terrestrial biodiversity is found in forests, many of the provisions under the Biodiversity Convention have – or should have – implications for forest management and protection measures. The Convention has established the principle of in situ conservation, requiring the parties to the convention to, *inter alia*, 'establish a system of protected areas or areas where special measures need to be taken to conserve biological diversity'; and 'promote the protection of ecosystems, natural habitats and the maintenance of viable populations of species in natural surroundings' (Article 8). Several other multilateral environmental agreements also promote the ecosystem approach and the principle of protected areas, including the Ramsar Convention on Wetlands of International Importance Especially as Waterfowl Habitat (1971); the Convention Concerning the Protection of World Cultural and Natural Heritage (1972); and the Bern Convention on the Conservation of European Wildlife and Natural Habitats (1979). Of the multilateral treaties that have consequences for forest policies, however, the Biodiversity Convention is clearly the most important due to its holistic approach to 'the conservation of biological diversity, the sustainable use of its components and the fair and equitable sharing of the benefits arising out of the utilisation of genetic resources' (Article 1).

In 1998, the parties to the Biodiversity Convention adopted a programme of work on forest biodiversity to clarify and elaborate on the convention's provisions pertaining to forestry. This programme was expanded in 2002. While the convention as such is legally binding on all ratifying states, the recommendations under the thematic programme on forest biodiversity are not. Those who had hoped to see the forest biodiversity programme set the stage for a more productive negotiation arena than the UNFF have been disappointed, however. The divisions separating states into camps for and against stricter international forest policies are reproduced in the forest biodiversity programme. The recommendations on forest policy to emerge from this programme so far echo in many ways the IPF/IFF proposals for action. The forest biodiversity programme has nevertheless reinforced the ecosystem approach to forest management and the principle of protected areas since the objectives of the programme are in line with the overarching objectives of the Biodiversity Convention. Compared to the IPF/IFF proposals for action, it also has more of an emphasis on practical action (Humphreys 2006: 192).

Regional criteria and indicator processes

As a supplement to negotiations in the UN, several regional, intergovernmental processes around the world were established to develop criteria and indicators for sustainable forest management. The scale of these processes varied from region to region. But states have agreed on nine sets of regionally tailored criteria and indicators for sustainable forest management, including the International Tropical Timber Organization (ITTO) criteria and indicators (adopted by 28 tropical timber-producing countries in 1992), the Pan-European criteria and indicators (adopted by 36 countries in 1993) and the Montreal-process criteria and indicators for non-European temperate and boreal forests (adopted by 12 countries in 1995). Although this common understanding of what constitutes sustainable forest management is valuable, it must be remembered that criteria and indicators are primarily used to exchange information and compare the state of the forests in different countries. They do not set out specific performance requirements, targets or measures for forest protection.

The widest ranging regional forest policy process takes place under the auspices of the Ministerial Conference on the Protection of Forest in Europe (Pan-European process). In that the EU lacks a common forest policy, the ministerial conferences in Europe have become the most important venue for European cooperation on forests. Ministers in charge of forestry from 46 European countries, including EU delegates, have, *inter alia*, developed common principles, criteria and guidelines for sustainable forest management.

International action to counter illegal logging

In the 1990s, the problem of illegal logging was known to governments, but it remained a non-issue in intergovernmental negotiations. As we have seen, cooperation on forest policy had hit rock bottom, with mistrust clouding the atmosphere between developed countries and forest-rich developing countries. After the turn of the century and several ambitious declarations to combat poverty and promote sustainable development (such as the UN Millennium Goals), tensions have eased somewhat and several new initiatives have been launched to address illegal logging. Illegal logging featured as a key element in the G8 Action Programme on Forests (1998–2002), and led to a series of regional Forest Law Enforcement and Governance (FLEG) conferences. The geographical regions covered by FLEG processes were East Asia and the Pacific (launched in Bali, Indonesia in September 2001), Africa (launched in Yaoundé, Cameroon in October 2003) and Europe and North Asia (launched in St. Petersburg, Russia in October 2005). These regional processes to counter illegal logging were initiated by the US State Department, which considered UN institutions like the UNFF too slow to deal with the complex issues involved (Humphreys 2006). Primarily as a result of the FLEG processes, however, institutions such as the UNFF and ITTO are beginning to address illegal logging.

To complement the FLEG processes, the EU committed in 2002 to developing an action plan to counter illegal logging and associated trade in forest products. As a major importer of tropical timber, the EU's objective was to develop supply-side measures to curtail the trade of illegally logged timber to the EU while providing assistance to producer countries to support such measures (Humphreys 2006: 156–59). This focus on trade led the EU to extend the FLEG acronym when developing what became known as the Forest Law Enforcement, Governance and Trade (FLEGT) action plan. The action plan was approved in 2003 and announces that the EU will develop voluntary partnership agreements with producer countries on timber licensing. Timber products from a partner country will only be allowed to the European market if they have a legality licence issued under a credible control system. Producer countries without a legality licence can continue to export timber to the EU, but the demand for licensed timber will, it is anticipated, likely persuade producer countries to join the scheme. As we saw above, what counts as legal and illegal logging varies from state to state, and the EU needs to agree with each producer country on a common definition of legality. Although the EU has concluded partnership agreements with a few producer countries, the implementation of the FLEGT action plan has been very slow. By contrast, in 2008 the US became the first state to legislate against the handling of timer which is illegal according to the laws of the country the timer originated from.

UN Framework Convention on Climate Change

Forests are recognised as important carbon reservoirs – or sinks. Reducing emissions from deforestation and forest degradation (REDD) has captured international attention as a potentially cost-effective climate change mitigation option. Forest loss, primarily tropical deforestation and forest degradation accounts for almost 20 per cent of global greenhouse gas emissions. The ability of a forest to capture and sequester CO_2 is acknowledged under the Climate Convention (UNFCCC 1992) and the Kyoto Protocol (1997). Annex 1 parties to the Kyoto Protocol may use *afforestation* (planting of new forests) and *reforestation* (planting of forests on lands that historically contained forests), measured as verifiable changes in carbon stocks since 1990, to meet their emission targets (UN 1997, article 3[3]). Conversely, deforestation in Annex 1 countries since 1990 may have a negative impact on their balance of carbon stocks. The clean development mechanism of the Kyoto Protocol allows emission credits for afforestation and reforestation projects during the first commitment period (2008–12), but not for projects related to forest protection and the sustainable management of existing forests.

REDD projects are not recognised under the clean development mechanism during the first commitment period, but there is a growing international consensus that a post-2012 UN climate-change treaty must include incentives to reduce greenhouse gas emissions from forests. At COP 13, held in Bali in December 2007, the parties to the Climate Convention agreed under the Bali Action Plan to consider: 'Policy approaches and positive incentives on issues relating to reducing emissions from deforestation and forest degradation in developing countries; and the role of conservation, sustainable management of forest and enhancement of forest carbon stocks in developing countries' (UNFCCC 2007, Decision 1b [iii]).

Sequestering may create stronger incentives for forest protection than do any of the soft law forest policy recommendations, although it could also stimulate uniform 'carbon plantations'. Viewing forests primarily as sinks – or carbon reservoirs – is different from appreciating their value in the full range of plant and animal species they accommodate. The planting of fast-growing monocultures of softwood would be the most cost-efficient way to lock up CO_2 and thereby claim emission credits, but this is certainly not a measure that could ensure species diversity. Carbon sequestration may even result in actions to *replace* natural grown forests with plantations, something that will almost certainly result in a loss of forest biodiversity. Similarly, substitution of biomass energy for fossil fuels – an implicit incentive of the Kyoto Protocol – could result in more intensive forestry at the expense of biodiversity conservation.

International Tropical Timber Organisation

The ITTO, headquartered in Yokohama, Japan, is another intergovernmental collaborative body. The organisation was established in 1986 to promote global trade in tropical timber and sustainable use of tropical forests. An opinion shared by many is that the ITTO has done more to achieve the former than the latter objective. The ITTO has 57 member countries divided into two caucuses: tropical timber producer countries

(31 members) and consumer countries (25 members). This intergovernmental organisation provides a forum for producer and consumer countries to discuss, exchange data and develop policies on issues relating to international trade in tropical timber and sustainable use of tropical forests. Its members represent about 90 per cent of world trade in tropical timber and covers 80 per cent of the world's tropical forests. One of ITTO's tasks is to implement the International Tropical Timber Agreement, a trade agreement which also has provisions on forest conservation. The agreement was first negotiated in 1983, while the latest successor agreement was negotiated in 2006. This chapter will not detail ITTO's activities, but one discussion is particularly interesting for the direction taken by international forest governance. At the close of the 1980s, the British delegation to ITTO tabled a proposal from several environmental organisations to investigate setting up a government-backed scheme for certification of sustainable forest management (Humphreys 1996; Gale 1998). A large majority of ITTO member states dismissed the proposal, but that was a decision that would have repercussions for forestry around the world. The refusal of the ITTO to discuss forest certification was what was needed to convince WWF and other non-governmental organisations of the overriding need to pursue a forest certification scheme outside intergovernmental negotiation processes, as we shall return to.

Some results, but no problem solving

As we have seen, unlike other areas of concerted action dealt with in this book, there is no single framework convention with protocols and supplementary provisions on forest management and conservation. What we have instead is a fragmented regime, based upon a number of agreements, processes and initiatives in different arenas. To begin with, there is the cluster of non-legally binding agreements and policy proposals on forests, which we could call soft international law. A number of multilateral environmental agreements supplement the body of soft law on forests with legally binding provisions pertaining to forest management and protection, notably the Biodiversity Convention. Finally, the EU, the UN Food and Agriculture Organization (FAO) and other intergovernmental organisations have increasing concern for forests. The biennial sessions of the FAO's Committee on Forestry, for example, bring together forestry experts to discuss technical and policy issues and advise the FAO and governments on appropriate action. How do all these agreements, processes and initiatives perform in practice? In terms of forest policy, intergovernmental collaboration has helped establish a regulatory structure with consequences for national forest management. A range of principles and guidelines have been devised to promote forest conservation and sustainable forest management. The following offers thumbnail sketches of some key policy outcomes.

- *An integrated ecosystem approach and protected areas.* All governments shall formulate and implement management strategies to protect and preserve unique, representative and sensitive forest types and ecosystems. Governments are also urged to develop methods for an ecosystem approach for all types of forest, both in protected areas and outside.
- *Deforestation and forest degradation.* Governments shall analyse historic and underlying causes of loss of forestland and implement national plans to combat deforestation and forest degradation.
- *Participation.* Another set of guidelines urges governments to promote participation of the public, indigenous populations, local communities and other affected interests in the management of forest resources.
- *Criteria and indicators for sustainable forest management.* Regional criteria and indicators for sustainable forest management shall be used in reports of the state of the forests. These criteria and indicators must not be confused with performance-based standards for well-managed forests. They are primarily a set of tools for exchanging information with other governments on the state of the forests.
- *International trade.* Governments shall implement measures to counter trade in timber products stemming from illegal logging, and promote trade in timber products originating from legal and sustainable sources.
- *National forest programmes.* Since the 1992 Rio Summit, the FAO has assumed a leading role in promoting national forest programmes. These programmes are recognised as a means to implement internationally agreed forest principles and guidelines. Governments shall formulate and implement national forest programmes which integrate forest conservation and sustainable forest management. These forest programmes shall enumerate appropriate institutional, legal and economic frameworks to promote sustainable forest management. They shall also set out mechanisms to safeguard property rights, fair distribution of benefits arising from the use of forest resources and access to forest for local communities and indigenous peoples. The private sector should be encouraged to develop and practise standards of sustainable forestry. A national forest programme does not necessarily address specific matters, but is a general instrument providing for a wide array of approaches to sustainable forest management in different states.

In sum, governments have agreed on a number of forest policy proposals, covering a wide range of issues. The problem with these guidelines is precisely their nature as rather weak policy recommendations, without binding legal force on states. Another weakness of the regulatory regime is the general fogginess of much of the wording. Governments are constantly urged to act 'to the degree possible', 'in accordance with own needs' and 'whenever appropriate'. It is easy to see in these guidelines the concessions governments with widely different interests felt compelled to make to achieve a settlement at all, as is often the case in international negotiations. The problem with regard to forest policy, however, is the positive aversion of the negotiating parties to compromise on important issues relating to forest conservation. Positions have been harder than in many other areas of negotiation. This has to do with the powerful economic and political interests connected with the exploitation of forests in many countries. Nor can problems of deforestation and forest degradation be solved by developing new technology or employing other innovations. Unlike the potential to develop technological solutions to such problems as climate change and air pollution, there are no technologies that can fix the problems of deforestation and land-use change. We are left then with general formulations and insufficient clarity on the balance between use and preservation of forests.

Although forest regulations are weak in legal terms, they do exert pressure on governments to act on the recommendations. And we have seen the growing concern in many states to see sustainable forestry practices in place. The principles on which there is agreement can be said to have *normative force* in favour of conservation and sustainable use of forests. National decision makers will, to some extent, feel obliged to enact the recommendations even though non-compliance cannot be punished. But there is a long way to go before the international community manages to solve the problems of deforestation and degradation of forests. Although many countries have passed laws and regulations on sustainable forest management, powerful economic structures and economic realities often stand in the way of new management practices. As noted, deforestation is driven by several interacting socio-economic and political factors, including the conversion of forests to agricultural land, urbanisation, commercial logging, mining, urbanisation and infrastructure development. In many developing countries, forest destruction is also related to corruption, organised crime and informal alliances between publically employed 'timber barons' and timber companies. Corruption includes bribery, granting of falsified logging rights, underreporting of illegal logging and deficient reports of illegal activity. Several studies show that control of forest resources in some tropical countries confers political power because public officials tend to reward accomplices with contracts and favourable economic terms (see e.g. Dauvergne 2001). Many countries have passed laws to combat illegal logging and promote sustainable forestry, while informal power structures frequently prevent the problems from finding a solution, leaving the destruction of natural resources to continue unabated. There is little to indicate a significant reduction in deforestation in the foreseeable future. The pressure to transform natural forests into plantations for production of, among other things, palm oil and soya beans, is if anything on the rise, helped by increasing demand for biofuel in the US and EU. Palm oil is used to produce biodiesel. In addition, large areas of Amazonian rain forest are being cleared to cultivate soya beans, which many US farmers have given up because they can earn more from growing maize for ethanol production, a component of biofuel.

Forest certification: an alternative to a global forest treaty?

One of the promising initiatives affecting forest management practices around the world is forest certification. When the ITTO threw out the forest certification proposal and the Rio Summit's created the toothless Forest Principles, the environmental organisations were fed up with all the talk about forests – and little action. In 1993, primarily at the initiative of the WWF, the Forest Stewardship Council (FSC) was officially founded by environmental organisations, timber traders, indigenous peoples' groups, forest worker organisations and other stakeholders. By creating a market-based certification programme, the WWF wanted to circumvent multilateral negotiations that were seen as arduous and non-productive (Gulbrandsen 2004). The FSC was formed to promote sustainable forest practices and to encourage retailers and consumers to support such practices by buying certified forest products. It developed principles and criteria for its definition of 'well-managed forests', including tenure and use rights and responsibilities, indigenous peoples' and workers' rights, use of forest products and services to maximise economic viability and environmental and social benefits, maintenance of forests with high conservation value, environmental impact, monitoring and assessment, and planning and management of plantations. These principles and criteria are elaborated upon and specified for each country or region in national or regional FSC working groups, through a process in which ecological, economic and social stakeholders have, in principle, equal decision-making powers. The FSC's international board approves national standards consistent with the scheme's principles, criteria and procedural rules. In areas where national standards remain incomplete or non-existent, FSC-accredited certifiers may assess operations against locally adapted 'generic' standards.

The ultimate decision-making authority of the FSC rests with its membership, comprising over 800 organisations and individuals as of 2010. The members are separated into environmental, social and economic chambers, which each control one-third of the total voting rights in the general assembly. In addition, each chamber has voting parity between stakeholders from developing and developed countries. The chambers each elect three representatives to the FSC's board of directors. Anyone can in principle apply for membership, but the FSC prohibits the participation of governments in the organisation. In 2002, the FSC changed membership rules to allow government-owned and government-controlled companies to apply for membership in its economic chamber. The international secretariat manages operational issues and carries out the mandates of the membership and the board of directors. In summary, the FSC's governance structure is designed to ensure that no specific interests are allowed to dominate rulemaking in the programme.

The national forestry interest organisations and landowner associations of several countries responded to the creation of the FSC by establishing producer-dominated certification schemes. The FSC and its supporters succeeded in creating demand for certification, but many forest companies and forest owners distrusted the scheme because it was initiated and promoted by the WWF and other environmental organisations. Equally important, forest companies and landowners disliked its relatively stringent environmental and social standards, which they claimed were applied with inflexibility. Thus forest industry and landowner associations in Europe, the US, Canada and elsewhere were motivated to establish schemes with less stringent environmental and social standards. In 1999, European landowner associations joined forces to create the Pan-European Forest Certification Council – PEFC (now the Programme for the Endorsement of Forest Certification), to facilitate the mutual recognition of national programmes. They were later joined by landowner- and industry-dominated programmes in Canada, the US and a few tropical countries, thus turning the PEFC into a global competitor to the FSC.

Unlike the FSC, the PEFC regulations state that national forest owner and industry associations are the appropriate initiators of standard-setting activities. Although all relevant stakeholders shall be invited to participate in the standard-setting process, landowner and industry associations have significant influence in determining the relevant parties in this process. The international PEFC Council is composed of national members primarily representing forest owner associations and other forestry organisations. It approves national schemes if they are developed in conformity with the PEFC's rules and regulations. The PEFC does not have a global set of principles and criteria stipulating general environmental and social requirements for forestry operations. It does have a set of basic procedural and substantive requirements for national-level certification programmes, but many of the specific requirements for forest operations are left to the discretion of national member programmes.

Forest certification potentially offers an alternative, fast-track route to ameliorate environmental problems that states have not been willing or able to address. A few observations about forest certification can serve to illustrate the potential and limits of private transnational governance programmes (Gulbrandsen 2010). First, the certified forest area worldwide has increased steeply since the inception of the FSC in 1993. By mid-2009, FSC- and PEFC-certified lands totalled 325 million hectares or approximately 8.3 per cent of the world's forest cover (UNECE/FAO 2009). Accomplishing this level of uptake in less than two decades is evidence of the success of non-state governance in the forest sector. However, an examination of adoption patterns around the world shows that certified lands are skewed in favour of temperate and boreal forests. The certified forestland in developing countries only represent about 10 to 20 per cent of the world total certified area, and many tropical countries are lacking any type of certification scheme.

Second, patterns of adoption show that the producer-backed PEFC programme has outperformed the non-governmental organisation-supported

FSC programme in several countries and regions. By the end of 2009, the PEFC had certified more than twice as much forestland as that certified by the FSC (UNECE/FAO 2009). The wider producer acceptance of the PEFC is an indication that producers, not surprisingly, tend to prefer participation in programmes with less stringent and prescriptive standard than FSC offers. On the other hand, market preference for the FSC has in many cases given forest companies and landowners an incentive to seek FSC certification. In general, the FSC is strongest in the timer market, whereas the PEFC has the upper hand in the pulp and paper market (Auld *et al.* 2008: 193).

Third, an unintended consequence of certification is the favouring of large operations and forest companies at the expense of non-industrial owners practising small-scale forestry. Because of economies of scale, it is easier for large forest companies to participate in certification programmes and comply with management rules. The problem of high transaction costs has spurred efforts to form specialised programmes to reduce entry barriers for smallholders. While this problem in part explains the formation of the PEFC by European landowner associations, the FSC is the only programme that has developed a social strategy to improve access for smallholders in developing countries and to address the special needs of forest communities, indigenous peoples and forest workers.

Fourth, reviews of auditing reports issued by third-party certifiers show significant attention begin paid to improvements in internal monitoring and auditing in forest organisations. These studies also indicate that forest holdings have had to attend to ecological aspects of their management more carefully following certification (Rametsteiner and Simula 2003). But we still know too little about the capacity of forest certification to change on-the-ground practices in ways that reverse or ameliorate environmental degradation in forestry. Moreover, issues of scale represent a significant hurdle in using certification as a tool to address environmental problems that are rarely contained within a single forest, such as management of large predators requiring large habitats (Auld *et al.* 2008: 199). Certification does not offer forest protection at the landscape level; protection on an individually certified tract can lead to higher pressure for extraction on non-certified lands. In regard to reducing pressure for deforestation, there is also broad agreement that certification provided an inadequate counterbalance to greater economic incentives for land-use conversion (Gullison 2003; Auld *et al.* 2008: 199).

In sum, forest certification has been a great success in terms of the level of producer and market uptake, but there is clearly a dilemma in setting stringent standards that would compel producers to undertake management reforms they otherwise would not pursue, while also ensuring broad-scale participation. In addition, as a voluntary policy instrument, certification cannot deliver forest protection at the landscape level or contribute significantly to reducing deforestation. With regard to the decision-making rights of non-state actors, a situation with two competing governance models has emerged. Whereas environmental, social and economic stakeholders participate on a level playing field in the FSC, landowners and forest companies tend to dominate rule-making and governance in PEFC-endorsed national programmes. These two models reflect different views of who ought to be accountable to whom and for what in forest governance. Whereas many forest managers and landowners maintain that they are primarily accountable to industry peers and national governments, environmental and social groups claim that forests are global commons which ought to be co-managed by a range of stakeholders.

Conclusions

The last two decades have seen the emergence of a body of soft law on forests, comprising several political agreements and a number of policy recommendations. Supplementing this soft law is a number of multilateral environmental agreements, notably the Biodiversity Convention, with legally binding provisions pertaining to the use and management of forests. In sum, the totality of soft and hard law pertaining to forests could be said to constitute a fragmented forest regime. Although this regime is weak in legal terms (*regulative strength*), it does exert normative pressure on governments to act on the commitments and recommendations (*normative strength*). However, there is little evidence to suggest that the forest regime has changed how key actors perceive the problems of deforestation and forest degradation or changed perceptions about how the problems can be addressed (*cognitive strength*).

Moving from the *output* to the *outcome* indicator, we noted how the rather weak policy recommendations of the forest regime mean that we should not expect significant behavioural effects from the regime. Powerful economic and political interests represent a major obstacle standing in the way of changing harmful forestry practices in many countries. It appears that market-based forest certification schemes, which emerged partly in response to the lack of progress in intergovernmental forest policy processes, have been more effective in changing on-the-ground practices among their members than has any set of intergovernmental recommendations. That said, we still know too little about the problem-solving effectiveness of non-state certification programmes. Because it may take many years, even decades, to observe the biophysical *impact* of an environmental institution, it may be premature to draw any conclusions about the impact indictor.

International collaboration on global forest policy, enshrined in the UNFF, has some major challenges to overcome. Negotiations have stalled. The biannual meetings are ritualistic and predictable. Delegates convene, exchange pleasantries, table their demands, complain about lack of progress, and issue woolly recommendations, providing a topic for coming discussions about what it was one actually agreed to on the last occasion. Forest-rich developing countries remain entrenched in their positions on financial assistance and undiluted sovereignty over their own forests, but the willingness of developed countries to bow to these demands in the forest negotiations is scant. Perhaps it is time to realise that the UNFF track will probably never succeed in agreeing on a legally binding global forest agreement. As the evidence shows, more could be done through regional alliances, something the US has been campaigning for in the field of illegal logging, through environmentalist pressure, and through forest certification schemes and other market-based instruments. And given that most of the world's terrestrial biodiversity is found in forests, perhaps it is time to realise that the Biodiversity Convention would probably be a better arena for negotiating a global forests agreement than would the UNFF.

Whether negotiated under the auspices of the Biodiversity Convention or the UNFF, however, a global forest agreement must be combined with other instruments and measures. Because the causes of deforestation and forest degradation are multiple and complex, there are no simple solutions to the problems. Market-based action will not succeed on its own, but nor will governmental regulations. A combination of market-based schemes, government regulation, international payment mechanisms to reduce deforestation and forest degradation, and action against illegal logging could, on the other hand, do much to improve the situation – if these instruments are synergistic, have an emphasis on practical action, and are seen in light of an integrated approach to resolve environmental and socio-economic problems.

Bibliography

Auld, G., Gulbrandsen, L.H. and McDermott, C. (2008) 'Certification schemes and the impacts on forests and forestry', *Annual Review of Environment and Resources*, 33: 187–211.

Dauvergne, P. (2001) *Loggers and Degradation in the Asia-Pacific: corporations and environmental management*, Cambridge, UK: Cambridge University Press.

Dimitrov, R. (2005) 'Hostage to norms: states, institutions and global forest politics', *Global Environmental Politics*, 5: 1–24.

Gale, F. (1998) *The Tropical Timber Trade Regime*, New York: St. Martin Press.

Geist, H. and Lambin, E. (2002) 'Proximate causes and underlying driving forces of tropical deforestation', *BioScience*, 52: 143–50.

Gulbrandsen, L.H. (2004) 'Overlapping public and private governance: can forest certification fill the gaps in the global forest regime?', *Global Environmental Politics*, 4: 75–99.

——(2010) *Transnational Environmental Governance: the emergence and effects of the certification of forests and fisheries*, Cheltenham, UK: Edward Elgar.

Gullison, R.E. (2003) 'Does forest certification conserve biodiversity?', *Oryx*, 37: 153–65.

Humphreys, D. (1996) *Forest Politics: the evolution of international cooperation*, London: Earthscan.

——(2006) *Logjam: deforestation and the crisis of global governance*, London: Earthscan.

Rametsteiner, J. and Simula, M. (2003) 'Forest certification – an instrument to promote sustainable forest management?', *Journal of Environmental Management*, 67: 87–98.

UNECE/FAO (United Nations Economic Commission for Europe/FAO) (2009) *Forest Products Annual Market Review 2008–2009*, ECE/TIM/SP/24, New York and Geneva: United Nations.

UNFCCC (United Nations Framework Convention on Climate Change) (2007) *Report of the Conference of the Parties on Its Thirteenth Session, Held in Bali from 3 to 15 December 2007. Addendum. Part Two: Action Taken by the Conference of the Parties at Its Thirteenth Session*, FCCC/CP/2007/6/Add.1.

Part V

Conclusions

11 Ideals and practice in international environmental politics

Steinar Andresen, Elin Lerum Boasson and Geir Hønneland

Environmental problems are complex and have different characteristics along various dimensions. The level of interests for states as well as the public varies over time and issue area, but in general more 'visible' environmental problems attract most attention. Looking at the big picture, though, the perception of environmental challenges has changed quite radically; in some areas, it has been possible to change the behaviour significantly of those targeted. As more and more environmental issues are tackled through international political collaboration, there is a growing tendency towards internationalisation.

In this concluding chapter we shall review the current status in the international environmental effort. We compare notes on the environmental challenges presented in the three main parts of the book on air pollution, stewardship of the seas and finally nature conservation and biodiversity. What characterises the various multilateral environmental agreements (MEAs) – or regimes – within each of these major areas? What are their similarities and differences? How well do they perform and how can it be explained? To round off we discuss what can be done to strengthen international cooperation in the field of the environment and the possibilities of achieving this.

Air pollution: advanced regimes, but varied success

We present three types of international cooperation in the field of air pollution in part II of the book. They target long-range transboundary air pollution, ozone-depleting substances and greenhouse gases, respectively. In terms of the nature of these problems, long-range air pollution threatens natural processes. When water acidity grows, fish suffer; when forests are destroyed, flora and fauna suffer. Ozone-depleting gases destroy the natural shield that protects animals and humans from the harmful ultraviolet rays of the sun. Greenhouse gases strengthen the natural layer of water vapour and other gases that regulate the climate on earth. That alters the climate and conditions of life of plants, animals and humans. Although long-range air pollution is a global problem, the impact of the actual emissions is primarily regional rather than global. Although the US and Canada are participants, the regime dealing with this problem is primarily a European regional venture. The two other problems are both truly global. States which emit long-range pollutants tend to escape the adverse effects themselves, thereby creating 'importers' and 'exporters' of pollution. In contrast, emissions which harm the ozone layer and climate harm the source country as much as everyone else. The emission of ozone-depleting substances implicate only a small number of manufacturers and sectors of society, while many stakeholders are involved in the two other problem areas, particularly climate change. It is also relatively easy to find quite inexpensive replacement substances for those which damage the ozone layer. This, combined with the relatively small stakes involved, make this problem stand out as a rather 'benign' one. Regional air pollution and the climate problem are, however, mainly a secondary effect of the most conventional factor inputs in modern industry, transport and heating, that is, fossil fuels like oil, coal and gas. These fossil fuels have played an absolutely decisive role in shaping modern societies as we know them today. While it is relatively inexpensive in most cases to reduce long-range air pollution by removing pollutants from gases and tailpipe exhaust, it is often technically demanding and expensive to reduce greenhouse gas emissions. Since it is hard to remove greenhouse gases and difficult for manufacturers and private consumers to switch energy sources, climate change stands out as clearly the most 'malign' among the three environmental problems. The problem is even harder to solve because powerful commercial interests stand to gain from increasing emissions. Many of these have opposed efforts to formulate climate measures both nationally and internationally. In short, while climate change stands out as very malign, long-range air pollution represents both malign and benign characteristics while ozone stands out as a rather benign problem.

The outcomes of the three regimes differ with respect to normative, cognitive and regulative aspects. To start with the normative aspects, the cooperation on long-range air pollution builds on a relatively modest and vague ambition to combat the problem, but as noted this has been considerably strengthened and specified over time. The ozone regime seeks to phase out harmful substances, a very strong normative message. The Climate Convention includes a long-term ambition to stabilise atmospheric greenhouse gases. Both global regimes differentiate obligations between developed and developing nations. The normative mechanism of 'shaming' and 'prize' is utilised in the three regimes as they collect data and publish country performance tables.

In terms of the cognitive dimension, international cooperation in all three issue areas came about as a political response to scientific findings. Comprehensive scientific bodies have been established under each of the regimes, dominated by natural scientists, but experts in the social sciences and economics are increasingly important. Procedures have been established to facilitate communication between the scientific and political bodies. Consultative scientific panels are increasingly important for specifying ozone-depleting substances and long-range air pollution and their advice has to a large extent been adhered to. This has not been the case for the climate negotiations, primarily due to the significant political and economic counter-forces. All three regimes have strong cognitive mechanisms. Despite significant differences in persuasive power and influence, over time scientists have defined the premises for the political work and not the least shaped public perceptions about these challenges.

In terms of regulations, efforts to reduce emissions of long-range air pollutants started in the 1970s, ozone-related work in the 1980s and cooperation on the climate in the early 1990s. All these regimes started out with rather weak and general framework conventions without targets and timetables. Over time, however, they have all become more specific, ambitions and binding through the adoption of protocols. Regarding long-range air pollution, the Gothenburg Protocol of 1999 represents a very sophisticated and ambitious regional regime. Turning to ozone, the ozone regime probably represents the most sophisticated and ambitious environmental regimes at the global level. The climate regime represents a novel approach through the adoption and use of the market-based flexible mechanisms. The goals fleshed out in the Kyoto Protocol, however, are rather modest and efforts to specify new obligations and procedures when the Protocol expires in 2012 have so far proven futile.

Differentiation of emission commitments is a key feature in these regimes, but it is done somewhat differently. The ozone regime gave developing countries more time to reach their targets. Commitments to reduce long-range air pollutants are differentiated according to biological tolerance thresholds. The climate regime imposes emission targets on developed countries, and even these are differentiated. Because of the flexibility inherent in the climate commitments, domestic action is but one way of meeting them. Rich countries can help fund emission-reducing projects in poorer countries. How this complicated system works in practice is a disputed question. Nor is the ozone regime only focused on domestic measures, though the means by which it has brought poorer countries on board differ from those of the climate regime. First, it is possible to ban the export and import of controlled substances. Second, a fund has been created to facilitate the funding of developing countries. Inasmuch as collaboration on air pollution is regional, with greater similarity between countries, there is no need for arrangements like these here.

Also when it comes to penalties, there are significant differences. The long-range air pollution regime disposes only over normative, not legal penalties. If a country fails to meet its commitments under the ozone regime, it can be warned and threatened with expulsion, but these sanctions have not been used to any extent. It could, alternatively, be liable to an export ban. The Kyoto Protocol includes heavier commitments among the possible sanctions, but what this means in practice is unclear considering the uncertain fate of the Kyoto Protocol.

With regard to outcome, all three regimes have spurred substantial change in perceptions of the problem and national policies, but there are significant differences when it comes to the effect on actual industry and consumer practices and their actual impact on the environmental problems. The ozone regime stands out as a particularly successful and effective agreement. In terms of how this can be explained, this is due both to its strong problem-solving ability as well as the nature of the problem. On the one hand it has a highly sophisticated and elaborate approach, but the problem has also been relatively easy to tackle. Industry responded quickly, offering alternative, less harmful products, which also earned them good money. Major industries almost behaved like campaigners, a rare thing in international environmental cooperation. Economic support to developing countries enhanced the agreement's effectiveness, helping to curb almost 95 per cent of emissions of ozone-depleting substances. The strong and consensual input from the scientists, individual leadership and not least the 'pusher' role played by the US also contribute to explain this regime's high effectiveness. But because already released substances will remain in the atmosphere for a long time, the problem is far from solved.

The performance of the long-range air pollution regime is more varied, and the different nature of the problems at hand contributes to shed light on these differences. Most success can be noted for in the field of sulphur abatements where emissions have dropped by some 65 per cent, leading to a significant reduction in acidification-related damage in Europe. To some extent this can be explained by the fact that technology to deal with this problem was present at an early stage. As NOx and volatile organic compound emissions emanate from a much more varied group of sources, they have been more difficult to deal with, rendering lower goal attainment. Overall, however, the regime has achieved significant results, but they cannot all be attributed directly to measures under the Convention; the changed positions by Germany and the UK, the strengthened role of the EU as well as the fall of communism in Eastern Europe also influenced the result. However, the situation would no doubt have been less positive in the absence of the regime. The sophisticated and strong scientific input, not least through the development of the critical loads approach as well as the interplay between hard and soft law and the flexibility of the regulatory structure have all contributed to enhancing the problem-solving ability of the regime. Nevertheless, critical loads in the environment are still exceeded in vulnerable areas.

Turning to the climate change regime, the picture is more pessimistic. True, this issue has come to be regarded as one of the most pressing challenges facing humanity and manifold climate policies have emerged. But actual emissions are still on the rise. The countries with most significant emission reductions over the last two decades are the economies in transition in Eastern Europe, and this is unrelated to the climate regime. The most positive development that can at least to some extent be linked to the Kyoto Protocol is falling emissions in key EU countries. Despite the emergence of organisations, national regulations and voluntary schemes in a large number of countries, total greenhouse gas emission rates are increasing fast. It can probably be argued that emissions would have increased even more without the climate regime, but this does not help much as emissions are still way too high compared to scientific advice. The main reason for failure to address the problem effectively is the malign nature of the issue. However, other factors make a difference as well, not the least the laggard role of the US, and the reluctance of dominant developing countries such as China strongly reduces the problem-solving ability of the regime. The EU has had ambitions to stand forward as a leader, but has not been able to generate a critical mass of followers. The regime is quite advanced both in terms of institutional design (flexible mechanisms) as well as scientific input, but this has so far not been sufficient to turn the negative emission trend and the very future of the climate regime is at present uncertain.

Although all three regimes address emissions into the same element – air – they seem to be relatively independent of one another. The natural connections between issue area – some of the ozone-depleting gases affect the climate, for instance, and long-range air pollutants can reduce the effect of human-induced climate change – have not made much difference to the respective negotiation processes. The regimes were all negotiated under the auspices of the UN, but because they are affiliated to the UN in different ways, there is little cross-coordination and cooperation. Still, there is evidence of cross-fertilisation in terms of approach, starting with framework conventions and adding protocols at later stages.

Despite certain structural dissimilarities, the regimes have all changed perceptions of these environmental problems because of the large body of reliable evidence they have accumulated. Cooperation to address climate problems is less effective than the other agreements, because the challenges require social change of a completely different order than the other forms of air pollution.

Management of the marine environment: from accepted over-exploitation to the precautionary principle

The third part of the book presented the main principles of the law of the sea with reference to the protection of the marine environment, common efforts to reduce North Sea pollution and regional fishery management regimes. While the three regimes working to reduce air pollution emerged relatively independently, the marine environment regimes enjoy closer ties. International fishery bodies and the partnerships to reduce North Sea pollution follow in many ways from the law of the sea, especially the Law of the Sea Convention and (in the fisheries sector) the Fish Stocks Agreement. The law of the sea delineates who has right of access to the sea and how resources should be shared. Rather than an environmental regime, it was initially about distributing rights among nation-states. While rights and obligations under the law of the sea apply equally to all countries, marine resource management is not conceived in terms of global cooperation at the political level. But the law does prescribe regional cooperation. This was instrumental both in the establishment of an intergovernmental partnership to tackle pollution of the North Sea and of regional fisheries regimes. The international *global* regime issues rules and principles concerning marine pollution and fishery management, but international policy is specified and enforced at the regional level. While this book has discussed regional fisheries regimes in general, it has limited itself to the joint European effort to curb marine pollution.

Several global conventions related to the law of the sea were in place as early as the late 1950s. In 1982, a comprehensive convention on the law of the sea was created. All areas of the world's seas are covered along with the atmosphere above, the seabed and its subsoil below. In all essential respects it replaced the former conventions. There were instances of bilateral and multilateral fishery management alliances before the global, convention-based law of the sea, but they were not particularly important vehicles until after the 1982 convention. Dumping and land-based emissions of nutrients and other environmental pollutants in the North Sea were addressed by three European institutional arrangements: the North Sea Conferences, OSPAR and EU. The first international steps to address North Sea pollution were taken by the Oslo and Paris conventions of the early 1970s. They merged to become the 1992 OSPAR Convention. The first North Sea Conference was arranged in 1984, but the EU would not develop a concrete policy on marine pollution until the 1990s.

The seas are more than a vital larder for people; they are complex ecosystems, sensitive to human activity in many guises. The seas are also interdependent: changes in one marine environment are likely to affect others. Fishing was not considered a serious threat to the planet's fish stocks until the 1950s and 1960s when fishing technology became so efficient entire stocks were virtually wiped out. By the early 1970s, it was clear that dumping and pollution were affecting marine life. The impact of pollution from a country could be felt far from the original source. But although ocean currents are capable of ferrying pollutants over very large distances, the regional implications are generally the worst. Because the marine ecosystem is complex and our knowledge of how species interact is limited, it will probably be impossible to understand fully causes and effects by scientific studies and observations alone. That said, it is easier to monitor the impact of fishing on the viability of individual stocks than to ascertain the total impact of countless toxins on marine ecosystems. Fishing stocks nearly to extinction has obvious economic implications, but it is not always as easy to predict the consequences of marine pollution. A great many players are implicated in the pollution of the seas, and even more are affected, while the industry responsible for depleting the stocks in the first place has to suffer the economic consequences. The conduct of one country's fishing fleet can be extremely detrimental to the fishing activities of others.

In normative terms, two objectives underpin the international management of the world's seas. One is to promote the sensible use of marine resources, the second to protect the marine environment against pollution. As the Law of the Sea Convention points out, states make use of the planet's fisheries resources for the benefit of mankind as a whole but not to the detriment of future generations' enjoyment of the same benefits. This is usually referred to as maximum sustainable yield. The 1995 Fish Stocks Agreement strengthens the requirement for precaution. In the absence of adequate scientific information, the precautionary approach requires states to choose the approach that exposes the stock to the least risk. The law of the sea urges states to minimise marine pollution and take counter-measures to prevent pollution of the marine environment from all potential sources of pollution. This was spelled out in greater detail by OSPAR and the North Sea Conferences, both of which embody the precautionary principle. Agreement was reached in 1995 to reduce the concentration of the most toxic substances to the background levels of naturally occurring substances, and eliminate entirely man-made compounds by 2020. Performance reports on the different countries have also been published.

While cognitive elements in the international marine management regimes at the global level are few, there are obvious cognitive mechanisms in regional arrangements for both fisheries management and conservation of the marine environment. The International Council for the Exploration of the Sea (ICES) was established as early as 1902 and advises today both the EU and numerous regional fisheries management bodies, including the North-East Atlantic Fisheries Commission and Norwegian–Russian Fisheries Commission. The latter sets the quotas for the most important fish stocks in the Barents Sea on the basis of scientific advice. The ICES has served as a model for similar organisations in other parts of the world, including the north-western and southern Atlantic, Pacific and Antarctic Oceans. The North Sea regime on dumping and pollution conducts scientific studies as well. This has been a particularly significant aspect of OSPAR. Relations between political and scientific circles have varied somewhat over time, however.

The Law of the Sea Convention gives sea-bordering states sovereignty over marine resources inside 200 nautical miles from the shore, that is, inside the so-called economic zones. Importantly, the Law of the Sea Convention also makes flag states responsible for regulating and controlling pollution from ships. Both in the field of fisheries management and pollution of the North Sea, detailed regulations have been produced. These are enshrined in OSPAR and EU directives, but not in the North

Sea collaboration. OSPAR's bans on dumping and waste incineration at sea along with permitted discharge levels of hazardous substances have been particularly important. The EU's IPPC Directive and Water Directive specify in even greater detail permitted discharge levels.

The law of the sea gives coastal states the right to enforce the rules by monitoring activities and issuing penalties. The right of coastal states to inspect foreign ships in the economic zones was strengthened with the extension of the enforcement right to beyond the 200-mile zone and the emergence of regional systems of port state control in recent years. Although such control is conducted by national authorities, it must be considered a strong additional regulatory mechanism. The law of the sea does not give coastal states as much power to enforce pollution and dumping restrictions. Neither the North Sea collaboration nor OSPAR have strong regulatory enforcement procedures, while the EU directives do empower the Commission to prosecute states for failing to implement the regulations.

The world's oceans are everywhere facing challenges, and the management of the marine environment is founded on a common global regulatory regime. In practice, though, matters are mostly addressed at the regional level. When it comes to what counts as morally acceptable conduct, perceptions have changed significantly in recent decades. The depletion of marine resources and use of the sea as a rubbish tip didn't use to raise an eyebrow. Although the mentality has changed, in terms of actual behaviour and despite some positive developments, a lot remains to be desired. Since the connections between human activity and changes in the natural marine environment are still in many cases unknown to science, it is also difficult to determine what has been achieved with any accuracy.

Before the economic zones were created, international fisheries bodies were incapable of effective management. The emergence of regional fisheries bodies is itself a tangible outcome of (the global) law of the sea. At the regulatory level, the most significant difference from the 1970s is the use of quotas as the preferred vehicle in international fisheries policy. Where governments usually failed to achieve consensus on international fishing limits, it is easier today because coastal states now have an 'ownership stake' in the fish. Normative pressure and the cognitive elements of the regional fisheries arrangements have amplified the effect and led to smaller catches and a more selective extraction of the commercial species. What's more, the precautionary principle, which was introduced in the mid-1990s, prompted the formulation of longer-term management strategies. Both the EU's common fisheries policy and Norwegian–Russian Fisheries Commission set multi-year rotating quotas. They provide for a more predictable regulatory environment for the industry and are also supposed to keep catches within reasonably certain biological limits.

Despite improvements, fishing fleets still have too many vessels, too technologically sophisticated vessels, and too little fish to go around. The economic zones have had a distributive effect by facilitating a massive transfer of resources from long-distance fishing states to coastal states, but without reducing overfishing to the same extent. Today, about a quarter of the fish stocks in the world's oceans are over-fished or have simply collapsed, though it could have been worse if the international community had not done anything.

The North Sea Conferences have strengthened OSPAR and the EU's regulatory regime, but also the law of the sea in a wider sense. The provisions of the law of the sea have not affected marine pollution to the same degree as fisheries management, not least because of the widespread use of 'flags of convenience' which allows flag states to avoid liability for pollution from ships. In that sense the shipping industry has succeeded in undermining the effectiveness of international regulations in the area. In Europe, OSPAR, the North Sea Conferences and later the EU have countered these developments not unsuccessfully. There is little doubt that the three institutional arrangements have complemented one another in such a way as to strengthen the effectiveness of marine environment policy in Europe. The impact of the North Sea Conferences has been principally normative. The non-binding North Sea declarations have gradually been adopted by OSPAR and the EU, and become regulatory and legally binding. At the latest North Sea Conference, in 2006, the parties could declare 'mission accomplished' insofar as most of the issue areas had been taken over by other collaborative bodies. While dumping and waste incineration at sea are now things of the past, land-based discharges of hazardous environmental substances and nutrients have fallen appreciably. Without the multilateral input, these achievements would probably not have been possible, so we can be pleased with the results. Quite a lot remains to be done, however, before the pollution problems are solved completely.

The discussion above illustrates the strong correlation between the provisions of the law of the sea and the two types of regional regimes, particularly fisheries management. Here, the law of the sea sets out general norms and regulatory frameworks, while regional fisheries regimes work cognitively and regulatively, especially in the setting of quotas. The North Sea collaboration has also worked normatively, while OSPAR and EU directives have supplied more specified rules. Apart from this, the North Sea partnership and OSPAR have had links to research bodies, and this has worked cognitively. In both areas, the international regimes have been crucial. All the same, the remaining challenges are still substantial.

Conservation and biological diversity: a global responsibility or national resource?

Part IV of the book presented the wider international effort to conserve biological diversity and the more specific efforts associated with crop genetic diversity in agriculture and forest management. In a certain sense, the Biodiversity Convention is the key document since it aims at regulating biodiversity per se. It has shaped both of the two more specific regimes, but the relationship is far from as close as that between general (global) and regional fisheries management. The global reach of the regimes on biological diversity has highlighted the clash of interests between North and South. Negotiations have been complicated further by very different natural, social, institutional and economic conditions in the various countries.

Biological diversity is being lost at an enormous rate; the estimated cost is in the region of $250 billion annually. The degradation of the natural environment affects a great many human activities and living conditions. The driving forces are numerous and different in nature, but include agriculture, forestry, industrial expansion and pollution, to mention a few. The majority of land-based biological diversity is found in tropical areas in the poorer regions of the world. Many prosperous countries are home to the industries which want to exploit these areas and the environmental groups which want to preserve natural values. Many developing countries have resisted the internationalisation of environmental management by, among other things, insisting on their sovereign right to manage their own forests.

Forests and agricultural biodiversity are two subareas of biological diversity. It is estimated that as much as 90 per cent of global, land-based biodiversity resides in forests, mainly in tropical rainforests. Vast swathes of tropical rainforest are lost every year to commercial logging, illegal logging, forest clearance for agriculture and industrial incursion. Forestry is not the only activity to threaten forest biology then. The agricultural crop genetic diversity regime is about ensuring the basis of all food production. For millennia, farmers the world over have created a rich diversity of crops with a wide range of attributes. Modernisation of agriculture, with the development of genetically homogeneous varieties, is causing rapid loss of biodiversity. In addition, it is increasingly difficult for farmers to obtain and use seeds of many crop varieties because a powerful multinational seed industry is constantly and successfully pressing for stronger regulations.

As Chapter 1 pointed out, the first nature conservation efforts were fuelled by a romantic view of nature and by nation-state consolidation both in Europe and the US. Traditionally, threats against biodiversity and especially commercially exploited species were conceived as national challenges. Nonetheless, conservation was the first issue area to attract political attention at the international level. During the 1970s, several agreements regulating the preservation and management of selected species and habitats pressed developments forward. In the 1980s, the preservation of biological diversity was increasingly viewed as a global responsibility. This global approach found expression in the 1992 Biodiversity Convention. That biodiversity today can be seen as an economic resource basis, a national attribute or global responsibility is a source of tension and makes international cooperation more difficult.

The management of crop genetic diversity was first addressed in the 1980s, but the Biodiversity Convention changed the direction of these initial efforts. A binding agreement was needed. After a lengthy negotiation process under the FAO, the Plant Treaty was adopted in 2001. The emergence of an international forestry regime under the auspices of the UN can also be linked to the process around the Biodiversity Convention. Although the international community has been unable to agree on an international treaty, several principles on sustainable forest management have been formulated.

The outcome of the regimes differs along all dimensions, normative, cognitive and regulative, but all are clearly weaker on the cognitive and regulative dimensions than the other environmental agreements discussed in this book. The Biodiversity Convention rests on a threefold normative basis: ensure preservation of biodiversity and sustainable use and equitable distribution of benefits arising from the use of genetic resources. Biodiversity is highlighted as a key value for which humanity as a whole shares a common global responsibility, but it does not spell out any overriding goal for the international effort. High levels of generality and many, often incompatible targets, actually weaken the normative message and also reduce the chances of reaching the objectives. In the meantime, an ambitious target was proposed to reduce the annual loss of biodiversity significantly by 2010. This was a short-term and diffusely worded goal, not least because we don't know what the annual loss is today, or what it would have been without human interference.

As mentioned above, principles and guidelines were formulated to facilitate sustainable forest management, but they contain no clear or unambiguously normative message. In terms of genetic diversity in nature and crop genetic diversity in agriculture, the international bodies have concluded that the industrial world has a greater responsibility to ensure diversity than developing countries. There is no corresponding framework for the forestry sector, however. The Plant Treaty promotes the value of preserving and sustainably using crop genetic diversity as a means of sustaining global food security. It develops the norms in the Biodiversity Convention to enable their application in the field of crop genetic diversity in agriculture.

In terms of the cognitive dimension, the different approaches have different ideas about the causes, impacts and likely solutions to the problems. According to the Biodiversity Convention, preservation and sustainable use are both necessary. Access to resources is a central aspect of the Plant Treaty because without access the crops cannot be used or preserved for posterity. In this connection, the treaty highlights the importance of the rights of farmers, though what it means in practice is not entirely clear. The forest regime lacks a corresponding superstructure, though the voluntary certification schemes suggest the active use of market mechanisms. Environmentalists have been the architects of the forest certification scheme. The scheme came about outside the UN system and is based on an entirely different rationale than the other regimes discussed above. Rather than governments monitoring forest owners' management practices, an independent body decides whether to award an 'environmental certificate'. In an increasingly environmentally aware market, the idea goes, a certificate is supposed to boost market shares and prices. In this approach, governments are not the main actors, but forest owners, environmental organisations and, not least, consumers.

The international endeavour under the Biodiversity Convention has not significantly added to what we know of the pervasiveness and importance of different types of biological diversity or of how different ecosystems interact globally. The focus on ecosystem services pinpoints biological interdependencies and connections, but these tend to be local, not international. The Biodiversity Convention also lacks methods for balancing conservation and sustainable use. And there are no scientific bodies for the various types of biodiversity either. Thus, also the forest initiatives lack robust cognitive underpinning. Although the science produced by the FAO is important, the lack of expert scientific bodies devoted to these processes is a major failing in this issue area.

There are very few binding rules in the Biodiversity Convention. The most tangible governmental responsibility is to formulate action plans and identify what needs to be done to protect and preserve biodiversity. In the absence of obligations, there can obviously be no penalties or sanction mechanisms. And since the Forest Principles are not embodied in any convention, the rules are even weaker here. The Plant Treaty stands out in establishing a global set of rules aimed at simplifying access to crop genetic diversity.

What can we say about the performance of these agreements and principles in terms of their stated objectives? If we look at general biodiversity, there is some evidence of significant outcomes, with respect to changing perceptions of the challenges as well as emergence of national policies. Most countries have formulated biodiversity preservation strategies and action plans, and there has been a healthy rise in the designation of biodiversity-protected areas. The international community has failed, however, to cement a conception of biodiversity as an environmental problem which can and should be dealt with globally. Although 192 states have acceded to the convention, they do not necessarily see global policy making as the best way to protect biodiversity. Concerning impact, the results are meagre. Biodiversity is being lost a hundred to a thousand times faster than the natural rate of extinction without human interference, and there is nothing to suggest the rate is slowing down. The lack of progress in the development of more binding protocols could express the tenacious hold of conceptions of biodiversity as a national resource. Disappointing performance results can also be explained by weak cognitive mechanisms, disparate targets and vague regulations. Seen in this light, the disheartening situation is not surprising if we look at the actual state of biodiversity. Complicated patenting rules and trading regulations make it even more challenging to find schemes with the capacity to promote an even-handed distribution of benefits and burdens among countries.

The stress in the international principles of the importance of conserving forest biodiversity could explain why these issues have attracted wider attention in recent years. The forest certification schemes have been a worldwide success to judge from their increasing uptake. It is hard to say how and to what extent this success in terms of outcome has affected the quality of forest management in general. The certification system has encouraged environmental action in the forestry sector, though mostly in affluent countries rather than the South which is where most of the biodiversity is found. Although certification cannot solve the formidable challenges of sustainable forest management, it has made public opinion 'greener' in the prosperous countries. Over the longer term, the same could happen in the forest-rich countries of the South.

The Plant Treaty entered into force in 2004 and the funding strategy is still not in place. If experience is anything to go by, it will be some time before we can say anything meaningful about its achievements. There are, nonetheless, several local level initiatives, often run by local organisations, which appear to be profiting from the international system in promoting the policy that assuring farmers' rights is vital for preserving crop genetic diversity. At the moment, little progress has been made to secure a sustainable use of crop genetic diversity in practice, and only a handful of countries have developed a regulatory framework for the purpose. On the other hand, the multilateral system under the auspices of the treaty is well under way. Annually, more than 100,000 plant specimens are transferred. A benefit sharing fund is in place and distributing funds to promising projects in the South, supporting farmers in the conservation and sustainable use of crop genetic diversity. The conservation of biodiversity in gene banks has also improved.

The three themes addressed in this part of the book are closely related. Despite the wider focus on biodiversity, the Biodiversity Convention has not had much effect on actual progress in forest management and crop genetic diversity in agriculture. The agreements and principles are weak in the area of cognitive mechanisms and their normative base is also unclear. The forest certification schemes stand out in virtue of their reliance on market mechanisms, which could explain why the forest is one of the most talked about ecosystems in recent years. The Plant Treaty is also unusual in having clear rules, but it is still too early to pronounce on the possible impact.

At the end of the day, environmental politics is all about preserving biodiversity and the viability of ecosystems, species and genes. It will therefore often be possible to connect each of the nine themes we have raised in this book to the discussion about conserving biodiversity. Nor is there any doubt that air pollution and management of the marine environment affect natural processes. The Biodiversity Convention borders not only on a large assortment of international environmentally related agreements; it stands in opposition to the global economic alliance represented by the World Trade Organization (WTO).

Varied success – various explanations

The environmental questions we have discussed give rise to different types of political conflict, and there are different reasons why they can be difficult to resolve. Having said that, our review of the different MEAs gives us a platform for assessing why some of the regimes perform better than others and what the most likely explanatory factors could be. What counts most, norms and values, a good cognitive setup or stringent, concise legal provisions? Perhaps the form of the agreement is not that important; perhaps what determines whether effective solutions can be found is the complexity or structure of the problems and the problem-solving will and ability of the members of the regime.

Regarding biodiversity, the international community's ability to solve the problems has been limited, we concluded, despite certain heartening moves. For emissions to air, the situation is much more encouraging. While two of the MEAs, especially regarding ozone, but also long-range air pollution, have enabled solutions to be found for these problems, the biggest challenges, those to do with the climate, are still unresolved. We need to remember, though, that concern over climate change came later than concern over the other two issue areas. And these regimes needed time to become effective. The challenges associated with climate change, however, are also much more 'malign' and hence effectiveness can be expected to be lower. In the area of stewardship of the marine environment, there has been a distinct normative shift towards greater caution in the marine environment and fisheries. The practical results, though, are mixed. There is evidence of declining marine pollution, at least in areas like the North Sea. The number of collapsed fish stocks from overfishing is rising, however.

Only a minority of experts and observers disputes the sense of handling ozone and climate problems at the global level. The problems and challenges of protecting the natural environment and biological diversity are not similarly global, however. A general global approach might make sense, but because the problems are so numerous, complicated and different in different parts of the world, it would necessarily have to be diffuse. Regional additions to the global framework could therefore be useful for moving the process forward. Indeed, this is what the regimes concerned with the management of the marine environment prefer. The major legal instruments are global, while the actual management proceeds at the regional level. Obligations can be fleshed out for the different regions and issue areas. Long-range air pollution is specifically defined as a regional problem.

The international air pollution regimes stand out with their strong scientific basis. This has possibly helped raise ozone and climate issues to the status of global challenges. There are links between all three regulatory arrangements and the scientific community, and political negotiations have driven the work forward. While the IPCC is the most comprehensive joint scientific body by far, it has not resulted in equally ambitious political objectives. Nevertheless, strong scientific relations have strengthened the legitimacy and authority of decision-making in international climate work and the other two types of regime. Agreements covering the management of the marine environment have clear links to scientific bodies, another effectiveness-raising aspect of those regimes. The lack of cognitive mechanisms – both globally and regionally – has undermined joint efforts in the field of biodiversity.

The normative basis of the two most practically effective collaborative arrangements in the area of air pollution is not as clear as that found in the climate regime. This does not appear to have had any adverse affect on the agreements. Performance may simply not depend as much on the normative basis. On the other hand, the normative shift given by the adoption of the precautionary approach in fisheries management has been positive. In the issue areas of marine pollution and long-range air pollution, naming leaders and laggards has evidently had a normative impact.

It is probably no coincidence that the most successful collaboration, on ozone, also has the clearest, most ambitious and detailed rules. However, this problem was also fairly easy to deal with and in contrast to the climate change regime the US was a pusher in the ozone regime, strengthening its problem-solving ability. The collaboration on long-range air pollution has also performed better thanks to detailed rules and obligations, while weaker obligations and sanction mechanisms have pared down the efficiency of the international climate effort. Quota trade and the other flexible mechanisms represent new and interesting approaches, but the impact is uncertain and these approaches cannot solve the climate problem alone anyway. Moreover, there has been a problem of generating leadership in the climate regime. The Plant Treaty is looking to create a similar set of global rules to regulate the exchange of genetic resources, but it is too early to pass judgement on how effective it will turn out to be. With regard to the North Sea collaboration, the rules have been tightened over time, making it one of the most successful arrangements we have discussed. The links between the 'soft-law' approach of the North Sea Conferences and the binding legal approach of OSPAR is important in explaining achievements so far. The weak rules of the biodiversity regime, and the lack of robust and clear cognitive underpinning, help explain its relatively poor performance. Moreover, this is also an exceedingly malign problem with deep-seated political conflicts and little or no leadership by key actors.

That is, although the wording of the agreements obviously affects how environmental problems are perceived and tackled, it is vital to take account of the essential nature of the problems as well as the problem-solving ability to understand why some regimes perform better than others. The difference between ozone and the climate, which we explained above, can serve as a useful illustration. For climate change, the deep political and economic fault lines separating North and South and setting off parts of the industrialised world against one another make it more difficult to build a stable, effective international regime. The North Sea arrangement shows, however, how international collaboration can succeed in reducing pollution significantly even when the initial cost of reducing the emission of many of the substances is very high, not the least due to a creative institutional set-up.

Our conclusions regarding the performance of the international regime on biodiversity were rather negative, but there are some encouraging developments regarding forest management, such as the market-based certification scheme for sustainable forest management. It is interesting to see what non-governmental players managed to achieve where the UN and traditional inter-governmental cooperation failed. But what explains the general lack of progress? We need here to take a closer look at the complexity and general political divisions in this issue area. Here too, relations between rich and poor countries are typically antagonistic. Cooperation has not been eased by forest rich developing countries, often with weak systems of government, claiming national jurisdiction over these areas. Relations with international trade bodies, of which not least the US is a major participant, complicates matters further, especially when the rules of the WTO and Agreement on Trade-related Aspects of Intellectual Property Rights are more specific than the typically woolly phraseology of the Biodiversity Convention.

All in all, the normative, cognitive and regulatory factors inherent in the regulatory regimes do have an effect. While the significance of norms is not given, the cognitive factor and not least the rules that are formulated, have a great effect on how the agreements work. The agreements are not, however, put together in a vacuum. They are frequently and largely a reflection of the underlying problems one is attempting to regulate. If the problems are complex and politically divisive, the collaborative schemes will often be weak. As we have seen, though, there are exceptions. In the next section we shall therefore ask how we can make future agreements more effective.

Can the agreements be better?

The comparison of the different collaborative arrangements reveals no magic performance-boosting formula. Environmental problems are dissimilar and the agreements obviously need to be configured to do as good a job with the basic problems as possible. In the work ahead, international environmental politics faces several fundamental questions. Can steps be taken at the general level to improve the effectiveness of the international work on environmental policy? In which cases would it be right to establish strong global regulatory regimes to solve environmental problems, and when would regional cooperation be more appropriate? These questions have been discussed by experts and politicians in recent years (e.g. Najam *et al.* 2006). Would it be possible to do something to the way agreements are designed to make them more effective? Although there is no common standard, there are a few general factors which could make a difference.

In light of the discussion, a well-developed system of *scientific cooperation* is obviously an advantage. The relevant scientific communities also need to reach a consensus on problem diagnosis. If the problems can be diagnosed and solutions suggested, it would ease cooperation, and good systems need to be in place to facilitate communication and information exchange (Andresen *et al.* 2000). Scientific knowledge and creation of a common perception of a problem, however, is only one factor decision makers have to take into account. As we have seen in the climate-related regime, a high score on this dimension is no guarantee of success. On the other hand, international climate collaboration shows how cognitive mechanisms can change perceptions of the problem. Moreover, we have seen how good scientific cooperation strengthens the normative and regulatory content of the international effort to deal with air pollution over time. There is therefore little doubt that a strong cognitive content is likely to increase effectiveness, and this may even be a necessary – although far from sufficient – component in a successful regime.

We have also touched on the importance of the *level* at which problem-mitigating steps take place, that is, global, regional or a mixture of the two. Not many environmental problems are genuinely global. There is a discernible preference for the global agreement. But we would advise against this tendency. It is hard enough to agree on anything but general principles at this level because there are so many incompatible interests. While the global reach is important for wider legitimacy, the more practical, tangible mechanisms are often easier to operate at the regional level. If environmental problems are amenable to regional action, practical results will be more likely. There are gains to be made from combining global and regional regimes.

We have seen that a specific and encompassing regulatory output increases the outcome and impact of a regime. Having precise and ambitious obligations is often important for practical results, although it is also important to underpin the goals with strong political and institutional efforts as we have seen for example in the North Sea collaboration. One of the reasons for the weakness of the biodiversity regime is the low level of specificity of goals. Thus, whenever politically feasible, it is important to aim for precise, but also realistic targets.

Another way of improving international agreements could be to strengthen the rules for monitoring, verification and sanctions, which are underdeveloped in most regimes. The challenges are bigger when it comes to sanctioning governments that fail to meet their obligations. There are two main approaches, carrot and stick. The carrot translates into an offer of assistance and support and is deployed when the reason for defaulting is lack of capacity. The stick, in contrast, is brought out when the means are in place, but not the will to use them. The ozone regime has combined both quite successfully. It might be beneficial in fisheries management to use softer, normative responses in addition to the rather stringent regulations. Despite the apparent good performance of the various air pollution regimes in the area of verification and sanctions, it would be too simplistic to advise replicating these global systems in other areas of cooperation. It's easier at the regional level when the knowledge basis is sound and there are fewer differences and divisions between the participating countries. It also explains why it is difficult to get verification and sanction mechanisms to work satisfactorily under the agreements on biological diversity.

When such strict rules are not politically possible to establish, normative systems or 'naming and shaming' have often proven quite effective. Links with scientific work and records of governmental performance have improved the surveillance and verification systems, especially regarding air pollution agreements.

A prominent feature of all international cooperation is the voluntary nature of participation. It is up to the individual government to decide whether to join in – commitments can't be forced on an unwilling government. Negotiations therefore tend to stop at what the 'least enthusiastic' parties are willing to accept. To put it in a few words, it is one of the main barriers to achieving strong international environmental regimes. Both in the literature and political debates advocates of a strong international line would like to see the unanimity principle or consensus approach dropped in favour of a majority vote. The EU stands out in having a majority vote procedure, but it does not seem feasible at present to transfer this approach to the global level.

There has also been some discussion in political and expert circles of the need for overarching approaches to improve international environmental efforts. It was a key issue at the 2002 Johannesburg Summit. The system is too complicated and needs a stronger, unified organisation. There should be a 'World Environmental Organisation' after the model of the WTO. This idea for a less inflated, more streamlined approach is fascinating and intuitively appealing. The number of agreements has grown enormously in the past few years, along with the degree of overlap. Many of these agreements have little or no impact at all. What's more, the many negotiations and mutually inconsistent commitments and obligations strain what resources most developing countries have to spend on environmental matters. Whether this is a good idea or not is not something we would like to say at the present moment, but it would probably not have been an 'abracadabra' given the diversity and complexity of most environmental problems and sharp political divisions. At present, the idea seems to be politically dead due to opposition from the US and key developing countries (Andresen 2007).

The number of environmental players is rising. There are more environmental organisations with a global reach and the business community has established its own international environmental organisations. Many of the major international corporations have authored and adopted principles on sustainable development which, they say, will inform their global business activities. We have also seen a sharp rise in governments working with non-governmental organisations (NGOs) on environmental questions. The forest certification scheme is a typical example of this type of partnership. Some are enthusiastic to the potential of such partnerships while others remain to be convinced whether NGOs can do a better job than governments in developing flexible and practical partnerships and see the partnerships as more likely to produce talk than action. It is too early to say which side is right, though the practical outcomes seem relatively limited so far. Over the longer term, however, a change here could strengthen the effect of international political cooperation on environmental issues.

In conclusion, we want to emphasise that while the cognitive, normative and regulative composition of international environmental agreements is important, it is not possible to 'design' our way out of the real, profound political conflicts in international political collaboration. At the end of the day, the direction of international environmental politics will depend on political capacity and will within the international community.

Bibliography

Andresen, S. (2007) 'The effectiveness of UN environmental institutions', *International Environmental Agreements: politics, law and economics*, 7: 317–36.

Andresen, S., Skodvin, T., Underdal, A. and Wettestad, J. (2000) *Science and Politics in International Environmental Regimes: between integrity and involvement*, Manchester and New York: Manchester University Press.

Najam, A., Papa, M. and Taiyab, N. (2006) *Global Environmental Governance: a reform agenda*, Winnipeg: International Institute for Sustainable Development.

Index

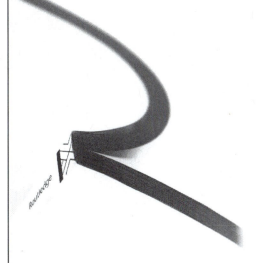